Companion to the

Calendar

Companion to the
Calendar

A Guide to the
Saints and Mysteries of
the Christian Calendar

Mary Ellen Hynes

LITURGY
TRAINING
PUBLICATIONS

This book is dedicated to the memory of my father, Frank Cronin.

Many people helped to assemble the information contained in this book. I wish to thank Peter Mazar; Archimandrite Hilary Madison of the Orthodox Church in America, Diocese of the Midwest; and Dave Beck of Native American Educational Services. Thanks also to the staffs of Rosary College, Loyola University and Oak Park Public Libraries. Assistance was provided by Tariq Asghar, Reverend John Boivin, Janet Campbell, Jeanne Crapo, OP, Mary Momper Cronin, John Hynes, Paul Messick, CFC, Christine Ondrla and Susan Brownell Thompson.
— *Mary Ellen Hynes*

MARY ELLEN HYNES is a free-lance writer and editor, and has been a contributor to *At Home with the Word* (LTP).

Companion to the Calendar was initiated and guided by Peter Mazar with editorial assistance from Sarah Huck.

Liturgy Training Publications gratefully acknowledges James Wilbur and Deborah Levine, who read parts of the text and made suggestions.

This book was designed by Lisa Grayson and typeset by Mark Hollopeter in Sabon and Futura Black. The cover was designed by Mary Bowers. Printed in the United States of America.

10 09 08 07 06 9 8 7 6 5

ISBN-10: 1-56854-011-6
ISBN-13: 978-1-56854-011-5
COMCAL

How many things
    by season season'd are
to their right praise
    and true perfection!

— William Shakespeare, *The Merchant of Venice* (Act V, Scene I)

Contents

Foreword

I MAGINE you were living aeons ago, back in the Stone Age, in a cave, a yurt, a tent. What is your smallest unit of time? No watch, no alarm clock, no church bells, no 6:00 news. No seconds, no minutes, no hours. What then? Alone with Mother Nature, how do you count time?

"Sunrise, sunset," sings Tevye in *Fiddler on the Roof*. Yes, the *day* is the smallest natural unit of time we can count. The Book of Genesis opens with the cosmic story of creation, a majestic poem whose seven distinctive stanzas are *days*, each representing a complete category signified in a primal unit of time. By an infinite word, we hear the Timeless One creating time.

Primitive people place little emphasis on exact noon — it takes some geometry and a sunny day to calculate noon — and even less on midnight. How could you tell it *is* precisely midnight? Rather, they count "sunset, sunrise," as the sun's orb disappears in the west and reappears in the east on the local horizon. The day is a solar design. God made the greater luminary to rule the day.

And God made the smaller luminary to rule the night. The *month* cycle is reckoned at night as the new moon returns faithfully more or less every 29 days. Four lunar phases divide almost neatly into four seven-day units. Is this the origin of the *week?* Nobody really knows, but we happily celebrate the week as a convenient and beautiful short cycle that reflects the days of creation.

What of the *year?* Twelve moon cycles do not form a full year, but four seasons do. They are rather well-marked. The summer solstice, the longest day (in the Northern Hemisphere), rises in the northeast and sets in the northwest and makes the shortest night. Ah! Midsummer night! The occasion for a bonfire! And for the church to celebrate the Birth of John the Baptist.

After Midsummer, days start declining until nights are equal to days (equinox means equal-night) and the sun is seen rising and setting almost due east and due west. Now we remember the Archangel Michael and the equitable weighing of souls in the spiritual harvest. It was once a day to celebrate a new year and a new resolve.

From then on, the days continue declining toward the winter solstice with its somber days and long, dark nights. In dark faith, we celebrate the coming of the Lord on clouds of glory, in the timeless aeon. These are also the days dedicated by the church to the mystery of the Incarnation in the birth of Jesus.

When the Roman New Year was kept on March 1, January and February were counted as the 11th and 12th months. This is the time of year when days gradually lengthen again until that joyous season of new life we call Lent or spring, another equipoise marked by the vernal equinox. Passover and Easter, each in its own way, now celebrate the opening of a sacred door, a passage through the waters onto spiritual liberation.

Can a 12-month *lunar* year of only 354 days be combined with the four-square *solar* year of a few hours more than 365 days? A lunar year runs short by 11 or 12 days. In the course of time, the cumulative difference completely disorders the months in relation to the solar-based agricultural seasons. To correct this, the Jewish calendar has worked out a cycle of 19 years with seven "leap years" that add a 13th month repeating the 12th. Thus the Jewish year remains a *luni-solar* year.

Was the 12-month calendar adopted to allow three months to each quarter? Who knows? It is not as simple as that. While day and year are solar concepts, our present months remain lunar, but, as it were, solarized.

By 46 BCE, the Roman calendar had run so far out of sync with the sun that Julius Caesar had to reform it, hence the Julian calendar, still kept today by some of the Orthodox churches. With its short February and a leap year patch-up, the Julian solar year and its lunar-inspired 12-month structure have been commonly accepted — in various forms — since before the time of Christ. Although Caesar's astronomers thought the calendar would now work perfectly, they overshot the mark by ten days in 1600 years.

Meanwhile, Mother Nature continued in her own sweet time to circle the year, and 1600 years after Caesar, it fell upon Pope Gregory XIII to implement a new reform, hence the Gregorian Calendar, initiated in 1582 and now widely accepted as the international civil calendar.

The great Christian feast of Easter is obviously associated with "Brother Sun" in the solar year, but it is also based upon the moon's phases. Western Christians celebrate Easter, counting from the spring equinox (solar), waiting until the full moon (lunar) and until the following Sunday (weekly). Every year, Easter, Pentecost and the movable feasts come on different calendar dates. Thus, "Sister Moon" adds to the interest and variety of each recurring year.

One more exquisite detail. Christ's victory over death is a "movable feast." But his birth, associated with the dark days and the promise of light near the winter solstice, is celebrated just as that of everyone born of a woman, of a human mother, on a particular day of a particular month — for Jesus the 25th day of December and/or the 6th of January.

So much for the greater feasts of the year. What about the lesser days? The custom of celebrating a martyr's anniversary is ancient. About the year 155, Polycarp, the elderly bishop of Smyrna, was betrayed, taken before the proconsul in the stadium, in the presence of a hostile crowd, and commanded to curse Christ.

"I have served him for 86 years," answered the old man, "and he has done me no wrong. How can I blaspheme my king and savior?" From a letter that has survived, we know that the church of Smyrna continued to remember the witness of their beloved Polycarp with a yearly remembrance in the liturgy.

From early times, we also know that, on his or her anniversary date, the eucharist was celebrated on a martyr's own tomb, thus joining the witness of followers to the death and victory of their savior. How does this differ from a family celebrating a birthday with a happy get-together, a song and a cake? Only in that the song is a hymn, the sacred meal is spiritual nourishment, and the feast celebrates a "birthday in heaven."

The memorial service of a holy person recalls the day of his or her death. Only three have a feast for their birth as well: Jesus, his mother Mary, and his cousin John the Baptist. Can you suggest why? Look into Luke.

Should we worry about exact historical dates for the saints? Perhaps all we need to know is that we had a great brother or sister in the faith, a hero who went before us, lived a good, interesting life, and died a valuable death in God's arms. So? Let us throw a church party to remember Cecilia, Martin, Elizabeth Ann, Maximilian. Do they hide Christ? By no means. Rather, they paint in vivid colors how the words of Christ's gospel have been lived by varied individuals, and how we can be encouraged to do the same, each in our own way.

As a tapestry, the Christian year shows a pattern of greater, movable feasts, designed on times of harvest, while lesser feasts, recalling good people's anniversaries set by custom or history, are woven here and there on particular days of the month.

The year has only 365 days, not nearly enough to count the "hundred and forty-four thousand" holy people (Revelation 14:1) who have gone before us in refreshment, light and peace, and who shine like stars "ad olam," for ever. More descendants in faith than Abraham could even attempt to count!

— *Adé Bethune*

Introduction

THIS book gathers uncomplicated and accurate information on the Christian calendar. It is intended for parents and teachers and catechists. Mary Ellen Hynes has accomplished a remarkable job of synthesis. With her audiences in mind, she has "winnowed" her diverse sources by deciding what to emphasize and what to ignore. Then she packaged this research into brief, spirited and (it's hoped) useful entries for households, schools and parishes.

You have in your hands a superb resource book. It includes the observances that are found on LTP's annual poster calendar called *The Year of Grace*. *Companion to the Calendar* answers all sorts of "who," "what" and "why" questions: Why is Lent 40 days long? What is the origin of April Fools' Day? Who was Kateri Tekakwitha? The language here is straightforward. Terms are defined. Entries are cross-referenced where appropriate. Like a dictionary, this book belongs close at hand.

But *Companion to the Calendar* can be more than a reference tool. As its title suggests, it can be a daily companion in the home and classroom. Entries can be read aloud before the evening meal or at the beginning of the school day. A few ribbons or paper clips can be used to keep your place in the sections of this book. It can be set on a stand and left open to the day or season.

This book is divided into five sections: "The Week," "The Seasons," "The Days," "Jewish Festivals" and "Muslim Festivals."

The Lord's Day receives first place on the Christian calendar and in this book as well, in the section called "The Week." Here also are reasons for Friday fasting and Sabbath rest.

"The Seasons" deals with Advent, Christmastime, Lent, the Paschal Triduum, Eastertime and the two spans of Ordinary Time, as well as the festival days and other observances that belong to these seasons. Here you will find the "movable feasts" — the days that depend on the date of Easter. The final days of Advent and the Christmastime feasts (such as Christmas Day and Epiphany) are here, too, although most of these have fixed calendar dates. The observances proper to each season are discussed in a seasonal context.

The section of the book called "The Days" includes everything with a fixed date in the year — the saints' days and national holidays (except, as mentioned, the special observances of Advent and Christmastime). Here you can find information about all saints' days and "fixed date" feasts of the Roman Catholic calendar for the United States of America. Obligatory Canadian observances also have been included.

The Roman calendar does not have remembrance days for the Jewish prophets and many other people whose stories are told in the Hebrew scriptures. The Byzantine calendar does, however, and so these have been added to this book. The old Roman martyrology (a list of "what happened on this day" in Christian and biblical times) notes a few people that the Byzantine calendar does not; their days have been included as well.

"The Days" includes information about the national holidays of the United States and Canada — for example, Labor Day, Thanksgiving Day and Mother's Day. For several modern-day peacemakers, such as Oscar Romero, there are brief biographical sketches on the anniversaries of their deaths (or of their births, if these are commonly observed). In this section are the dates of the equinoxes and solstices, as well as the year's best meteor showers.

A few days are here just for fun. Most of these are feast days of the church that have become folk festivals somewhere in the world. "The Three Freezing Saints" (May 11–13) are an example. Those days bring together the springtime anxiety of farmers and the memorials of martyrs.

Information about Jewish holidays and Muslim holidays is located in two separate sections. The dates of these festivals change from year to year, but they can be found on most desk calendars and on *The Year of Grace* calendar. (Note, however, that the English spelling of the names of these holidays can vary from publication to publication.)

Companion to the Calendar, like the calendar itself, is divided into separate days. Lacking, therefore, is "the big picture" — an overview of history or of the development of the Christian calendar. Some of the recommended resources (a list begins on page 203) can help counter this limitation.

To tell the story of a biblical saint, often scripture is retold. But the name of the book of the Bible containing the story is given first. It is usually a good idea to read the story directly from the Bible.

Putting facts about the saints into print is risky and difficult — for all sorts of reasons. One is that sometimes people's names get confused. For example, for centuries now the stories of Mary Magdalene have gotten mixed up with stories of other women in the gospels. The various men named James also have gotten confused with one another. *Companion to the Calendar* can be helpful in sorting out these identities.

Another difficulty is that names change from language to language. We know many of the apostles by an English version of a Latin version of a Greek version of an Aramaic name. Some people are known to us by several names. For example, on October 1 the church remembers "St. Thérèse of the Child Jesus," which is the name she took as a Carmelite nun. She was baptized Marie Françoise Martin. Many people know her as Thérèse of Lisieux (the city in France where her convent was located). Because of her writings, we also call her "The Little Flower."

If a saint's year of birth and death are known, they are given, but many dates are unknown, even for people whose lives are well documented. Estimated years are indicated by the prefix "c," meaning *circa,* which is Latin for "around." The term "BCE" (Before the Common Era) is used to date the prophets and saints of the Jewish scriptures.

In describing a season or in telling about a saint, sometimes a great deal of interesting information had to be left out. This process of simplification has the potential for lapsing into inaccuracy. For example, there are saints who held opinions or did things that were eccentric or even wicked. It's not difficult to find among the writings of the saints firm support for slavery, for persecution and for forced conversions, but such views have not been included here.

Saints are easy targets for criticism. They have their human weaknesses. They err. Sometimes they commit crimes. The title is not a badge of perfection. Often enough, and well enough too, sainthood is a reminder that Christ came to call not the righteous but sinners.

There's no denying that the sanctoral cycle is not fully representative of the human race. There are too few women, too many religious founders, too few married people. However, there is a wonderful mix of nationalities, and there is also another kind of marvelous blending: The calendar juxtaposes great figures from Christian history (Catherine of Siena, Martin of Tours) alongside prophets of social justice (Vincent de Paul, Frances Xavier Cabrini), sparked with near-legendary characters whose stories are rich with scriptural imagery (Lucy, George). The company of heaven will keep us amazed.

Any book filled with facts is bound to have errors. If you find a problem, please tell us. Because each entry had to be brief, often the task was to determine what *not* to write about. Maybe something was left out that you feel is too fascinating or important to omit. We can't change the church's roster of saints and feast days, but surely there are other peacemakers and prophets whose stories belong in this book. Please tell us. Drop us a note about how you use this book and how it can be made more useful.

— Peter Mazar

The Week

Some people think that the number seven became holy as a symbol of creation. In ancient times people knew that there were seven celestial bodies that seemed to move in the heavens. These were the sun, the moon, and the planets Mars, Mercury, Jupiter, Venus and Saturn. (Neptune, Uranus or Pluto were not able to be seen until the invention of the telescope.)

The Jewish people keep a seven-day week. Each day begins at sunset, not at midnight. The days of the week are called "first day," "second day," and so on. The seventh day alone has a special name. It is called the Sabbath, the day of rest.

According to the first chapter of the Book of Genesis, God created the world and all of its creatures in six days. On the seventh day — the Sabbath — God rested. According to God's law, which is set forth in the books of Exodus, Leviticus, Numbers and Deuteronomy, the people are commanded "to remember to keep holy the Sabbath day." The Sabbath begins at sundown on Friday night and ends at sundown on Saturday. It is the holiest day.

The Romans thought a seven-day week that included at least one day of rest was a good idea. They named the days after the sun, moon and planets. In the English language we still have "Sun's Day" and "Moon's Day," and "Saturn's Day." But the other days got named after Norse gods: Tiw's Day, Woden's Day, Thor's Day and Freya's Day.

The "Sun's Day," the first day of the week, is also called the Lord's Day, the weekly feast day for Christians. On Sundays we gather for the eucharist, which is a joyful banquet with the risen Lord and our sacrifice of praise offered to God.

Why is Sunday so joyful for us? On this day God began the work of creation. On this day Jesus was raised from the dead and the Holy Spirit was poured out upon the disciples. Sunday is the best day for baptism and eucharist. Sunday is our holiest day.

Some Christians call the Lord's Day "the eighth day of the week" — the day that leaps out from the other seven days. Sunday is the wonderful day that can give us a taste of heaven's own timelessness. It is a day to "play heaven."

Friday, the sixth day, is the day God created humans — completing creation. Friday is also the day on which Jesus died so that we might be brought back to the innocence of Eden. Christians are called to prepare for the Lord's Day by keeping Fridays with extra prayer, fasting and works of charity.

One reason it's customary to fast from eating meat on Fridays is to show respect for the animals, who also were created on the sixth day. By not eating meat, we give thanks to God, the creator of all living things. Each week the prayer, fasting and charity of Friday can become the "first course" of our Sunday feast.

The Seasons

Advent

Winter is a dangerous season for people who live in cold climates. Farm animals often are killed by the bad weather. In some places, roads get muddy and become rutted, making travel difficult. Cold weather lowers our resistance to infection. Before modern medicines were invented, most human deaths resulted from bacterial infections. In times past, some families would run out of food or fuel during winter. People had to work closely together to help each other survive.

The coming of winter can be a frightening time because the nights are growing longer. The prophet Isaiah (May 9) used the example of falling leaves to speak about our longing for God at this season. "We all fade like a leaf, and our wrongdoings, like the wind, take us away. For you have hidden your face from us."

Advent is a season to name our fears. We struggle with them. With God's help, we see beyond them. We can do none of this alone. Like people who help each other through the winter, we keep Advent together, as a church. That's the only way to make it through safely.

One of our helpmates during Advent is the Blessed Virgin Mary. During Advent we remember the expectation of Mary, when she waited for the birth of her child. Through the message of an angel, she heard God's word and kept it. She was filled with the Holy Spirit, and in her body the body of Christ came to be.

Waiting for the birth of a child is a lot like Advent. There is a strange mix of happiness and contentment, along with nervousness and fear. Advent is a season of waiting. Keeping Advent well is practice for all the other times in our lives when we must wait.

For what is the church waiting during Advent? The 25th chapter of the Book of Isaiah tells us one reason: We wait for the day when God will remove the veil that separates people and nations from one another. When that happens, we shall see things as they really are.

Another of our Advent companions is John the Baptist. He prepared the way for Jesus. He lived in the wilderness, and people were so fascinated with him that they went there to hear him speak. John said what they didn't want to hear: He told people what was wrong with them and what was wrong with the nation. Imagine John standing in a shopping mall during December. What might he say to us?

Like John's preaching, the message of Advent can be hard to take. But unless we face it, we are not ready for the coming of Christ.

The season of Advent begins on the fourth Sunday before Christmas. At Christmas we will welcome the coming of Christ. During Advent we do whatever is necessary to make ready for Christ's coming.

In preparation for Christmas we invite others to feast with us. We write cards to keep in touch. We clean house. We shop. We attend rehearsals. And every so often we take a break so we can remember why we're doing all this work. Whatever we do, we also do it for others.

Advertisers make the mistake of beginning the Christmas celebration too early. If we imitate them we can get overloaded. That takes the fun (and the point) out of both the preparations and the celebrations. Christmastime begins on December 25 and lasts for several weeks afterward. There will be plenty of time for parties and concerts and caroling and all the other joys of that season.

But for now, it is Advent. Advent has its own joys. Some people gather each evening for prayer.

They may light the candles of an Advent wreath or open the little doors of an Advent calendar. They might keep the saints' days in Advent as a way of preparing for Christmas. Many people get the Christmas tree and lights and other decorations repaired and ready so that on Christmas Eve all these wonderful things can be used to welcome the Savior.

In the quiet of Advent we make ready to hear angel songs. In the darkness we prepare to be dazzled by the star of Bethlehem.

The Third Sunday of Advent
Gaudete Sunday

Each Mass has its own "entrance antiphon." This is a sentence or two, most often from the scriptures. We can sing it at the beginning of Mass (although, in our country, we usually begin Mass by singing a hymn instead of the antiphon). Years ago, people gave a title to each Sunday's Mass. The title came from the first Latin word of the day's antiphon.

The entrance antiphon for the Third Sunday of Advent begins, "Rejoice in the Lord always." These words are from St. Paul's Letter to the Philippians. In Latin, "rejoice" is *gaudete* (gow-DAY-tay). So today is called Gaudete Sunday.

Why should we rejoice on this day in the middle of Advent? The antiphon tells us why: "Rejoice in the Lord always. Again I say, rejoice! The Lord is near."

The Wednesday, Friday and Saturday
after the Third Sunday of Advent
Winter Ember Days

All Wednesdays and Fridays of the year used to be fasting days. On these days people tried to pray more, give more to charity, and eat less. Many people still keep this custom.

Near the beginning of each of the four seasons, a Sunday was set aside for thanksgiving to God.

People gave thanks for whatever was being harvested from the land at that time of year. The Saturday night vigil before a "thanksgiving Sunday" was well attended, and people fasted and prayed in a special way on the Wednesday and Friday before the Sunday. These Wednesdays, Fridays and Saturdays came to be called "Ember Days." (The word "ember" means "season.")

The Wednesday, Friday and Saturday before the Fourth Sunday of Advent were the winter Ember Days. In lands around the Mediterranean Sea, olives are harvested at this time of year. So the winter Ember Days were days of thanksgiving for the olive harvest.

Olive oil was just about the only type of oil that people had. People illuminated their homes with oil lamps. They used olive oil to soothe cuts and bruises. Athletes used it to loosen up their muscles, and wealthy people mixed it with perfume to make themselves smell better. And, of course, people used olive oil in cooking, just as we do today. So these Ember Days at the beginning of winter were important in countries where olives grew.

It's interesting that the Jewish festival of Hanukkah (page 197), which comes at this time of year, also includes rejoicing in the olive harvest. Of course, each part of the world has its own seasons and its own harvests. In 1969, the bishops of each country were asked to move the Ember Days to times when these days would make the most sense in their part of the world.

The bishops of the United States have not yet set special dates for the Ember Days. Many people try to fast and pray and give extra charity on the three weekdays before Thanksgiving.

Christmas, too, is a harvest festival. That's why we bake and serve so many good, rich foods. Perhaps keeping the Twelve Days of Christmas is like saying a long grace after the meals that have fed us in the past year, and like saying a long grace before the meals that will feed us in the year to come. Extra prayer, fasting and giving of charity during Advent is a way to give thanks for — and to share — our daily bread.

The O Antiphons

The final week of Advent is here. If Advent is like the nighttime, these last days are like the hours before dawn. All nature is waiting for the sunrise. If Advent is like a woman's pregnancy, now the baby is kicking in her womb. Soon the child will be born.

The last week of Advent is a time of special prayer. The church sings the O Antiphons. These are beautiful chants that are sung at Evening Prayer. There is an antiphon for each night from December 17 to December 23. They are called O Antiphons because each one begins with the word "O."

The antiphons include many of the titles of Christ, such as "Lord," "lawgiver" and "sun of justice." The song "O come, O come, Emmanuel" is a version of the O Antiphons that many people know and love.

December 17

O Wisdom

> *O Wisdom, O holy Word of God,*
> *you govern all creation*
> *with your strong yet tender care.*
> *Come and show your people*
> *the way to salvation.*

According to a Jewish tradition, Lady Wisdom is the source of knowledge. She brings us peace and health. Wisdom was present with God since before time began. The whole of the universe was set in order by her.

Since then, the world, so beautifully ordered at creation, has become confused by sin. As a result of sin, we misunderstand each other. We fight. Our lives are unbalanced. Sickness brings sorrow to our world. Death takes us away.

But soon will come the day when Lady Wisdom will rule over us once again. Soon will come knowledge and healing and the resurrection of all who have died.

O come, O Wisdom from on high,
Who governs all things tenderly;
To us the path of knowledge show
And teach us in your ways to go.
   Rejoice, rejoice,
   Emmanuel shall come to you, O Israel.

December 18

O Adonai

> *O sacred Lord of ancient Israel,*
> *who showed yourself to Moses*
> *in the burning bush,*
> *who gave him your holy law on Sinai*
> *   mountain:*
> *Come, stretch out your mighty hand*
> *to set us free.*

On Mount Sinai, God spoke to Moses from a burning bush. Moses learned God's name. The name means, "I am who am." Out of respect, we do not say God's name. Instead we say "Adonai" (Ah-doe-NYE). This word means "Lord." To call God Adonai reminds us of God's mighty acts of love and protection.

We Christians call Jesus our Lord. When we say that Jesus Christ is Lord, we are saying that Jesus is God. Jesus will lead us to freedom and new life.

In the birth of Christ, God comes to us. God will not appear in power and might, like the roaring fire of the burning bush or the lightning and thunder on Mount Sinai.

This time, God will appear humble and weak. God will be born in our image that we might be reborn in God's image.

O come, O come, great Lord of might,
Who to your tribes on Sinai's height
In ancient times once gave the law
In cloud and majesty and awe.
   Rejoice, rejoice,
   Emmanuel shall come to you, O Israel.

December 19
O Flower of Jesse

O Flower of Jesse's stem,
you have been raised up as a sign for all peoples;
the powerful stand silent in your presence;
the nations bow down in worship before you.
Come, let nothing keep you
from coming to our aid.

Jesse was the father of King David. As the gospels of Matthew and Luke explain, Jesus was descended from David. So the title "flower of Jesse" praises Jesus as our monarch.

But Jesus is a different kind of monarch than any other before or since. Jesus is the royal ruler of all peoples. The holy nation he rules is just and peaceful. And all who are baptized will receive Jesus' crown.

Even the mighty of this world who do injustice on earth will understand that some day. So we have been promised. We eagerly wait for that day.

O come, O Flower of Jesse's root,
Before whom all the world stands mute.
We trust your mighty pow'r to save
And give us vict'ry o'er the grave.
    Rejoice, rejoice,
    Emmanuel shall come to you, O Israel.

December 20
O Key of David

O Key of David, O royal Power of Israel,
controlling at your will the gate of heaven:
Come, break down the prison walls of death
for those who dwell in darkness
and the shadow of death,
and lead your captive people into freedom.

During Advent we puzzle over the writings of the prophets. What sort of person will the Anointed One be? How is it that we stay locked up in prisons of selfishness, greed and fear? Why do the dead stay dead? Is this the way it will be for ever?

But the day is coming when the mysteries will be unlocked. The Lord Jesus Christ, the Key of David, will open the gate of heaven. Christ will call each of the dead by name, "Arise, my love, my lovely one, and come away."

O come, O Key of David, come
And open wide our heav'nly home.
Make safe the way that leads on high,
And close the path to misery.
    Rejoice, rejoice,
    Emmanuel shall come to you, O Israel.

December 21
O Dawn

O Radiant Dawn,
splendor of eternal light, sun of justice:
Come, shine on those who dwell in darkness
and the shadow of death.

Thank God for the darkness of winter, for through it we can know that Christ is our sun. Soon the light will return to the earth. Days will grow longer and winter will pass over into spring.

O come, O Dayspring, come with cheer;
O Sun of justice, now draw near.
Disperse the gloomy clouds of night,
And death's dark shadow put to flight.
    Rejoice, rejoice,
    Emmanuel shall come to you, O Israel.

December 22
O King

O King of all the nations,
the only joy of every human heart;
O keystone of the mighty arch of humankind:
Come and save the creature
you fashioned from the dust.

There is a splendid image in today's O Antiphon. Human beings are imagined to be blocks in an arch. If you take just one block out of an arch, the whole thing crumbles. Every block is necessary.

That makes building an arch difficult. Until the final, topmost stone is put in place, an arch is unstable. This final block is called the keystone.

The prophets promised that the ruler of the Jews would be honored by all peoples. Divisions between nations would end. Everyone would gather as friends in Jerusalem to keep an endless festival. Everyone would lean on each other and depend on one another, kept secure by God, the keystone.

O come, O Keystone, come and bind
In one the hearts of humankind.
Come bid our sad divisions cease,
And be for us the king of peace.
   Rejoice, rejoice,
   Emmanuel shall come to you, O Israel.

December 23
O Emmanuel

O Emmanuel, king and lawgiver,
desire of the nations, Savior of all people:
Come and set us free, Lord our God.

"Emmanuel" means God with us, God right in our midst! God's Son is our Emmanuel. God's Son comes to save us so that we can live with God forever.

Emmanuel is our lawgiver, who comes to bring justice and freedom. Everything will be set right not only for ourselves and our families and our nation, but for all the nations of the world.

And so we pray with the prophet Isaiah: "Let justice descend, O heavens, like dew from above. Like gentle rain let the skies drop it down. Let the earth open and salvation bud forth."

O come, O come, Emmanuel,
And ransom captive Israel
That mourns in lonely exile here
Until the Son of God appear.
   Rejoice, rejoice,
   Emmanuel shall come to you, O Israel.

December 24
After sundown
Christmas Vigil

On Christmas Eve the church sings, "Today you will know the Lord is coming, and in the morning you will see God's glory." Tonight is a time of wonder and promise and great blessedness. We hover between Advent and Christmas, between expectation and fulfillment.

For centuries, the day before Christmas was a fast day. People would wait until nightfall to break the fast. It was also a day of abstinence. Meat was not eaten out of respect for the animals, who were the first to see their newborn Lord lying in their own manger. Many families do not eat meat tonight, but serve fish and other seafood. A feast of fish reminds us that the Messiah will slaughter the great scaly sea beast, Leviathan, who is death itself. Then everyone will be invited to sit down to supper together. Imagine that! Heaven will be like a fish fry.

The customs of this night may look a bit different in each country, but they are often more alike than unlike. In many households a loaf of bread is broken and dipped in honey and then shared with kisses and wishes for a sweet Christmas. Sometimes this bread looks like the unleavened bread of communion. Sometimes it is rich and yeasty and filled with fruit. And sometimes it isn't bread at all but a porridge of grains and sweet berries. We are reminded in this ritual that Bethlehem means "the house of bread." The newborn Christ is placed in a manger, a feed trough, to be our bread of life.

On this night we are welcomed back to paradise. The angel who barred our way to the garden puts aside the flaming sword. The angel throws open the gates of Eden and leads us back to the tree. Then creation joins with all the company of heaven to sing glory to God.

In Finland, paradise is represented by a canopy of straw and stars set over the dining table. In Italy the *ceppo*, the nativity scene, is shaped like a candle-lit tower hung with fruits and flowers and filled with gifts. The custom of the Christmas tree began in villages in Austria and Germany, but about a century ago it spread among Christians in many lands.

The strongest and most ancient tradition of the tree is that it is lit for the first time tonight. We make a great burst of light to welcome the Lord. Then Advent is over and our Christmas festival is here at last.

From Christmas Eve
until the feast
of the Baptism of the Lord

Christmas Season

In the Northern Hemisphere, during the last week of December and the first weeks of January, the days ever-so-slowly begin to lengthen. That is when the church keeps Christmas.

In these merry days we Christians welcome our Lord, who comes as a tiny child, in mercy and gentleness and compassion. But make no mistake. This newborn is our God and Lord, our savior and our judge. And so we sing out loud, "Joy to the world, the Lord is come!" In the words of Psalm 96, "O sing to the Lord a new song! Sing to the Lord, all the earth! Then shall all the trees of the forest sing for joy before the Lord, who comes to judge the world with justice, who comes to judge the people with truth."

To announce God's epiphany — the glorious appearing of heaven on earth — we give gifts and greetings. We drive away the winter with lights and flowers. We gather around the shining tree of life, and we open our homes to every guest.

But the keeping of Christmas is not easy. On the day after December 25, the *after*-Christmas sales begin, as if Christmas were over. But it's not over. It's just begun! We Christians have to rely on our own resources when it comes to keeping our festivals.

And we have so many days to keep! There's the feast of Stephen, when "Good King Wenceslas looked out." There's St. John's Day, when people toast each other's good health. There's the feast of the Holy Innocents, the sad day of the season.

Christmastime includes the New Year celebration, when we ring out troubles and ring in blessings. Then there's Epiphany, the merriest day of our merry Christmastime, when we follow a star to our heart's desire.

The Christmas season ends on the feast of the Baptism of the Lord. Usually that falls on the second Sunday in January. But the season echoes again on February 2, Candlemas, when we praise Christ, the light of the world. Think how much we'd miss if we ended Christmas on December 25.

Advent and Christmastime — the preparation and the celebration — bring us from the old year to a new. The Christian year is not a circle, leading nowhere. Rather, our years form a twisted spiral, like the ladder of angels in Jacob's dream. The ladder of the year leads us out of time, ever upward into God's bright eternity.

December 25
Solemnity of

The Birth of the Lord: Christmas

> Christ the Lord is born today;
> today the Savior has appeared.
> Earth echoes songs of angel choirs
> and archangels' joyful praise.
> Today on earth Christ's friends exult:
> Glory to God in the highest, alleluia.

St. Augustine (August 28) said that "God became human so that humans might become God." What an amazing thing to say! At Christmas the church sings about the "marvelous exchange": We share in Christ because Christ shares in us.

This "exchange" keeps happening. God became human so that humans might become God — right now. Today. Sometimes people say that Christmas is Jesus' birthday. But the church doesn't call Christmas a birthday. Christmas is "the Birth of the Lord." So when we sing, "Christ is born today," we really mean what we sing. Today. Imagine that.

St. Leo (November 10) puzzled over the mystery of "today." He said that the body of Christ is our body. It is the church's body. If on this day we sing that Christ is born, it is our own new birth in baptism that we sing about. All of us, the living and the dead, are born in Christ.

The third chapter of the First Letter of John speaks of this mystery:

> You may be sure that everyone who does right has been born of Christ. See what love the Father has given us, that we should be called children of God. And that is what we are.

There are four Masses in celebration of the Birth of the Lord: one for the vigil, one for the night, one for dawn and one for daytime. Beginning with sunset on Christmas Eve, we make holy the four corners of the day — sundown, midnight, sunrise and noonday.

Christmas comes at the time of year that daytime stops growing shorter and begins, slowly at first, to grow longer. The Northern Hemisphere takes its first step back to spring. That is why so many of the signs of Christmas are full of life. In the dead of winter we celebrate with greens and bright flowers and shining lights.

The word Christmas means "the feast of Christ." That's a good name for December 25 and for the season that begins this day. The fullness of Christ is celebrated. At Christmas we remember the birth of Jesus in Bethlehem. We rejoice that we are born in Christ and that Christ is born in us. And we look forward to the day when we shall see Christ face to face.

> For lo! The days are hast'ning on,
>   by prophets seen of old,
> When with the ever-circling years
>   shall come the time foretold,
> When peace shall over all the earth
>   its ancient splendors fling,
> And all the world give back the song
>   which now the angels sing.

December 26 – January 6
The Twelve Days of Christmas

> When Christmas's tide
>   comes in like a bride
> With holly and ivy clad,
> Twelve Days in the year
>   much mirth and good cheer
> In every household is had.

Christmas is not a day but a season! It lasts from Christmas Day until the feast of the Baptism of the Lord.

In the year 567 the church council of Tours called the 13 days between December 25 and January 6 a festival season. Up until that time the only other joyful church season was the 50 days between Easter Sunday and Pentecost.

Almost everyone knows the carol "The Twelve Days of Christmas." In England they begin counting the 12 days on December 26, making January 6 the 12th day. The stroke of midnight on New Year's Eve is the center point. In most of Europe they begin counting the 12 days on December 25. That makes January 6 the 13th day. Either way, we have a "baker's dozen" of days for announcing the good news of the birth of Christ.

A Ukrainian carol speaks of "the three feasts of guests," Christmas Day, New Year's Day and Epiphany. These solemnities are the high points of the holy Twelve Days.

Christmastime is meant for hospitality, gift-giving, caroling and storytelling. We set this time aside to relax and be merry after weeks of preparation. We do only the work that is absolutely needed so that we can enjoy these festival days with our families and friends, and so that we can make sure that everyone is able to take part.

Some families make it their custom during this time to cluster around the Christmas crib for prayers each evening. The Christmas tree is lighted each night while folks pray and sing carols. On Christmas Day the figures of the Magi are placed far away from the crib, then moved a little closer every day until Epiphany, when they arrive in

Bethlehem. The Christmas story can be told and retold in plays and pageants.

An old proverb says that "a guest in the home is Christ in the home." Maybe the most important Christmas customs are to invite guests and to be a guest.

The Sunday within the Octave of Christmas
Feast of
The Holy Family

From Christmas Day to New Year's Day is the Christmas octave. Octaves are eight-day weeks. Of course, an ordinary week is seven days. It's what we expect. But eight days? That's something strange and wonderful.

In Christian symbolism, eight days represent eternity. Maybe that's because an eight-day period begins and ends on the same day of the week. (Christmas and New Year's always fall on the same day of the week.) Christmastime is a season to live with one foot in eternity.

Christmastime is filled with feast days. The first Sunday of the season is the feast of the Holy Family. (Unless, of course, Christmas Day is itself a Sunday. Then the feast is kept on December 30.)

Holy Family Day is a favorite time for family reunions. Students are home from school and many people have extra days off from work. Like every day of Christmastime, it's an occasion for feasting and caroling and relaxing. Some people say that the nicest part about Christmastime weekends is that there's finally some time to sit back and enjoy the decorations and music and good company.

January 1
The Octave of Christmas

Solemnity of
Mary, Mother of God

(See also New Year's Day, January 1, page 27.)

Some people think that Christmas is one holiday and New Year's is another holiday, but the church keeps the first of January as one of the days of Christmastime. The rejoicing of December 25 belongs to January 1 as well.

The gospel for Mass today is short. But it gives us several reasons to rejoice. And it also gives us the reasons for the many different titles that the first of January has had over the years.

The gospel, from the second chapter of Luke, is a continuation of the story we began at Midnight Mass on Christmas. Today we hear that the shepherds did what the angels told them to do. They found Mary and Joseph and the newborn Jesus. Then they went to tell their neighbors that a savior was born.

Mary treasured what was said about her child. In joy, the shepherds sang the angels' song of glory in heaven and peace on earth. Eight days after his birth, Jesus was circumcised and received his name, which means "savior."

Today is the World Day of Prayer for Peace. For some churches, today is the feast of the Holy Name of Jesus or the feast of the Circumcision. For Roman Catholics, today is the solemnity of Mary, the Mother of God. This solemnity is over 1500 years old on the church's calendar. We celebrate today the fulfillment of the promise made to Mary by the angel Gabriel. God's child is now her child. Mary is the mother of God.

In the U. S. A. and Canada,
the Sunday after January 1
Solemnity of
The Epiphany of the Lord

(See also the Twelfth Day of Christmas, page 10.)

It's hard to talk about Epiphany without sounding like we're exaggerating. Today is a day of superlatives. Epiphany is the grandest, merriest, brightest and best day of Christmastime.

Today we celebrate three wonders: The Magi offer the Lord gifts of gold, frankincense and myrrh. The Lord comes to the Jordan River to be baptized by John. The Lord turns water into wine at the wedding feast in Cana.

Epiphany means "appearance" and "revelation" and "manifestation." In the gospel stories of Epiphany, we hear that God appears in creation. God is revealed in a star, in the waters of a river, in the shining skies, on the wings of a dove, in stone jars of everyday water.

In many families, a famous Epiphany tradition is to have a party in honor of the visit of the Magi. A special cake — in which a bean or coin has been hidden — is served. The lucky person who finds the bean or coin in her or his slice of cake is crowned queen or king for the evening! This person leads everyone in the dancing and procession that tops off the fun.

The monarch has two major responsibilities. One is to host the Carnival party before Lent begins. The other is to lead the blessing of the home for the new year. The numerals of the year are written with chalk over the front door. The initials of the legendary names of the Magi are added — Caspar, Melchior and Balthasar. The home is dedicated to hospitality.

In a sense, at Epiphany all of us are queens and kings. In baptism we were anointed to be God's royal people. Now the star shines over us, we who are baptized, we who bear the name of Christ.

January 6
The Twelfth Day of Christmas

January 6 is the ancient day of Epiphany. Among Roman Catholics in the United States and Canada, Epiphany is now kept on the first Sunday after January 1. In Europe and Latin America and in many of the Christian churches of North America, Epiphany is celebrated on its ancient day.

Many Christians have special traditions for Twelfth Night. In some countries, children receive gifts on this day to remind them of the gifts given to Jesus by the Magi. In Puerto Rico on the eve of January 6 (which they call "Three Kings Day"), children fill their shoes with hay for the camels and horses (and in some places, even elephants) of the Magi. The next day the hay is gone and the children find the shoes filled with candy and toys.

In Italy a fairy godmother named Befana leaves people surprises. (Her name comes from the word Epiphany.) A cranky fellow named Rodolfo joins her, threatening to punish people who need to mend their ways. Befana had wanted to join the Magi in their search for the newborn Christ, but she lost courage at the last minute. So now she goes house to house in search of Christ. She sees Christ in everyone she meets, and she teaches us to do the same.

From Epiphany to Shrove Tuesday
Carnival

Carnival marks the time between winter and spring, and between two liturgical seasons, Christmastime and Lent. The last day of Carnival is Mardi Gras or Shrove Tuesday (page 12), which is the day before Ash Wednesday, when Lent begins. The name Carnival comes from the Latin words for "farewell to the flesh," or perhaps it can be translated "putting meat aside." People do whatever they can to make ready for Lent's fasting.

In winter the weather can be miserable for long stretches of time. Perhaps that encourages people to cultivate their "inner world," the world of fantasy and imagination. Carnival is a season for music, plays, art, and also for wild behavior and for wearing disguises. People try to get the wildness out of their systems before the serious and reflective season of Lent starts.

Carnival festivals have become major tourist attractions in many cities of the world. Italy begins its *Carnevale* as soon as Christmastime is over. In many places the dusty Christmas decorations get left up and then get smothered with Carnival decorations. In the city of Rio de Janeiro, in Brazil, street dancers move to the rhythm of drums under showers of confetti. German cities such as Mainz, Cologne and Dusseldorf hold *Karneval* parades with elaborate floats. In Munich masqueraders dance with decorated hoops. In cities along the Gulf Coast of the United States, Carnival is an old tradition.

The masks and costumes worn during Carnival have a special meaning for Christians. During Lent, when we let go of little comforts, we find that our masks are stripped away. Perhaps when we fast we discover grumpiness just under the surface. Or we find that something in us doesn't really want to give to the poor. These discoveries about ourselves are the way we begin in some small measure to know that we need a Savior.

But for now we revel in hiding from our true selves for a while longer. There are discoveries to be made even while wearing a mask.

The Sunday after Epiphany
(or, if Epiphany is kept on January 7 or 8,
the Monday after Epiphany)
Feast of
The Baptism of the Lord

When Advent began we heard the words of Isaiah: "O that you would tear open the heavens and come down!" Today God answers this prayer. Jesus goes into the Jordan River to be baptized by John. Suddenly the skies open. God's Spirit comes down in the form of a dove. Then God speaks for everyone to hear: "This is my beloved."

In the fifth century, Bishop Maximus of Turin wrote that we have every reason to celebrate this day with the joy of Christmas: "At Jesus' birth his mother Mary held her child close to her heart. So today the Father holds his beloved Son for all people to adore. Jesus is baptized so all Christians may follow him with confidence."

In Hebrew the name of Jesus is Joshua. This name means Savior. A thousand years before the time of Jesus, in the days of the Exodus, after Moses died a man named Joshua (September 1) became the leader of the Hebrew people. Joshua led the people through the Jordan River and into the Promised Land.

Our Savior Jesus is a new Joshua. Jesus leads us into the Jordan of baptism. We pass through the water to enter a new life. Sweetened dairy foods such as cheesecake and eggnog are customary during Christmastime in honor of our Savior, who leads us into "a land flowing with milk and honey."

From the day after the feast
of the Baptism of the Lord
until the day before Ash Wednesday
Ordinary Time

There are five church seasons: Advent, Christmastime, Lent, the Paschal Triduum (a three-day season), and Eastertime. There are two blocks of Ordinary Time. First, in winter come the weeks between Christmastime and Lent. Then, in summer and fall come the weeks between Eastertime and Advent. That's over half the year! On most days in Ordinary Time, green vestments are worn.

Ordinary Time isn't a season, just a way to describe the weeks between seasons. The word "ordinary" means regular, plain, run-of-the-mill. It also has another meaning. It means "counted." "Ordinal" numbers are first, second, third, fourth and so on.

We count each week. There's the first week in Ordinary Time, which begins right after the feast of the Baptism of the Lord. The 34th week of Ordinary Time comes right before Advent begins. We count the Sundays, too. The Sunday after the Baptism of the Lord is called the "Second Sunday in Ordinary Time" because it begins the second week in Ordinary Time. We do all this counting to keep track of the weeks so we know which scriptures to read when we assemble for the liturgy.

Each year at Sunday Mass during Ordinary Time we read bit by bit through one of the gospels. One year we read through the Gospel of Matthew. The next year we read Mark's gospel. The next year Luke's gospel is read; then we read through Matthew's gospel again.

The church's biggest feast during these winter weeks of Ordinary Time is the Presentation of the Lord, on February 2. Like Carnival, the Presentation is a turning point. We look back to Christmastime. We look forward to Lent and Easter.

Mardi Gras/Shrove Tuesday

The last day before Lent is a weird mix of happiness and sadness. We say goodbye to the joys of winter. We look forward to the coming of Easter. Perhaps the people who keep this day the most wildly are the ones who intend to keep Lent the most seriously.

In England, today is Shrove Tuesday, and another word for Carnival (the festive time before Lent) is "Shrovetide." "Shrive" is an old word for having your sins forgiven. People would get ready for Lent by celebrating the sacrament of reconciliation and by asking forgiveness of one another. Then they would keep the disciplines of Lent as their penance. Lenten penance is a sign of sorrow for injustices and an act of thanksgiving for pardon.

That was the serious business of Shrovetide. Another task during Carnival was the eating up of Lent's forbidden foods.

For over a thousand years, most Christians kept Lent by not eating animal products. It's unusual that a custom would be kept by Christians in both the East and West, but that's how important this tradition was. It probably began out of necessity. The coming warm weather would spoil foods in storage. Also, late winter and early spring are the animals' birthing season. By not eating animal products at this time of year, people helped a new generation get off to a healthy start.

Christians thought that by not eating animal products during Lent, they could better resemble Noah and his family aboard the ark. They could help prepare the world for a new creation.

At Carnival all meat, butter, cheese and eggs got used up in a final feast before the lenten fast. Making pancakes and doughnuts uses up a lot of these ingredients. Russians call the days before Lent "Butter Week." In some countries, the last day before Lent is called Doughnut Day or Pancake Day. The Irish call it "Ash Eve." The French call it Mardi Gras, which means Fat Tuesday.

In Venice, at midnight on Ash Wednesday Eve, a straw figure named Carnevale, whose body has been stuffed with fireworks, is burned in a fire in St. Mark's Plaza. In some places last year's Palm Sunday branches are burned with an effigy of old man winter, and so Lent's ashes get made at the same time that winter burns up.

From Ash Wednesday
until sundown on Holy Thursday

Lent

Lent is the 40-day season of preparation for the Paschal Triduum. The 40 days are counted from the First Sunday of Lent until Holy Thursday. (Lent ends on Holy Thursday.) The four days between Ash Wednesday and the First Sunday are an introduction to the season. The readings at Mass on these days were chosen to teach us about the three lenten disciplines of prayer, fasting and almsgiving.

Why 40 days? The number 40 calls to mind the 40 days of rain during Noah's flood, when evil drowned and the earth was washed clean. It also calls to mind the 40 years the Hebrew people traveled through the desert to the promised land. We fast for 40 days because Moses and Elijah and Jesus fasted 40 days in the wilderness to prepare them for their work.

The days of Lent are often compared to a journey. That means that at the end of Lent we expect to find ourselves somewhere different than where we started. That's why the stories of the journey of father Abraham (see October 9) and mother Sarah (see August 19) and other scriptures about journeys are an important part of Lent. On the final Sunday of Lent we will come to our destination. We will enter Jerusalem, the holy city.

The word "Lent" comes from the same root as the word "lengthen." It's an old word for springtime, when daytime lengthens rapidly. Together with the Paschal Triduum (page 16) and Eastertime (page 19), Lent is the church's spring.

Two groups of Christians are particularly important during Lent. First, there are the catechumens who have been chosen to be baptized this coming Easter. During Lent they make their final preparations. Second, there are baptized people who are in some way returning to the church. During Lent we try to join in praying for these people and for all of us.

Every Lent we come back to our baptism. We struggle with the hard questions we were asked: Do you reject Satan? Do you believe in God? Do you believe in the church? We stand alongside the people who are soon to be baptized. With them we look into that frightening water. In the sixth chapter of the Letter to the Romans, St. Paul tells us that we die in the water of baptism! We die in the hope that we will be raised with Christ.

At baptism, Christians take on three lifelong disciplines. These are prayer, fasting and almsgiving. They help us remain faithful to our baptismal promises. Each of these disciplines can take many forms. Prayer is communication with God. Fasting is self-denial, self-control, simple living. Almsgiving is giving to those in need. We share our goods, our money, our talents and time.

These three disciplines function best when they are done together. They balance each other. The word itself, "discipline," reminds us that we are "disciples" of Christ. Another word for prayer, fasting and almsgiving is "exercise." Exercise does little good unless it's done according to a schedule that we stick to. If we make excuses not to exercise, if we cheat on the program, then we won't get results.

The same can be said for prayer, fasting and almsgiving. Lent is the season to renew good ways to practice these three kinds of activity. Most Christians find that, in time, these three exercises transform their way of life.

This is the season to give the earth and ourselves a spring cleaning. This is the season to turn away from our wanderings and to travel home to God.

The seventh Wednesday before Easter
Ash Wednesday

The Forty Days of Lent begin on the Sunday after Ash Wednesday. The 40th and final day will be Holy Thursday.

Today is the beginning of the lenten fast. A good beginning is important. On Ash Wednesday and the three days afterward the scripture readings focus on prayer, fasting and almsgiving (the giving of charity). In Ash Wednesday's gospel (from the sixth chapter of St. Matthew), Jesus offers advice about the disciplines. Notice that Jesus doesn't say "*if* you fast." Jesus says "*when* you fast."

Many Christians struggle with Jesus' commandment to pray, fast and give alms. People want to know how. What are the traditions? How can these be adapted to the ways we live now? There is no one right way to keep Lent. St. Catherine of Siena (April 29) said that those who practice self-denial "are happier to see people walking in many different ways than to see just one way."

Lenten fasting usually means eating and drinking less than usual. During Lent many people eat just one full meal a day. Fasting also includes abstinence. That means not eating certain kinds of food, such as meat. The traditional lenten diet is mostly grains, legumes and vegetables. This is good, healthy eating.

Lenten fasting also means less entertainment, less music, less nonsense. We try to do things consciously, deliberately. People with health problems usually do not fast. Young people are gradually initiated into lenten fasting, depending on their age and ability.

The Book of Tobit says, "Prayer with fasting is good. But better than both is almsgiving with justice. Giving a little to the poor with justice is better than giving a lot with injustice." Justice is a goal of the Christian disciplines. We forget ourselves. We live for others. Eventually, living simply and justly and kindly becomes our way of life.

In the language of the church, this is called "mortification," which means "death to self." Mortification is one reason ashes are put on our foreheads at the beginning of the lenten fast. Ashes are what's left over after something burns up. For Ash Wednesday the church burns up the palms and branches left from last Palm Sunday. When Lent is nearly over we will have fresh green palms again, and the cycle will be complete.

Smearing ashes on our foreheads in the form of a cross is an odd thing to do. It makes us stick out. It makes us dirty. It mars our appearance. Ashes represent death. In the past, people put ashes on their faces when someone near to them died. It was a way to remind those around them to treat them with understanding. For a while at least they would be overwhelmed with death.

Ash Wednesday is a kind of slap in the face to bring us to our senses. "Remember, human, you are dust and to dust you will return." That's what God said to Adam and Eve when they were banished from paradise. We hear these words today.

However, the words "you are dust" don't reveal the whole truth about human beings. The cross on our foreheads tells us that there is more to be said. But today these words are enough, or even more than enough. They send us off on our lenten journey, perhaps a bit scared, but in search of compassion and hope and a better idea of the truth.

Often celebrated on the First Sunday of Lent
The rite of election

All year long there are adults and children in the parish who are getting ready for baptism. These people are called catechumens. This is a Greek word that means "someone who is taught by word of mouth." Catechumens are taught to become Christians. They are learning a way of life. That takes time and experimentation and questioning. Sometimes in the process it's two steps forward and one step back.

Each year, usually, some of the catechumens are ready for baptism at Easter. This process of determining who is ready is called "election." The catechumens who will be baptized this coming Easter are called "the elect." "Elect" means "chosen."

The elect are chosen by the bishop. Usually on the First Sunday of Lent the catechumens go to the cathedral along with their godparents and teachers and other members of the parish. These people give witness to the bishop that the chosen catechumens are worthy and ready to be baptized. The bishop says to the catechumens, "I now declare you to be members of the elect, to be initiated into the sacred mysteries at the next Easter Vigil."

Baptism, confirmation and eucharist are the "sacred mysteries" that the bishop spoke about. These are the Easter sacraments. The elect keep Lent as the final preparation before these sacraments. The members of the parish pray for them. They fast with them. And they celebrate the three scrutiny rites with them (page 15).

Catechumens and the elect bring the parish a tremendous gift. They remind the already baptized what a great responsibility it is to be a Christian. They work hard to prepare for their initiation into the mysteries of the church. When we see the eagerness of the soon-to-be-baptized, how can any of us take the Easter sacraments for granted?

The Wednesday, Friday and Saturday
after the First Sunday of Lent
Spring Ember Days

Lent comes when the winter food supplies are at their lowest. In many places, fasting during Lent used to be a matter of life or death. People fasted to make the food supply hold out longer. If everyone fasted together, the community had a better chance of surviving.

On the old Roman Catholic calendar, the springtime Ember Days fell during the first full week of Lent. The spring Ember Days were a fast within a fast.

The word "ember" means "season." There were four sets of Ember Days, one set for each season. During these days people fasted in thanksgiving for whatever was being harvested at that time of year. In 1969 the church's calendar was reformed. Now the Ember Days are supposed to be scheduled by the bishops of each country to match the actual times of harvests and other occasions for prayer.

In Mediterranean lands, where the Ember Days originated, salad greens are plentiful in early springtime, but were once unavailable for much of the rest of the year. Because these foods can now be obtained year round, it's hard to imagine how welcome they were in springtime. They have become part of the celebrations of the season.

For example, the first food eaten during the Jewish Passover meal is a sprig of fresh green parsley or lettuce. Many Italian Christian families consider Easter incomplete without *mâché,* also called lamb's lettuce. Northern European Christians gather the shoots of nettles and scallions. Springtime salad greens may be many people's first dose of Vitamin C since the fall.

Bishop John Chrysostom (September 13) called fasting a "medicine" for the church. Real fasting can make us healthier. We get back to basics. We lay off junk foods. When we fast, the limited foods we allow ourselves need to count for something. Like salad greens, lenten foods can be low fat, low salt, high fiber, rich in vitamins, simple and good. And for that we give thanks.

Often celebrated on the Third, Fourth and Fifth Sundays of Lent

The scrutiny rites

The word scrutiny means "search." The lenten scrutinies are rites of searching. They are meant to heal all that is weak or sinful in the hearts of the people chosen for baptism at Easter. These chosen people are called "the elect."

The scrutiny rites usually take place on the Third, Fourth and Fifth Sundays of Lent. When the scrutiny rites are celebrated, on the Third Sunday of Lent we hear about the Samaritan women who met and spoke with Jesus at a well. On the Fourth Sunday we hear about the cure of a man who was born blind. On the Fifth Sunday we hear about the raising of Lazarus from the dead. These stories are from the Gospel of John. Each story is about a "passover" — from dishonesty to truth, from blindness to sight, from death to life.

During a scrutiny rite, the elect step forward with their godparents. They bow their heads or kneel. Everyone in church prays for them. People ask God to give the elect a "sense of sin." That's a powerful gift — to know what sin is like, to understand the difference between good and evil.

The church prays that the elect will be free from Satan's power. This prayer is called an exorcism. The church knows too well that evil has power. But we know also that Christ can free us from this power.

The Fourth Sunday of Lent

Laetare Sunday

Each Mass has an entrance antiphon. This is a sentence or two most often from the scriptures that can be sung at the beginning of Mass. In times past, people gave a title to each Sunday's Mass from the first word (in Latin) of the day's antiphon.

The antiphon for the Fourth Sunday of Lent is from the 66th chapter of the Book of Isaiah. It begins, "Rejoice, Jerusalem! Come together, you who love her." In Latin, one of the words used for "rejoice" is *laetare.* So today is named Laetare Sunday.

In biblical poetry, the city of Jerusalem is called our mother. Perhaps this means that Jerusalem is the source of our life. Christian poets have said that on earth we feel homesick for heaven, for the new Jerusalem. Deep down, we want to go home.

In a wonderful and mysterious way, the Easter celebration is a homecoming. It is a march into heaven. Maybe that's why there are so many processions in the liturgies of these days. Today, on the Fourth Sunday of Lent, we are halfway to Easter.

The Sixth Sunday of Lent
(The Sunday before Easter)

Palm Sunday of the Passion of the Lord

Because there are four gospels, there are four accounts of the passion of the Lord. John's account is proclaimed every year on Good Friday. Today, the final Sunday of Lent, we hear one of the other three accounts. The vestments this day are red, just as they are on Good Friday.

Most people call today Palm Sunday. It is a day for marching in processions. The gospels tell us that the people waved branches to welcome Jesus into Jerusalem. So today we too wave branches. The 40 days of Lent have been a time to travel in spirit to the holy city of Jerusalem. Today we enter the city.

Any kind of branch can be used in the processions today. Olive branches are traditional because, ever since Noah's flood, they have been symbols of peace and forgiveness. In cooler climates, forsythia bushes, which are related to olives, come into bloom during this season. In most churches, palm branches are blessed and waved today. The Gospel of John mentions them specifically.

In the Middle East, date palm trees grow in the incredible heat. In fact, they need several months of very high temperatures (100 degrees or more) to produce their sweet fruit. In warm climates people plant palms in cemeteries as a sign that life is stronger than death. For the same reason, people in northern countries plant pussy willows and evergreens. Then they cut branches from these plants for the Palm Sunday procession.

In our country, most churches buy palms from florists. But there are places where people gather their own home-grown branches to bring to church. No matter where the palms and branches come from, they are all signs of life and resurrection. This Sunday is the last Sunday before the Paschal Triduum, our Passover festival. The branches help us to welcome the Passover.

From sundown on Holy Thursday until sundown on Easter Sunday

The Paschal Triduum

We Christians are a people of sacramental signs. We search for signs of Christ in everything around us. In doing this, we take our cue from the gospels. Jesus said that he can be found in the hungry, the thirsty, the stranger, the sick. Even the stars in the sky can lead us to find the Lord.

We can learn to see in all the seasons — in winter rest or the autumn harvest, in a snowstorm's fury or a rain shower's gentleness — signs of what the reign of God must be like. If we keep our eyes open to wonder, the turning of the year is filled with parables.

Once each year, at Easter, it seems as if all the signs point in the same direction: Easter is the first Sunday after the first full moon after the spring equinox. Why is this astounding day so important to us?

When the spring equinox comes, daytime grows longer than night. Springtime begins. When the moon is full, it rises in the east at the same time the sun sets in the west. So there is never a moment when either the sun or the full moon isn't shining in the heavens.

Friday, Saturday and Sunday, too, are important signs for us. Friday is the sixth day of the week, when God made the first human beings. Saturday is the Sabbath, when God rested. On Sunday the week begins once again. It is the day God said, "Let there be light."

Friday is the day of Jesus' death. On the Sabbath Jesus rested in the tomb. On Sunday God raised Jesus from the dead. That is why we call Sunday the Lord's Day.

Every year, on the Sunday after the first full moon of spring, we Christians keep the Lord's Day with all our might. In English we name this Sunday "Easter," from an ancient word for the first light of dawn. In most other languages, the word for Easter is based on the Hebrew word for Passover, *Pesach* (page 199). That's where we get the English word "paschal."

On the Friday and Saturday before Easter Sunday we fast, rest and keep watch. We put aside meals, entertainment, our jobs, schooling and hobbies. We do what we can to come together with others in prayer. Then, in the night between Holy Saturday and Easter Sunday, our fasting ends and the feast begins.

This is the best time of the year for baptism. Like the rising sun or the full moon, like the coming of spring, baptism is a sign of our Passover. For us, baptism is a new creation rising from chaos. It is an escape from slavery through the sea. It is death and burial and resurrection in Christ.

The fast and the feast together—Good Friday, Holy Saturday and Easter Sunday—are called the Paschal Triduum, which means "the Three Days of Passover."

These three days are begun and ended not from midnight to midnight but from sunset to sunset, in the Jewish manner of reckoning days. That way these three days match more closely the days of creation. The Triduum is the year's heart—the three days of the death, burial and resurrection of Christ. It is the Passover of the Lord.

Holy Thursday

Holy Thursday until sundown is the final day of Lent, the 40th day of the 40 days. But at sundown Lent ends and the Paschal Triduum begins.

This morning, the people of the diocese gather around the bishop for the Chrism Mass. (In some dioceses, the Mass takes place earlier in Lent.) The oil of the sick and the oil of catechumens are blessed and the sacred chrism is consecrated. After the Chrism Mass, the oils are sent out to the parishes of the diocese. The oils are sometimes called the Easter gifts of the bishop to the people. Chrism is needed for the baptisms that will take place on Easter Eve.

Chrism is a mixture of olive oil and perfume. After people are baptized, they are anointed with chrism. Chrism is the sacramental sign of the gift of the Holy Spirit. The olive oil reminds us of Noah's dove, who returned to the ark with an olive branch. When Noah saw the branch, he knew the earth was dry and it was time to leave the ark. Perfume is a sign of the Spirit, which invisibly works to make us, in the words of St. Paul, the "aroma of Christ."

On Holy Thursday evening, we gather together and do something strange. We wash feet.

The Gospel of John tells us that on the night before Jesus died, while he was at supper, he got up and washed the feet of his disciples. In the Middle East, where people's feet easily became dusty, this washing was an act of hospitality. But because rich people usually had servants do it, the apostle Peter was embarrassed and told Jesus not to do it. But Jesus warned Peter, "Unless I wash you, you can have no share with me." Then Jesus said, "I have given you an example. You should do for each other what I have done for you."

On Holy Thursday night we follow the Lord's command. On this night the church collects the lenten alms, which are the money and goods for the poor that we have been putting aside throughout Lent. We celebrate the Lord's Supper, and then we keep watch with Christ. The three days of the death, burial and resurrection of the Lord have begun.

Good Friday

This day is part of something bigger than itself. It is the first day of the Paschal Triduum. The liturgical services of Good Friday have no formal beginnings or endings, no greetings or dismissals. The services are all part of the single, three-day liturgy of the Triduum.

The main service on Good Friday is usually held in the afternoon. This is the time when the lambs were slaughtered in the Temple in Jerusalem to prepare for the Passover feast. This is the time when Jesus died.

The service begins in silence. For a few moments everyone kneels or lies flat on the ground. Then everyone rises. A prayer is read. The traditional prayer for this day is very old. It reminds us that this is the day God created the very first humans from clay.

John's account of the passion is heard today. This account is in many ways different from those in the other three gospels. John shows us how God's glory is seen in the suffering and death of Jesus. We hear that Jesus was buried like a monarch, with a hundred pounds of sweet-smelling myrrh. The tomb was in a garden. Perhaps John is telling us that, because of the death, burial and resurrection of the Lord, we are welcome back to paradise.

On Good Friday the gathered church prays for the world and all its peoples. We do this every day, but today the prayer takes an ancient form, with kneeling and standing so that even the movement of our bodies becomes part of the prayer.

A large wooden cross is carried into church. Then, in most parishes, everyone comes forward in procession to honor the holy wood, "on which hung the Savior of the world." The cross is surrounded with candles and fragrant incense. People keep watch near it.

In mystery, we say that this wood is the cross on which Jesus died. We also say that this is the tree of life in Eden. This is the ark that saved Noah and his family and the creatures huddled inside. This is the staff that Moses held up to split the waters of the Red Sea. Is it any wonder that people call this Friday "good"?

People fast on Good Friday and Holy Saturday. This is called the "paschal fast." Before a big event or after a tragedy, most people lose their appetites. That's one reason that members of the church fast during these days. We're filled with anticipation.

Another reason for the fasting is to remind us of Adam and Eve in paradise. God told them not to eat the fruit of a particular tree. On these days the children of Adam and Eve stand before the tree, the holy cross of Christ, and they refuse to eat.

Holy Saturday

The paschal Sabbath lasts from Good Friday sunset to Holy Saturday sunset. This is the middle day of the Triduum. It is perhaps the strangest, most mysterious, most puzzling day on the calendar.

In Latin, Holy Saturday is *Sabbatum Sanctum*, the Holy Sabbath. In the tomb, Jesus rested on the Sabbath. The church rests in Christ today. It's customary to keep Holy Saturday free from all kinds of work, even the preparation of food. That's one reason to continue the paschal fast this day.

At nightfall on Holy Saturday, the blessed Sabbath is over. The first day of the week begins. After the Sabbath, according to custom, the first work to be done is to make a fire and to kindle the evening lamp. That is what the church does. That is how the Easter Vigil begins.

On this night, every member of the church is asked to gather with the soon-to-be-baptized. We keep watch together. We settle down and listen to the paschal scriptures. St. Augustine (August 28) said that, on this night above all other nights, the church keeps watch for the Lord and the Lord keeps watch over the church.

The first Sunday after the first full moon after the vernal equinox
Easter Sunday

Easter is the Sunday of Sundays, the solemnity of solemnities, the last day of the Paschal Triduum and the first of the Fifty Days of Eastertime. We celebrate the death, burial and resurrection — the passover — of Christ. At baptism we became a sharer in Christ's passover. No matter what day we were baptized, Easter is the anniversary.

The church's heart and soul is found in Easter. It is the time of the most beloved scripture stories — of creation, Noah, the Exodus, of Daniel in the lion's den, of Queen Esther saving her people, of Jonah in the belly of a fish. And, of course, at Easter the church tells the gospels of the passion and resurrection of our Lord.

Easter is filled with songs and customs and foods that remind us of these stories. For instance, dyeing eggs in rainbow colors can be a celebration of the promise made to Noah and all the animals after the great flood. Sprinkling ourselves with Easter water can speak to us of the Israelites marching through the Red Sea from slavery to freedom.

Egg hunts in gardens are also an Easter week custom. At Jesus' tomb the angel had asked the women, "Why do you look for the living among the dead?" An egg hunt is a search for life. Like the holy women, we discover that life has conquered death.

The word "Easter" comes from the same root as the words "star" and "east." It means "dawn light." This word has become a wonderful way to describe the Christian Passover. In the words of Psalm 118: "This is the day the Lord has made. Let us rejoice and be glad in it."

From Easter Sunday until Pentecost

Easter Season

Eastertime is the 50-day celebration that flows from the Triduum. It is the church's most ancient and most beautiful season. These are springtime days of blossoming orchards, of open windows, of the great gladness of the awakening earth.

Fifty days are a "week of weeks," seven times seven, with a day added so Eastertime has eight Sundays—a mystical sign of eternity. Each week we have a Lord's Day. And each year we have Eastertime—50 days to sing alleluia, 50 days to live as if God's rule of justice and peace were fully with us.

In times past another word for Eastertime was "Pentecost." Now we use that word to mean the last day of Eastertime, but "Pentecost" can mean "fifty days" or "fiftieth day." The ascension of the Lord and the sending of the Holy Spirit are celebrated on two solemnities of the season, but they also are celebrated throughout Eastertime. We can't really separate these wonders. The Lord's incarnation, epiphany, passion, death, burial, resurrection, ascension and the gift of the Spirit are one mystery, called the "paschal mystery," mystery of the Passover of the Lord.

Every Eastertime there are lilacs and irises, the first strawberries and asparagus and rhubarb. According to the gospels, the risen Christ is found by a lake shore or on a mountaintop as well as behind closed doors. According to the Acts of the Apostles, the first thing the Holy Spirit does is send the disciples out into the streets.

Each Eastertime there's May Day and Mother's Day. There are confirmations, first communions, graduations and weddings. There's spring fever and spring cleaning. Amusement parks open. Beaches open. Finally there are hours of daylight after supper time.

We can expect to meet the risen Christ in bird songs each dawn and dusk, in renewing our friendships with neighbors, in the aroma of a crabapple tree, in the teamwork necessary for our Eastertime activities. Like the Lord's Day each week, Eastertime is for recreation that "re-creates" us.

During Eastertime the church reads through the Acts of the Apostles, which is the sequel to Luke's gospel. This book is a kind of family history of the first Christians. John's gospel is also read during Eastertime. In this gospel Jesus calls himself the Good Shepherd, the Gateway, the Vine, the Way, the Truth and the Life.

Throughout these 50 days, the paschal candle burns brightly in church. The candle is a symbol of the risen body of Christ and the fire of the Spirit. During the rest of the year the candle is kept near the baptismal font. It is lit during baptisms. The newly baptized light their own candles from the paschal candle. During funerals the candle is put near the coffin. That way, throughout the year, the light of Easter shines on the dead.

The first eight days of Eastertime

Easter octave

The octave is the eight days from Easter Sunday to the Second Sunday of Easter. The days of the octave are called Easter Sunday, Easter Monday, Easter Tuesday, and on through the next Sunday, called the Second Sunday of Easter.

This octave is eight solemnities one after the other. Or maybe it's one single, eight-day-long solemnity. All through this time the church tells the gospel stories of the resurrection.

The people baptized during the Easter Vigil are given a beautiful new garment to wear. In times past, they would wear their baptismal clothes all through this week. That custom of beautiful clothing for the baptized became the custom of new clothes for everyone at Easter.

It's a Central European tradition to take an "Emmaus walk" during Easter week. People go out and speak with anyone they meet. This is done in remembrance of Cleopas and his companion (September 25), who met the risen Christ on their journey to Emmaus. When families take their Easter walks, parents drop treats from their pockets for the children to find. These Easter walks have now evolved into protest marches. Throughout central Europe this week, people march for a better environment, for better race relations, for fairer labor laws.

The second Sunday after the first full moon that falls after the vernal equinox according to the Julian calendar

Orthodox Pascha

There are a few differences between the way Eastern churches calculate the date of Easter and the way Western churches do. For one thing, many Eastern churches follow the Julian calendar. This calendar is 13 days behind the Gregorian calendar that most people follow. So, for instance, when it is April 3 on the Gregorian calendar it is March 21 on the Julian calendar.

Another difference is that Eastern churches say that the Christian Passover needs to come after the days of the Jewish Passover are over, just as the Lord's Day follows the Sabbath. The end result is that many Eastern churches (such as the Orthodox) usually keep Easter a week later than it is kept by Western churches (such as Roman Catholics and Protestants). But sometimes the Orthodox Easter is four or five weeks after the Western date, and sometimes, amazingly, all the churches keep Easter on the same Sunday.

Pascha (PAH-skuh) means "Passover." In the Latin, Greek and Slavic languages, *Pascha* is the word for Easter. *Pascha* is the greatest feast of the year. Most Eastern Christians really keep it that way. They prepare for *Pascha* by following the lenten fast strictly. As a part of the fast, they eat no meat, fish, butter, eggs, cheese or other animal products. Toward the end of Lent, houses are cleaned and decorated. Most importantly, people ask forgiveness from anyone they have wronged.

On the Thursday before Easter the church gathers to begin the sacred three days. Because it is important for everyone to be there, strangers and

newcomers are made welcome and encouraged to join in. The services last for hours. On Friday night people honor the shroud of Christ's burial. They carry it through the streets and then place it in a tomb. Then people keep watch near the shroud through Holy Saturday. (Eastern Christians call these days "Great Friday" and "Great Saturday.")

On Easter Eve toward midnight, or in some places at dawn on Easter Sunday, there is a procession around the church. Everyone gathers in front of the church. The cross is used to knock on the closed doors. Then the bells ring and the doors swing open. Everyone marches into church and sings, "Christ is risen from the dead, trampling down death by death, and to those in the tomb, Christ bestows life!"

At *Pascha* Christ is risen and we are risen with Christ. The holy cross opens the gates of paradise.

Maybe because the fast was so strict, the Easter feast is especially splendid. Red is considered the most beautiful color for Easter eggs because it is a token of the life-giving blood of Jesus. Lamb is a reminder of the paschal lamb that saved the Hebrew people from the angel of death. Sweetened dairy dishes are edible announcements that in baptism Christ has led us through the water to a promised land flowing with milk and honey.

The Fourth Sunday of Easter

Good Shepherd Sunday

Psalm 23 begins, "The Lord is my shepherd." This psalm is much loved, especially by people who are grieving or in trouble. Most people have never met a shepherd, and they rarely see sheep. And yet the image of God as our shepherd is strong and lasting. Springtime is the season lambs are born and grow strong. Perhaps that is why every Easter season brings us renewed acquaintance with our Good Shepherd.

The communion song for the Fourth Sunday of Easter gets right to the point: "The Good Shepherd is risen, alleluia!" The prophet Ezekiel (July 23) said that bad shepherds let wolves catch the sheep. Jesus said that he is the good shepherd who lays down his life for the sheep.

Rogation Days

Among farmers and herders and fruit-tree growers there is a natural anxiety at this time of year. Crops are planted. Trees bloom. A new generation of animals is born. What if it hails? What if there's a drought or a flood? A cold snap can kill newly emerged plants and newborn animals.

In the fifth century, Bishop Mamertus (May 11–13) of Vienne in Gaul (now France), held processions on the three days before Ascension Day. People marched through the fields and sang psalms. Farmers asked God to protect the crops and orchards and flocks.

These three days were called rogation days. (Another one falls on April 25, the feast of St. Mark.) The word "rogation" comes from the Latin word *rogare*, which means "to ask."

In 1969 the calendar was changed. Instead of all Roman Catholics keeping the rogation days on the three days before the Ascension, the bishops of each country now choose the most appropriate times of the year for keeping days of prayer. When there is a need, the bishops ask people to keep a rogation day.

In the United States, the memorial of St. Isidore the farmer is kept on May 15. In many places it has become a kind of rogation day. The Catholic Rural Life Conference sponsors the blessing of farmers and farmlands on this day.

The fortieth day of Eastertime
The Thursday after the Sixth Sunday of Easter
(In Canada, the Seventh Sunday of Easter)
Solemnity of
The Ascension of the Lord

The celebration of Easter is the oldest yearly festival of the church. We know this because we still have a few of the writings of second-century Christians, such as Bishop Polycarp of Smyrna (February 23). When he was young he was taught by some of Jesus' disciples.

On the night of the Jewish Passover, Polycarp celebrated in memory of the death and resurrection of Christ. Other groups of Christians celebrated on the Saturday night and Sunday that followed the Passover. In those earliest years of the church, once a year at Passover time Christians celebrated the fullness of Jesus — his birth and baptism, his life and teachings, his death and burial and resurrection. They celebrated the glory of Christ and the sending of the Holy Spirit.

Especially in the fourth and fifth centuries, new holy days were kept in celebration of gospel events. That's when most Christians started to celebrate Christmas, Epiphany, the Presentation, the Annunciation, the Birth of John the Baptist and many other festivals. This didn't happen everywhere at the same time. There were different ways of celebrating and different ways of calculating the seasons.

In the late fourth century many Christians began to celebrate a feast day in memory of the Ascension of the Lord. In most places this was kept on the 40th day of the 50 days of Easter rejoicing.

St. Paul wrote to the church in Ephesus: "The fullness of Christ fills all in all." That is what we celebrate on Ascension Day. This day is not about the absence of Christ. It is about Christ's presence. At the conclusion of Matthew's gospel, Jesus says, "I am with you always."

The nine days from Ascension until Pentecost
Pentecost novena

The Ascension of the Lord is kept on the 40th day of the Easter season. The giving of the Spirit is celebrated at Pentecost, the 50th and final day of Eastertime. The nine days from Ascension to Pentecost are called the "novena," which is the Latin word for the number nine. These final days of Eastertime are days of prayer for a new outpouring of the Spirit, a new Pentecost.

Pentecost Vigil

Pentecost became a time, like Easter, for baptism. In preparation for baptism, people kept watch through the night in prayer, in reading the scriptures and in singing psalms.

The vigil of Pentecost has an ancient heritage. Fifty days after Passover is the Jewish festival of Shavuot (see page 199). It is a celebration of the firstfruits of the spring harvest. It is also a celebration of the covenant God made with the Israelites during the exodus. After they escaped from slavery in Egypt, Moses led the people to Mount Sinai. There they pitched camp. Moses went up the mountain to meet God, and the people kept vigil down below. God gave the people their Law.

The church has special scriptures to read on Pentecost Eve. One of the readings is about the covenant on Mount Sinai. God appeared in fire and wind, in signs and wonders upon the mountain.

Luke tells us in the Book of Acts that people of many different nationalities came to Jerusalem to keep the festival of Shavuot. The disciples of Jesus were there, too. Suddenly they were filled with the Holy Spirit. They went out into the streets and began to preach the good news.

Like Easter Eve and Christmas Eve, Pentecost Eve is one of the holiest nights of the Christian year. In some places it is customary to decorate homes this night with roses and peonies and fresh green leaves in preparation for tomorrow. Years ago there was caroling and dancing outdoors near churches.

Like Christmas or like a wedding, Pentecost is a day for lights, flowers, garlands, wreaths and all sorts of decorations. These are joyful signs of welcome to beloved guests. On Pentecost Eve the church makes ready for the Holy Spirit. We prepare to welcome the presence of God.

The Eighth Sunday of Easter
The fiftieth and final day of Eastertime
Solemnity of

Pentecost (Whitsunday)

One of the biblical names for Pentecost is "the festival of firstfruits." A "firstfruit" is the first of a crop to ripen. These were offered to God in thanksgiving for the harvest.

We usually don't think of this time of year as a harvest season. But in mild climates, such as the lands around the Mediterranean, the apricots, cherries and strawberries are ripe now. So are wheat and other grains. The grain harvest is the principal harvest of the year, the crop that can feed people all year long if it is abundant enough. Even in the north, gardens yield asparagus, rhubarb, the first peas and spinach and other salad greens. Winter's fast has become springtime's feast.

In the First Letter to the Corinthians, St. Paul uses the imagery of Pentecost to speak of the resurrection of Jesus: "Christ has been raised from the dead, the firstfruits of those who have died. All will be made alive in Christ, but each in proper order: First Christ, then all those who belong to Christ."

The Jewish people keep the festival of firstfruits (page 199) 50 days after Passover. This day is called Shavuot (shuh-voo-OAT). Besides being a harvest festival, it is also a celebration of God's covenant with the people, made on Mount Sinai, when God gave Moses the holy law. Shavuot means "weeks" because it comes seven weeks plus a day (50 days, a "week of weeks") after Passover.

Christians celebrate Pentecost 50 days after Easter Sunday. Pentecost is a Greek word that means either "50 days" or "50th day." Pentecost sets a seal on the 50 days of Eastertime. It is a grand finale.

On Pentecost, Christians celebrate the outpouring of the Holy Spirit. The gospels speak often of the coming of the Spirit. John's gospel tells us that, when Jesus died, "he bowed his head and gave up his spirit." John tells us that the risen Christ breathed on the disciples and said, "Receive the

Holy Spirit." (This story is the gospel for Pentecost Day.)

In the Acts of the Apostles we hear today of a great outpouring of the Spirit, who descended in fire and wind on the disciples, just as God appeared to Moses on Mount Sinai. But that isn't the only time Luke tells us of the coming of the Spirit. The gospel is filled with stories. Luke tells us that John the Baptist was filled with the Holy Spirit even before he was born. Mary was filled with the Spirit. So were Elizabeth and Zechariah, John's parents. So were Simeon and Anna.

At Jesus' baptism, the Holy Spirit appeared in the form of a dove that descended on Jesus. In Luke's gospel, we hear over and over that Jesus was filled with the power of the Spirit. In the Acts of the Apostles, the descent of the Spirit happens over and over to the disciples. Pentecost is made new again at every baptism, every eucharist, every time two or more gather in Jesus' name.

From the day after Pentecost
until the day before Advent begins

Ordinary Time

There are about 32 weeks outside the five church seasons. These weeks are called "Ordinary Time," from the word "ordinal," meaning "counted." Each week is given a number to help us divide the scriptures into readings and to place these in an orderly book called the lectionary. We do the same thing with the church's prayers at Mass, ordered day by day in a book called the sacramentary.

Ordinary Time is a name for the weeks that come between the church seasons. The period of Ordinary Time that lasts from Eastertime until Advent spans over half the year. In the Northern Hemisphere, most of summer and autumn fall during these weeks. This is harvest time. In the gospels, Jesus often talked about the harvest as a symbol of what heaven might be like. Slowly but surely, as God's creatures grow ripe and then die, they will be harvested into heaven.

The Wednesday, Friday and Saturday
after Pentecost
Summer Ember Days

Years ago, the Wednesday, Friday and Saturday after Pentecost were the summer Ember Days. (The word "ember" means "season.") In the Middle East, north Africa and southern Europe, this is the season of the grain harvest. Barley, wheat, oats, millet and other grains grow ripe and need to be gathered in.

On the summer Ember Days, the church used to read several of the scriptures that tell of thanksgiving for the grain harvest. These were also the scriptures of the Jewish holiday of Shavuot (page 199), which is called "the festival of firstfruits." People would fast from eating on Ember Days as a way to thank God for the crops.

During Eastertime, even on Fridays there isn't any fasting. Psalms and songs have alleluias added. Throughout those 50 days the church rejoices. But Eastertime ends after Pentecost, and the weekly Friday fast begins again. The summer Ember Days were a reminder for people to return to the ordinary disciplines of Christian living. Like the summer sun, they can help us to grow healthy and strong.

The Sunday after Pentecost
Solemnity of
The Holy Trinity

Throughout the Easter Season we have been celebrating the work of the Trinity. Perhaps that is why the church celebrates the Holy Trinity on this first Lord's Day after Eastertime. It helps to remind us of what we celebrate every Lord's Day: The risen Christ sends the Holy Spirit to be God's presence in us and in all God's creation.

As Christians, we are called to begin and end whatever we say or do, "in the name of the Father, and of the Son, and of the Holy Spirit. Amen."

On the universal Roman calendar, the Thursday after the Solemnity of the Holy Trinity; in the U. S. A. and Canada, the Sunday after the Solemnity of the Holy Trinity

Solemnity of

The Body and Blood of Christ

Today's solemnity was first called *Corpus Christi,* which is Latin for "the Body of Christ." People in the Middle Ages wanted a joyful day to celebrate Jesus' gift of the eucharist. They created today's feast at a good time of year for processions and street fairs and other outdoor events.

The processions on this day were fantastic. In many towns the streets were lined with flowers. Often flowers and herbs were arranged into pictures and intricate designs. The bread of the Lord's Body was carried outdoors under a canopy. Bands played and many people joined in singing hymns of praise. These processions still take place in some towns in Latin America and in Europe.

Today, many Christians think that the best way to celebrate Jesus' gift of the eucharist is to put heart and soul into celebrating the eucharist well. That way every Lord's Day is a feast of the Body and Blood of Christ.

The third Friday after Pentecost

Solemnity of

The Sacred Heart of Jesus

In the Middle Ages this third Friday after Pentecost was celebrated among Roman Catholics in some places as a feast of the wounds of Christ. It became a kind of echo of Good Friday, the same way Corpus Christi was an echo of Holy Thursday.

Devotion to the passion of Christ often was very strong in the church of the Middle Ages. Remembering the suffering of Jesus helped people make sense of their own troubles. Gertrude the Great (November 16), who lived in the thirteenth century, said that Jesus appeared to her the way he had appeared to Thomas. He showed her his wounds. He taught her his love, which shone from his heart.

In the seventeenth century a false idea called Jansenism was becoming popular. People believed that human sinfulness was overpowering. No one was worthy of God's love, and few people would receive it.

Also at this time the devotion to the heart of Jesus grew strong. People said that Jesus wanted them to know his love. God's love was stronger than sin.

Margaret Mary Alacoque (October 16) said that she was chosen by Christ to spread devotion to the Sacred Heart. John Eudes (August 19) preached about the loving heart of Jesus. He composed a liturgy for a feast of the Sacred Heart. In the year 1765, 75 years after Margaret Mary died, Pope Clement XIII approved this devotion and set the feast of the Sacred Heart of Jesus on the church's calendar.

The Saturday after the Solemnity of the Sacred Heart of Jesus

Memorial of

The Immaculate Heart of Mary

The Sacred Heart of Jesus and the Immaculate Heart of Mary are honored in celebration of God's generous love. The First Letter of John says that "God is love." God's love gives value and purpose to every human life. Louis Grignion de Montfort, an emotional and powerful preacher in France, spread the devotion to the Immaculate Heart of Mary. He died in 1716 and was canonized in 1947.

Devotion to the Immaculate Heart of Mary has become a comfort and a promise that salvation is a gift of God open to all, not only to a select few. St. Paul tells us that "eye has not seen nor ear heard what is in store for those who love God."

*The Wednesday, Friday and Saturday
after September 14,
the feast of the Holy Cross*
Autumn Ember Days

The Ember Days were days of fasting and prayer to mark the turning of the seasons. They also were days of thanksgiving for the various harvests of the year. In many countries of the Northern Hemisphere, the autumn Ember Days came when the grape and apple and nut crops were ripe.

Nowadays we often think of wine as a special treat at festive meals. Perhaps the abuse of wine and other alcoholic drinks has caused us trouble. In times past, in grape-growing countries wine was thought of as an important source of nourishment. In those days the alcohol content of wine usually was lower than it is now, and people diluted wine with water before they drank it.

The grape harvest is a big event — and a lot of hard work. Once the grapes ripen, they have to be picked and processed quickly. In the old days, no matter what a person did for a living all year long, he or she was expected to pitch in to help with the harvest and the making of wine.

The church doesn't have an official harvest festival. Several days in late summer and fall have been christened as harvest festivals, such as the Assumption of Mary (August 15), Holy Cross Day (September 14), Michaelmas (September 29), All Saints (November 1) and Martinmas (November 11).

Ember Days were harvest festivals marked not by feasting but by fasting. Both are ways to give thanks to God. Many people keep the days before Thanksgiving Day with extra prayer and fasting and by giving gifts to the poor. Perhaps these days can be our autumn Ember Days.

*The Last Sunday in Ordinary Time
The Sunday before Advent begins*
Solemnity of
Christ the King

The solemnity of Christ the King is a fairly new feast day. Pope Pius XI put it on the calendar in 1925. He set it on the Sunday before All Saints' Day. Maybe it could have been called "All Saints' Sunday." In 1969 the feast was moved to the Sunday before the season of Advent begins.

The church uses the language of royalty as a symbol. Like a monarch, we are anointed at baptism. We become a royal people. We share in Jesus' crown. The kingdom we are called to announce is one of justice, self-sacrifice, peace and freedom.

We call Christ "the King." Maybe this word brings to mind power and wealth and authority. The gospels we hear today tell us something else. Jesus is crowned with thorns. His throne is the cross. We recognize our royal ruler in the hungry, the thirsty, the sick, the imprisoned. These are the kings and queens of heaven.

January

The first month of the year gets its name from the Roman god Janus, whose name means "gate." Janus has two faces. One looks behind, the other ahead. January is a month in which we look back in time and look ahead.

January is the month of Epiphany. That can be the merriest day of our merry Christmastime. In most churches in North America, Epiphany is kept on the first Lord's Day of the year. A Greek name for Epiphany is *ta phota,* which means "lights." It was Advent during most of December, when the days got as short as they can get. But now the light is growing. That's something hopeful to keep in mind. Even in the dead of winter, spring is on its way.

These winter days of growing light take us to Lent. They are Carnival days. Carnival (page 10) is the customary time of year for plays and puppet shows and circuses and all the human arts that can help drive the cold winter away. This is a season of hospitality. To people in need, wintertime hospitality can be a gift of life and light.

The third Monday in January
Martin Luther King Day (U. S. A.)

In 1929, millions of African Americans lived in the American South, where, because of racial prejudice, their freedom was limited by unfair laws. They had the poorest schools and were allowed to work only the worst jobs. At this time and place, Martin Luther King, Jr., was born. Unlike most blacks, King lived his early life in prosperity. His father was a respected Baptist minister in Atlanta.

King started college when he was only 15 years old. After college, he attended divinity school in Boston. He earned the highest grades in his class and served as president of the student body. When he graduated, he could have remained in the North to teach. Instead, King and his wife Coretta Scott decided to move back to the South.

They wanted to help change the unjust system. They settled in Montgomery, Alabama, where King became the minister of the Dexter Avenue Baptist Church.

At that time the Montgomery bus system did not allow black riders the same rights as white riders. To protest the unjust rules, King led a boycott of the bus system. He asked black riders to refuse to use the buses until the rules were changed. As a result of his action his house was dynamited and his family was threatened. However, in time the unjust rules were made more fair.

The bus boycott was powered by nonviolent resistance, which is gentle refusal to cooperate with unjust laws. King had learned about nonviolence from the teachings of Mohandas Gandhi of India (January 30). King began to lead nonviolent actions in other cities. He helped Americans realize that racism existed everywhere, not just in the South.

In 1964, King received the Nobel Peace Prize, a great international honor. Also, because of King and other civil rights leaders, important new laws were passed. They protected the civil rights of all Americans. In 1968, when he was 39 years old, Martin Luther King was shot and killed by a man who hated what he had done.

Martin Luther King, Jr., helped millions of Americans turn against racism and against violence. In 1983 a national holiday was declared in his honor. It falls on the third Monday in January. That day is on or soon after January 15, which is the day he was born. On Martin Luther King Day we take for our own these words of the prophet Amos: "Let justice roll down like waters and righteousness like an everflowing stream."

The second new moon after the winter solstice
Lunar New Year
(also called Chinese New Year, or *Tet* in Vietnamese)

The word "month" comes from the word "moon." The "months" of most ancient calendars were the 29½-day periods from one new moon to the next. That's how the Jewish and Muslim calendars work. The ancient calendars of the peoples of east Asia are organized like that, too.

Nowadays, most Asian countries keep the western calendar, in which New Year's Day is January 1. However, the Vietnamese and the Chinese people love their old New Year's festival, which begins on the second new moon after the winter solstice (December 21) — sometime between January 21 and February 19 on the western calendar. The Lunar New Year is celebrated in China and southeast Asia as the beginning of spring.

Chinese and Vietnamese communities around the world celebrate the Lunar New Year as a heritage festival. In North America you can join the celebration in New York, San Francisco, Vancouver, Los Angeles and other big cities that have east Asian populations.

In Chinese communities, a huge dragon — the symbol of prosperity and good luck — slithers through street parades held at night. It's made of bamboo covered in paper, silk and velvet, and it can be up to 125 feet long. A crew of dancers supports it from underneath. Firecrackers are set off and gongs clang to chase troubles away. The streets are packed with acrobats, lion dancers, floats, clowns and stilt walkers.

Red is the good luck color, the color of life. People hang red scrolls bearing wishes for a healthy and prosperous new year. Spring flowers are everywhere. Piles of oranges and sweet pastries are set up as signs of abundance.

The celebration lasts for two weeks, from the new moon until the full moon. In Baltimore, it includes a fashion show of traditional Chinese gowns. In San Francisco, the city with the largest North American Chinese community, more than 50,000 people celebrate outdoors. Drama, opera and athletic demonstrations are staged. The Golden Dragon Parade is held at sunset of the last day. Its dragon glitters with lights.

Gung Hay Fat Choy! Happy New Year!

1

The Octave Day of Christmas

Solemnity of
Mary, Mother of God
See page 9.

New Year's Day

On New Year's Eve, some people "pray in" the new year. Church bells peal out the old and ring in the new. With noisemakers and fireworks, people make a racket to try to scare away their troubles. The next morning, many people attend church services. It is the Roman Catholic Solemnity of Mary, the Mother of God, the Lutheran and Episcopalian feast of the Holy Name of Jesus and the Byzantine feast of the Circumcision of Jesus. In Greece January 1 is also St. Basil's Day (see January 2). A bread, *vasilopita,* is baked with a coin in it; whoever gets the coin is crowned queen or king for the new year. (The name Basil means "royalty.")

In some countries January 1 is the official day to exchange Christmastime gifts. Everywhere, feasting is customary. In Japan, where pink and red are colors of good fortune, a pink fish called red snapper is served. Strawberries are eaten as a taste of spring.

In many European countries, a dinner of roast pork is supposed to bring a bountiful year. Swedes drink a toast to the new year with *glögg* — hot spiced wine. In the southern and southwestern United States, black-eyed peas are cooked in a traditional New Year's dish called hoppin' John.

On this day people visit friends to settle any misunderstandings from the previous year. People also call on the folks they want to spend time with during the next year. In some families, parents bless their children. Many people pay a visit to their godparents.

Hospitality is the rule of the day. At the new year many people make a special effort to be loving and outgoing. Perhaps extra good will on this day is a Christmastime hope that this spirit will last all year long.

In the United States and Canada,
the Sunday after January 1
Solemnity of the
Epiphany of the Lord
See page 9.

The Sunday after Epiphany
(or, if Epiphany is kept on January 7 or 8,
the Monday after Epiphany)
Feast of the
Baptism of the Lord
See page 11.

Memorial of
Ss. Basil the Great and Gregory Nazianzen
Basil (329 – 379) and Gregory (329 – 390),
bishops, doctors of the church

These two bishops of the early church are remembered together because they had so much in common. Both were gifted writers and preachers who became great bishops. Each has been granted high honors by the churches of both the East and West. The two saints were also close friends.

Both saints were born in Cappadocia, in what is now southeastern Turkey. The two met as young students. They went on to Athens, Greece, to study law together. Soon after that, Basil visited monasteries. His travels helped him to decide that he wanted to be a monk. He founded the first monastery in Asia Minor (Turkey), on the banks of the Iris River.

Gregory became a bishop. Although he was shy and never comfortable in public, he was a famous preacher. He was also a brilliant writer.

Basil was made bishop of the city of Caesarea. He built a hospice to minister to the sick. He helped victims of drought and famine. He told any priests and monks who lived luxurious lives that they needed to live simply, as Jesus did.

When Basil preached, he challenged the people of his diocese to care for the poor. He said, "The money you keep locked away is the money of the poor. The acts of charity that you do not perform are so many injustices you commit."

Roman martyrology
St. Abel
the first to die

Abel was one of the sons of Adam and Eve (December 24). The story of Abel and his brother Cain is in chapter four of the Book of Genesis. Abel was a shepherd and Cain was a farmer. Cain was jealous and angry when he saw that his brother's offering to God had been honored, and so Cain murdered Abel.

Coming during Christmastime, St. Abel's Day can remind us of Christ, the Good Shepherd, who came into the world to lay down his life for his sheep. Like the feast of the Holy Innocents

(December 28), today calls us to pause in our celebration. We remember the mystery that human beings are capable of being jealous and hateful. But they are also capable of great goodness and justice and self-sacrifice.

Byzantine calendar

St. Malachi

prophet (fifth century BCE)

We don't know who Malachi was. All we know is that the last book of the Jewish Bible is called "Malachi." Because the word means "my messenger," Malachi may be a code word for a writer who wanted to remain unknown.

The prophecy of Malachi came at a time when many people did not worship with love or care. Harvests were lean. There were droughts, and locusts destroyed crops. Some of the people decided that God had given up on them.

The book's message is one of power and courage. It promises the coming of the messenger of the Lord. After that, it says, the Lord will appear like fire that purifies precious metals.

In the 11th chapter of the gospel of Matthew, Jesus explains to the crowds that John the Baptist is Elijah (see July 20), the messenger promised by Malachi to prepare the way for the Lord.

Quadrantid Meteor Shower

These are the longest nights of the year, but they are also some of the most brilliant. Tonight and tomorrow night are the best nights of the year to see meteors.

At this time each year the earth's orbit crosses the path of a batch of meteors floating in space. Meteors are small bits of rock left by a comet that once passed by. Some of these small rocks will fall into the earth's atmosphere where they will burn up. From the earth they look like "shooting stars."

Look for them in the night sky. If the sky is clear, early in the morning today and tomorrow you might be able to see about one meteor every minute. Because these days come near the solemnity of Epiphany, meteors can remind us of the Star of Bethlehem.

In the U. S. A., memorial of

St. Elizabeth Ann Seton

married woman, religious founder (1774–1821)

All her life, Elizabeth Ann Seton loved to conquer challenges. In a way, that was true even after her death. She is the first person to be declared a saint who was born in what would soon become the United States of America.

Elizabeth was born in New York City. Her parents were wealthy and well-educated Episcopalians. They believed in helping the poor, and they taught her to do so from the time she was a small child. She later married a successful businessman and they began a family. Elizabeth still found time to do important volunteer work. She founded the Society for the Relief of Poor Widows with Small Children.

By the time Elizabeth was 30 years old, her situation had changed completely. Her husband lost his business, grew seriously ill and died. Now she herself was a widow with young children. During her husband's illness, encouragement from Catholic friends had consoled her. She decided to become a Catholic, although in doing so she lost the support of her wealthy family. As a single parent with five children to care for, she had no way to earn a living.

However, soon she was invited to begin a school for young girls from poor families. The school she founded, near Baltimore, Maryland, was the first Catholic school in the United States. With 18 other dedicated women, Elizabeth went on to organize the first group of women religious in the United States, the Sisters of Charity.

Cheerfully, she started from scratch in the work of building Catholic education. That meant not only starting more schools but also training teachers and writing textbooks herself.

Elizabeth Ann Seton accomplished all this in a very short life. She died when she was in her late 40s. The Catholic school system that she founded now thrives all over North America.

In the U. S. A., memorial of

St. John Neumann
bishop, religious, missionary (1811 – 1860)

In 1836, a young man came on a boat from Europe to New York City. He wanted to be ordained a priest. He was only five feet, two inches tall. All he owned were the clothes on his back, plus a suitcase full of heavy books. His hat had been stolen on the boat.

John Neumann had already studied Latin, Greek, Hebrew and eight modern languages. Back home in what is now the Czech Republic, he had been told that new priests were not needed. He came to America in the hope that he could be of use.

The bishop of New York was delighted to put John to work. He assigned John to the mission parishes of Buffalo. John visited his German, French, Irish and Scottish parishioners on horseback. Many of them were immigrants like himself, and he spoke to them in their own languages. He visited the sick, taught catechism and trained teachers.

John served faithfully for four years, but it was a lonely life. Eventually he decided to enter the Redemptorist order so that he could live in a community. Soon he became the head of all the Redemptorist priests in America.

In 1852, John was appointed bishop of Philadelphia, which was at that time the biggest diocese in the United States. Many wealthy and influential Catholics lived there. Most of them didn't want John Neumann to be their bishop. They wanted someone more polished. John also faced opposition from the "Know-Nothings," a political group that tried to keep immigrants from coming to America.

John worked hard and was an excellent bishop. He set up Catholic schools for thousands of children. He visited every parish and mission in the huge diocese at least once every two years. He wrote articles for newspapers and magazines as a way to teach the faith. He even prepared catechisms and a Bible history for immigrants who spoke German.

John died at age 50. He is buried in St. Peter's Church in Philadelphia.

6

In the U. S. A. and Canada, optional memorial of

Bl. André Bessette
religious (1845 – 1937)

Brother André Bessette failed at many things that he tried. He was unable to manage as a shoemaker, baker, blacksmith or tinsmith. But he did have one amazing talent: When he prayed for the sick, they got well.

Born to a poor family in Quebec, André (or Albert, as he was called in childhood) was a frail boy. He was barely able to read. He and his nine brothers and sisters were left orphans when André was only 12 years old. That's when he began looking for a trade. He needed work to support himself.

After some time André found a job as the doorkeeper at a high school for boys in Montreal. He became a religious brother of the Congregation of the Holy Cross. For 40 years he cheerfully did his chores as a janitor and handyman during the day. But at night, great numbers of crippled, blind and dying people who had heard about his gift of prayer sought him out.

By the time he died at age 91, Brother André was known all over Canada. Half a million people are said to have filed past the coffin of this humble man. He always said he was living proof that "it is not necessary to have spent many years in college to love the good God."

André Bessette was given the title "Blessed" in 1982. This title means that he is close to being declared a saint.

The Twelfth Day of Christmas
See page 10.

7

Optional memorial of

St. Raymond of Penyafort
presbyter, religious (1175 – 1275)

Raymond lived for a century, and he earned acclaim throughout his life. But for all his great achievements, what made him a saint was a gentle and humble heart.

Born in Spain, Raymond was teaching at the University of Barcelona by the time he was 20 years old. He was a hero to his students. Then he moved to Italy to study law. He won fame for his great compassion for the poor.

Raymond was on his way to becoming a church official with great power. But at age 47 he decided to become a Dominican priest. He went through the same training as the other novices, who were half his age. Then he went to preach all over Europe to renew the faith of thousands of people.

A few years later, Raymond was called to Rome to be the pope's spiritual director. He urged the pope to have greater compassion for the poor. He also used his legal skills to organize a large mass of church laws that had never been collected in one place before. The system he designed was so logical that it was used for 700 years.

Raymond wanted a simple life. When he was made bishop, he became seriously ill and begged to be excused from that office. After recovering, he returned to the work he loved best: preaching and hearing confessions.

Shortly after that, to his shock, he was elected leader of the Dominican Order. During his two years of service he visited every house in the order. He called the priests to service and prayer. At age 65 he retired, saying that he was now too old for the job. But he continued to preach until he died 35 years later.

January

Julian Calendar Christmas Day

Shortly before Jesus was born, Roman mathematicians created a new calendar. It was called the Julian calendar because the emperor, Julius Caesar, ordered that it must be used throughout the Empire. The calendar is almost like the one we use today.

The Julian calendar was an improvement over the calendars used before it. Still, as the centuries passed, people noticed that something was wrong. The solstices and the equinoxes, which mark the beginnings of the seasons, were occurring a few days too late. By the year 1500, the seasons were 10 days off from where they started out in Caesar's time. If this was allowed to continue, eventually it would be summer on January 1!

Pope Gregory XIII asked his mathematicians to create a more accurate calendar. The result was the Gregorian calendar, named in his honor. That's the calendar we use today.

The new calendar was ready in 1582. But because of disagreements among the Protestant, Orthodox and Catholic churches, many countries didn't adopt it right away. England and its colonies didn't begin using the new calendar until 1752.

When a country started to keep time by the Gregorian calendar, they would need to skip ten days. For instance, the day after October 5 would become October 15. This confused some people, who thought their lives would be ten days shorter!

Many Orthodox churches still use the "old style" Julian calendar to set the dates of feasts. But almost all the countries of the world use the Gregorian calendar for business dealings. There is now a 13-day difference between the two calendars. So today, January 7 on the Gregorian calendar, is December 25, Christmas Day, on the Julian calendar.

In Russia, where most Christians are members of the Orthodox church, today is Christmas. People greet each other with the words *Khristos rozhdayetsia!* Christ is born!

Carnival begins
See page 10.

12

In Canada, memorial of
St. Marguerite Bourgeoys
missionary, religious founder (1620–1700)

Marguerite Bourgeoys (bor-ZHAY) was the daughter of a candle maker in Troyes, France. In her teens she joined the Sodality. Sodalists were women who lived at home with their families and devoted their time to Christian service. They helped homebound people and taught poor children.

At that time, the only children in France who were receiving an education were those whose parents could afford to pay a private tutor. Teaching children in classrooms was an exciting new idea. A new invention, blackboards, made this kind of teaching easier. Marguerite began teaching classes for children whose parents were poor.

In 1652, Marguerite was invited to teach in the colony of New France in Canada. After a long voyage on a leaky ship she began her work. Her first school building was a scrubbed-out stable.

On Marguerite's trips home to France, eager young women volunteered to return with her to Montreal. They knew this meant facing brutal cold and occasional battles between the French and the Native Americans, but they wanted to serve God. The community of women grew and branched out.

The bishop of Canada gave his approval to the work of the congregation. They were called the Sisters of Notre Dame of Montreal. In 1698 Marguerite and 23 other sisters were allowed to take their vows. Two years later she died at the age of 80.

Optional memorial of
St. Hilary
bishop, doctor of the church (c. 315 – 368)

Hilary may have become a saint because of one simple practice. He began every conversation and action with a prayer. He was able to do great things that way.

Hilary was born in the city of Poitiers in Gaul (now part of France). His parents were wealthy pagans, but he decided as a young man that he couldn't believe in a whole collection of gods. He believed there must be only one God who had created everything. Hilary discovered the scriptures and became a Christian.

At age 35 Hilary was chosen bishop of Poitiers. At that time bishops were elected by the local clergy and then acclaimed by all the people of the community. Hilary, a humble person, tried to decline the honor, but this made him seem like an even better choice to the people of his diocese.

Hilary soon became known as a wise leader. He was also a great speaker. Unfortunately, the emperor decided that Hilary was a troublemaker, and he had the bishop exiled. Hilary spent three years in Phrygia (now central Turkey). Although he suffered many hardships, he remained cheerful — which is the meaning of his name. He spent this time writing a great work on the Trinity. He also wrote the earliest known Latin hymns.

Finally, Hilary was allowed to return to Gaul. The whole city of Poitiers turned out to cheer him when he arrived. He spent the rest of his life writing. He has been honored with the title "Doctor of the Divinity of Christ" (the word "doctor" here means "wise teacher").

On the Scandinavian calendar
St. Knut
king, martyr (c. 1040 – 1086)

Knut (also called Canute) was king of Denmark. The Christian faith had been brought there centuries earlier, and Knut built churches all over the land with money from the royal treasury. He even donated his own crown to one of them.

Knut met with resistance to his work. Some of his subjects rebelled against paying taxes to the church. They were also angry because of unjust acts by some of the king's officials. During the rebellion Knut was murdered in one of the churches he had built.

In the Roman martyrology, which is a list of the saints and their days, St. Knut is remembered on January 19. But in Scandinavia he is remembered today for a very strange reason: Back in King Knut's time, the Christmas Season lasted for 40 days. Nobody worked from Christmas Day until Candlemas, February 2. Knut declared that 40 days was too long to be lazy. Everyone's Christmas vacation should last only 20 days, from December 25 to January 13.

This evolved into a party held on this day called "plundertime." All the candies and cookies on the Christmas tree are "plundered" from it and eaten. Then the tree is taken down, and everyone "dances the tree out the door." (In many homes they even throw it out a window.) The figure of St. Knut, dressed in rags and carrying a broom, may then appear to "sweep Christmas out."

January

15

Anniversary of the birth of
Martin Luther King, Jr.
(1929 – 1968)
See page 26.

17

Memorial of
St. Anthony
abbot (251 – 356)

Where's the quietest place you've ever been? What's the longest you've ever been silent? Anthony of Egypt lived in profound stillness for years at a time. In that stillness he heard the voice of God, which filled him with joy.

Anthony's parents were wealthy Christians who lived near Memphis in Upper Egypt. Before he reached age 20, they both had died. Anthony soon gave away to the poor everything he had inherited. Then he began a life of listening to God. He went to live in the quietest place he could find — a tomb in a cemetery in the desert. For more than ten years, the only people he talked to were a few other hermits. He would travel to where they lived. Then he would learn everything he could from them about how to pray.

Anthony later moved to an even more isolated place: an abandoned fort on a mountain. For 20 years, he saw no other humans. By this time, Anthony was a famous holy man. People who wanted him to be their leader settled in huts and caves around his fort. Anthony answered their call. He founded the first Christian monastery, the *Fayum*. Its monks lived apart, but they came together to worship. When all were gathered, it is said that Anthony stood out from the others because his face glowed with radiant happiness.

When Christians in Alexandria were thrown into prison for their faith, Anthony left his quiet life to console them. This showed boldness, because everyone knew who he was. Yet he was never arrested. When he returned to the desert, he founded another monastery. (1600 years later, people are still living in both monasteries Anthony began.) Then he retired to Mount Kolzim, near the Red Sea.

He wove mats, took care of his pets and worked in his garden for 45 years. He said that he needed no books because nature was a book that spoke to him constantly of God. He died when he was 105 years old.

In Mexico and other places in Central America, Anthony is a much loved saint. He is the patron of farm animals and pets. On his feast day children paint stripes or polka dots on livestock. They dress up chickens and cats in homemade clothes and collars of flowers. Then they lead the animals to the churchyard for a blessing. This is a good day for people everywhere to give thanks to God for their pets.

18-25
Christian Unity Octave

The word "octave" comes from the Latin word for eight. According to the first creation story in the Book of Genesis, God created the world in seven days. Seven is a number that represents wholeness and completion. The resurrection of Jesus was called the "eighth day" by the earliest Christians, because now life was lived in a whole new dimension of freedom.

The Church Unity Octave is eight days of special prayer for the reunion of all Christians. At the Last Supper Jesus prayed for his followers "that they all may be one." But Christians have sometimes forgotten that we are all one body with Christ as our head. We think of ourselves instead as Eastern or Western, Protestant or Catholic.

In recent years the churches have made important steps toward understanding each other. Pope John XXIII made history by inviting leaders of other Christian churches to the Vatican. When he called the Roman Catholic bishops to the Second Vatican Council, Anglicans, Methodists, Quakers, Congregationalists, Lutherans and Orthodox were included as observers. Nothing like this had ever been seen.

The churches have continued to work together toward greater harmony. But prayer is still needed so that the body of Christ on earth can be strong and united. That will help the people of the world hear the voice of Christ speaking clearly.

The church prays for Christian unity all during the year. But during the week of the Church Unity Octave we pray with special concern. We ask that all Christians might be able to work together.

The Church Unity Octave ends on January 25, the feast of the Conversion of St. Paul.

Optional memorial of
St. Fabian
pope, martyr (died c. 250)

It must have taken tremendous courage to be a Christian in a time of all-out persecution. Pope Fabian lived at such a time.

Not much is known about Fabian's life. He lived in Rome, and was not a priest when he was elected pope.

To appreciate Fabian, we need to understand his murderer, the emperor Decius. Roman emperors varied in their attitudes toward Christianity. The persecutions lasted for hundreds of years, but there were times and places of relative quiet within the empire.

Decius was one of the most bitter enemies of the new religion. He was determined to force all Christians to return to pagan worship. He demanded that people sign documents saying that they sacrificed to the pagan gods and had always done so. If they refused to sign, they might be placed in stadiums where the Romans could watch them being eaten by lions. Fabian was one of the first Christians to be martyred by Decius.

Optional memorial of
St. Sebastian
martyr (c. 288)

Sebastian was martyred in the third century. He was buried along the Appian Way in Rome. A church was built nearby in his honor. A century later he was already famous in some Christian communities. That's all we know about him for certain. However, according to legends, Sebastian was a young nobleman from Gaul. He felt great sympathy for Christians in prison. Though he didn't believe in military life, he became a soldier. This work gave him a chance to comfort the people who were about to be martyred.

Bowmen were ordered to kill him when the emperor found out that he was a Christian. (Paintings of Sebastian often show him being shot by arrows.) Left for dead after being shot, Sebastian was nursed back to health by another Christian. He lived to confront the emperor about the cruel way that Christians were being treated. Then he was executed—again.

Christians of the Middle Ages admired the way Sebastian found the strength to fight again after the first attempt on his life. Sebastian is therefore considered the patron saint of athletes.

Memorial of

St. Agnes

martyr (died c. 258)

Most of us know someone who died while still young. The value of a person's life can't be measured by the number of years she or he spends on earth. Some people live with more meaning and joy in one day than others do in years. Agnes was such a person; she lived a whole lifetime of love for God in just 13 years.

Although Agnes was young when she was martyred, her courage made a great impact on the people around her. A church was built over her tomb after her death. She may be the most famous of the early Roman martyrs.

A skull believed to be hers is still preserved in the church of St. John Lateran (see November 9) with relics of other martyrs.

According to legend, Agnes was very beautiful. When she refused a proposal of marriage from a pagan, the young man reported to the emperor that she was a Christian.

The name Agnes means "pure" in Greek. It sounds like the Latin word *agnus,* which means "lamb." Every year on this day, two lambs from a special flock are blessed in the Roman church that bears her name. At Eastertime, the soft wool from these lambs is sheared and made into vestments for bishops of the church.

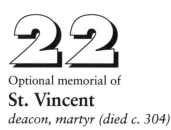

Optional memorial of

St. Vincent

deacon, martyr (died c. 304)

Vincent was born in Saragossa, Spain. As a young man, he was instructed in the faith by his bishop, Valerius. Valerius then ordained Vincent a deacon. Because Valerius had difficulty speaking, he entrusted to Vincent the important task of preaching. Vincent also instructed new Christians as Valerius had instructed him.

At this time the Roman emperor was persecuting Christians. Valerius and Vincent were highly visible Christians because they were leaders. Dacian, the brutal governor of Spain, threw them into prison. He hoped to shake their belief so that they would deny Christ. But, though starved and treated harshly, they would not give up their faith. This made Dacian furious.

When Dacian commanded the two to sacrifice to the pagan gods, Vincent spoke for both of them. He assured Dacian that they were ready to suffer everything for the one true God. Dacian sent Valerius into exile and had Vincent tortured. But the young deacon went to his death rather than renounce Christ.

When Vincent died, Dacian had the body left out for wild animals to devour, but according to legend, a raven guarded Vincent's remains. Because of this legend, paintings of Vincent often show him with a raven.

Vincent is the patron saint of the city of Lisbon in Portugal and is buried in the cathedral there.

Memorial of

St. Francis de Sales
bishop, religious founder, doctor of the church
(1567 – 1622)

The noble father of Francis de Sales had planned a brilliant career for him in the senate of Savoy in France. But Francis had other plans. Although he earned a degree in law in his early 20s, his heart's desire was to serve the poor and preach the gospel. He struggled gently to persuade his family to allow him to enter the priesthood.

Francis was offered the opportunity to become an official of the diocese of Geneva. His father gave in and allowed him to be ordained. Francis found his work challenging, to say the least.

People in one province of his large diocese were warring with one another. Francis traveled on foot through the area for several years, preaching and ministering to the people. During this time he endured many dangers. Once he was beaten by a mob. On another occasion he spent a winter night in a tree surrounded by a pack of wolves. Eventually he restored peace and a prayerful spirit to the diocese.

In 1602, Francis was appointed bishop of Geneva. He continued to travel constantly and took great joy in preaching and giving spiritual direction. He also loved teaching the children of his diocese, who followed him wherever he went.

Francis loved to counsel ordinary people about their prayer lives. He assured them that "saintliness is both desirable and possible." For them, Francis wrote *Introduction to the Devout Life.* It was translated into several languages and is still in print today.

Francis's last word before he died was the name of Jesus.

Feast of the

Conversion of St. Paul
apostle (For more about St. Paul, see June 29.)

The ninth chapter of the Acts of the Apostles tells the story of Paul's conversion to Christ. This story is so important that Luke includes it two other times in the Acts of the Apostles, and Paul tells the story in his own words in the first chapter of his Letter to the Galatians.

Before he became known as Paul, his name was Saul. He was a tentmaker from the city of Tarsus. Saul had studied to become a teacher. When Stephen (December 26), the first Christian martyr, was killed, Saul held the coats of those who threw the stones.

Saul set out for Damascus. He wanted to arrest any Christians who had escaped from Jerusalem after Stephen's death. Along the way, Saul was struck down to the ground and blinded. He heard the voice of Jesus. Jesus asked him, "Saul, Saul, why are you persecuting me?"

Saul was in shock. He allowed himself to be led to the home of Christians in Damascus. A holy man named Ananias prayed with him and his sight was restored. Saul went to an isolated spot to reflect on his new faith. Then he returned to Damascus and began preaching the gospel.

Everyone was astounded at the change in him. Now Saul was the one being persecuted. His friends feared for his life. They helped him to escape from Damascus by lowering him over the wall of the city in a basket.

Saul, who began to call himself by the Roman name of Paul, went out on missionary journeys. He crossed the Roman empire four times to bring the good news of Christ to the world.

January

Memorial of
Ss. Timothy and Titus
Timothy (died c. 97) and Titus (died c. 94),
bishops

We remember Paul's partners on this day after the feast of Paul's conversion. There was the married couple, Prisca and Aquila, who were Christian leaders in the cities of Ephesus and Rome. There was Chloe, a woman who was the head of a group of Christians in the city of Corinth.

There were Timothy and Titus, who traveled with Paul. Sometimes Paul would send one of them ahead as his messenger, or else he would ask one of them to stay behind when he moved on. That helped a new community establish itself.

Timothy and Titus served as Paul's representatives when he could not visit a community that needed him. Because they had some Gentile (non-Jewish) ancestry, both these young men seemed well-suited to bring the gospel to Gentile lands. Also, both were beloved friends of Paul.

Timothy's mother was Jewish, so he studied the scriptures while growing up. That early training helped him to understand Paul's message when the apostle first preached in Timothy's hometown of Lystra. Paul called Timothy a preacher; this was a high compliment.

Eventually, Timothy became the first bishop of Ephesus, a city in what is now Turkey. This meant that he carried responsibility for all the churches in the region. He was martyred for protesting the worship of pagan gods.

Titus was probably from Antioch, another city in Turkey. He served as Paul's secretary. He was a talented peacemaker, and he was sent by Paul to Corinth when there was a scandal in the community. He carried with him a stern letter from Paul.

Because Titus showed patience and tact, the Corinthians were able to accept Paul's scolding. Titus was so well respected in Corinth that he later returned there to ask for donations for needy members of the church.

Eventually Titus was named the bishop of the island of Crete. He worked very hard throughout his long life, and he died a peaceful death.

27

Optional memorial of
St. Angela Merici
religious founder (c. 1474 – 1540)

Angela Merici was born in Desenzano in Italy. She spent much of her early life grieving. By the time she reached her twenties, she had lost the five people closest to her. Her parents, her favorite sister, the uncle who raised her, and her best friend had all died. She could have spent her life in sorrow. But Angela saw that there was great need around her. In filling that need, she found new joy and hope.

Angela especially noticed the needs of the poor children of her town. Four friends came to live with her, and they began to teach religion to young girls.

The work went well. Angela designed a training program for teachers. Soon she was asked to begin a school in the city of Brescia. She also gave spiritual encouragement to a group of men and women there. They provided funds for the school.

In 1525 the pope tried to convince Angela to take charge of a congregation of nursing sisters, which was a job with great honor. But she didn't want so much fame. Even more important, she sensed that her true mission was to teach.

In time Angela gathered a group of young women. Some of them lived in community, but many others lived at home with their families. They wore simple clothing, prayed and studied together, and devoted their lives to teaching. They called themselves the Ursulines. They were to become the first teaching order of religious women. They chose Angela as the head of the group. She held that position for the last five years of her life.

The Ursulines flourish to this day and still have as their mission the education of young women.

Memorial of
St. Thomas Aquinas
presbyter, religious, doctor of the church
(c. 1225 – 1274)

The classmates of Thomas Aquinas had a nickname for him. They called him "the dumb Sicilian ox" because he was big, slow-moving and shy. They didn't realize until later that their classmate was fantastically intelligent.

Thomas's family was related to emperors. He was born in the family castle at Rocca Secca in Italy. His parents prepared him for a life of importance. Instead, humble Thomas joined the Dominicans, an order whose friars took a vow of poverty.

His family felt angry that Thomas would be begging for his living. His six older brothers, who were soldiers like their father, held him captive for more than a year while his mother and sisters tried to talk him into changing his mind. During this time, Thomas calmly read and studied. He also learned a great deal of the Bible by heart. Finally his family gave in and allowed him to return to the Dominicans.

Thomas kept quiet in his university classes because he did not like to show off his intellect. However, he was so brilliant that he became a professor at the University of Paris. He was also known as a great preacher.

In those years, just about everyone talked about religion. They got into big arguments over small matters. Some people insisted that the truth of spiritual things is different from the truth of material things and that only spiritual truths really mattered. But Thomas said to look in a mirror. Ask yourself, where does the body stop and the soul begin? How is it possible to separate spirit and matter?

In future years the ideas of Thomas Aquinas became the way that theology was taught in much of the church.

Thomas's writings fill 20 volumes. Perhaps he was able to produce so much in the midst of a busy life because of his deep prayer life. Celebrating the eucharist often moved him to tears. He treated everyone with patience and kindness. During his whole life he was never known to lose his temper or speak sarcastically about another person.

Thomas died at age 50. Because of his writings, Thomas has been honored with the title "Angelic Doctor" ("doctor" here means "teacher").

30

Anniversary of the death of
Mohandas Gandhi
(1869 – 1948)

Mohandas Karamchand Gandhi did something remarkable. When he started working in his homeland of India, most people of different classes and different religions didn't even speak to one another. Gandhi managed to unite the vast country. His work has had a great effect on the rest of the world, too.

Mohandas Gandhi was born in a town in western India. His parents were religious Hindus. Gandhi was shy. As a young man, he studied law in England. Visiting South Africa to help a client, Gandhi was mistreated because he was Indian. The experience changed his life. He and his family moved to South Africa, where he fought against injustice for the next 21 years.

In 1914 Gandhi and his family returned to India. The country was ruled by the British. Gandhi began to understand that most of the huge profits made in India were sent to Britain, while the people of India suffered in poverty. He saw that the people stayed powerless against this injustice because different religions fought one another and most people were divided into a rigid system of social classes.

The situation seemed hopeless. Gandhi managed to begin to change it by his own simple lifestyle. He learned how to spin cotton to make his own cloth so that he wouldn't have to buy cloth from England. He dressed like a member of the lowest social class, an "untouchable," even when he was meeting world leaders. He told the truth. He always announced his plans beforehand in the struggle against the British.

Gandhi's most important tool of change was nonviolence — protesting wrongs without doing injury. For the sake of nonviolence Gandhi was jailed, as were his wife and friends, and many of his followers died. But eventually India became an independent nation. Shortly after that happened, Gandhi was murdered.

Nonviolence has now become a tool of change in other countries. Martin Luther King, Jr. (page 26), brought the teachings of Gandhi to the American civil rights movement.

The Indian people honor Gandhi with the title of "Mahatma." This means "great soul." In their land, it is the highest compliment.

31

Memorial of

St. John Bosco

presbyter, religious founder (1815 – 1888)

To call others to Christ, John Bosco used everything he could think of, even acrobatic tricks and tightrope walking. His cleverness stood him in good stead. Many young people learned about God because of the care they received from John.

He was born in a small village in the Piedmont region of Italy. His father, a peasant farmer, died when John was only two years old, leaving the family very poor. When young John went away to the seminary at age 18, even the clothes on his back had been donated by people from his village.

John decided that his ministry would be in Turin, the closest city to his village. Turin was becoming an industrial town. Teenage boys would leave their poor families in the countryside and come into town searching for work. In the city these teenagers lived in terrible conditions.

Even before his ordination, John began taking a group of boys out to the country every Sunday for sports, a picnic, song and prayer. No one else cared about them. After John became a priest he housed boys who had nowhere else to live. Then he began programs to train them as shoemakers, tailors and printers. The training protected them from a harsh world they were too young to face.

Many of the boys and young men John assisted were troubled. Often they had experienced abuse or neglect. Somehow John called forth the best in them by affirming them and treating them kindly. This was considered a very unusual approach to teaching. Most teachers in those days thought that children must be forced to learn and punished severely when they didn't.

The number of young people in John's care grew ever larger. He had trouble finding assistants who understood his gentle teaching methods. Eventually he began an order of priests and an order of sisters. He also started a group of laypeople called Cooperators. All were trained especially for this work. Today these orders serve in schools, colleges, seminaries, hospitals and missions all over the world.

February

The second month of the year takes its name from the Latin word for "purification."

The ancient Roman calendar had ten months, March through December. (December means "tenth month.") There was no January and no February. These days were left off the calendar. Strange as it seems, people didn't feel the need to keep track of the days during winter.

The late winter period before March became a season, like Lent, of purification and renewal. When the Romans began using a 12-month calendar, the old names for the months continued to be used. The month before March got named for the season of purification.

The third Monday in February
Presidents' Day (U. S. A.)

Today is a celebration of the lives and works of President George Washington and President Abraham Lincoln. Years ago, many states observed the birthday of Abraham Lincoln on February 12 and that of George Washington on February 22. In 1971 the two observances were combined and moved to the third Monday of the month. That made it possible for many Americans to enjoy a three-day weekend.

1

Roman martyrology
St. Brigid of Ireland
religious founder (c. 450 – c. 525)

Many legends are told about Brigid. One of the loveliest is that she helps to chase away the winter and usher in the spring. Another story tells that, when she was only ten, she would give food and clothing from her household to poor people. She worked as a dairymaid and would give milk, butter and cheese from her master's cows to the needy. Her generosity made her much loved.

Brigid was born near Kildare in Ireland. Her mother, a sickly woman, was a Christian and a slave. When Brigid was young, she persuaded the Druid master to set her mother free. Brigid could then follow her heart's desire and give her life to God.

There were no convents in Ireland, so Brigid founded one, near Kildare. Here, and at the other communities she would begin throughout her life, providing for the poor was the most important work. "What is mine is theirs," she said.

Brigid's simple life of prayer and penance influenced the growth of the church all over Ireland. During her lifetime, her reputation for holiness spread through Europe. When she died, she was buried in Downpatrick, very close to the graves of St. Patrick and St. Columba. This was considered a great honor.

Brigid is one of the patron saints of Ireland. Irish farmers pray to the former dairyworker to protect their cattle from harm. Many Irish cottages and barns display St. Brigid's crosses, made of straw. In Ireland she is sometimes called St. Bride.

February

2

Feast of

The Presentation of the Lord: Candlemas

Today is 40 days after Christmas. In many places the nativity scene is left up until today. On this day it is decorated with the first flowers of spring before it is taken down and put away.

Today we celebrate a joyful event told in the second chapter of the Gospel of Luke. When Jesus was 40 days old, Mary and Joseph brought him to the Temple in Jerusalem to present him to the Lord. In the Temple Jesus was recognized by Anna and Simeon, two elderly people of great holiness. They were filled with joy. Simeon took Jesus in his arms. Old age embraced youth.

Simeon spoke a beautiful prayer: Now that he saw the Messiah, he could die in peace. Simeon also spoke of the sadness to come, which would pierce the heart of Mary.

Simeon called Jesus "a light to the nations." The light of Jesus' presence in the world has been celebrated on this day for many centuries.

On today's feast, enough candles are blessed to last the whole year. That's why today is also called "Candlemas." It is a feast of light. At church everyone joins in singing Simeon's song. In some parishes, the people light the candles and carry them all around the church and even out into the streets. We can carry the light of Christ to every corner of the world.

Groundhog Day

The Celtic people divided the year differently than we do now. For them, February 1 was the first day of spring. The first days of May, August and November marked the beginnings of the other seasons. That way of dividing the year makes a lot of sense in northern Europe, where the change in the length of days is dramatic.

St. Brigid's Day and Candlemas Day are associated with folklore about the arrival of spring, or at least the arrival of lengthening days.

German farmers say that on Candlemas the badger interrupts its winter nap to check the weather. If the day is sunny, the badger sees its shadow and gets scared, and then goes back to hibernate for six more weeks. The bright, cold days of winter aren't over yet. But if the day is cloudy, the badger cannot see its shadow. That means that hibernation is over and the cloudy, warmer weather of spring is about to arrive. Good news for the farmers!

German farmers who immigrated to Pennsylvania did not find badgers. They decided that groundhogs would provide the spring forecast, instead. So on Candlemas Day we wonder if the groundhog will see its shadow or if spring is coming soon.

3

Optional memorial of

St. Blase

bishop, martyr (died 316)

Blase was the bishop of Sebaste in Armenia. He was martyred during the persecution of Christians by the Roman emperor Lucinius.

Blase is said to have been a physician as well as a bishop. A legend tells that Blase saved the life of a boy who was choking on a fish bone. Blase is now the patron saint of all who have diseases of the throat.

On his feast day in many parishes of the United States, people have their throats blessed. It's no surprise that this custom coincides with the peak of the sore throat and flu season. Years ago, wintertime illnesses were very dangerous. Before the discovery of penicillin, a person could die from complications of a sore throat.

The tradition of blessing throats began at a time when the church's calendar was filled with blessings for the saints' days. Many of these are no longer practiced, but somehow, the custom of blessing throats survived. Two candles are tied in the shape of a cross, and the candles are touched to our necks. We can think of the blessing of our throats as a sign of God's care for every part of us.

Optional memorial of
St. Ansgar
bishop, missionary (801 – 865)

Accepting difficulties and disappointments with a spirit of faith and good cheer is sometimes what makes someone a saint. So it was with Ansgar. He was born near Amiens in France. As a boy he dreamed of traveling to dangerous, distant lands. He wanted to spread the gospel.

Ansgar became a monk. He loved preaching and working with poor people. King Harold, in exile from his country of Denmark, was so impressed with Ansgar that he asked the young monk to return there with him. Ansgar converted many Danish people to Christ. Soon King Bjorn of Sweden invited Ansgar and some companions to come to his country. During their stay they built the first Christian church in Sweden.

In the year 831 Ansgar became the first bishop of Hamburg in Germany. For the next 14 years he organized missions to the peoples of northern Europe. He built churches and even started a library. (Books were very rare in those days.) But

in 845 a tribe of fierce pirates, the Northmen, invaded Hamburg. With fire and sword they destroyed much of the area. It must have seemed to Ansgar that his work had been canceled out.

In time Ansgar was able to return to both Denmark and Sweden. When he did so, the people's faith was rekindled.

Bishop Ansgar continued to serve the poor. To imitate Jesus, he would wash the feet of his people and wait on them at meals. Because of missions to Sweden, Norway and Denmark he is called the apostle of Scandinavia.

Memorial of
St. Agatha
martyr (died c. 251)

Agatha died at Catania, on the island of Sicily, during the early Roman persecutions. Her tomb can still be visited in a network of catacombs on another island, Malta. After her capture she is said to have told her torturers, "To be a servant of Christ is to be truly free."

Agatha is one of the patrons of Sicily. For many centuries, Sicilians have prayed to St. Agatha when Mt. Etna, a volcano on their island, threatens to erupt.

Like many other early martyrs, Agatha is known to us only by her death. Stories about her life were not written down until several centuries later, so we have no way of knowing whether or not they are true. What we do know about Agatha, though, is that she must have been a person of outstanding faith and courage. We can tell this because she was held in such high esteem by the other Christians of her own community.

Agatha continues to be held in esteem. She is mentioned in the first eucharistic prayer of the Mass. In the sixth century two churches in Rome were given her name. Famous mosaics at Ravenna in Italy portray legendary scenes from her life.

Memorial of
St. Paul Miki and companions
Paul Miki, religious, missionary, martyr, and companions, martyrs (died 1597)

Most Americans know the town of Nagasaki, Japan, as one of the places where the atomic bomb was dropped during the Second World War. But for more than three centuries before that, Nagasaki was the site of a Christian community.

Paul Miki is one of a group of Christians who were martyred near Nagasaki. Paul himself was a Japanese-born Jesuit priest. He was a talented preacher and teacher.

Francis Xavier (December 3) had brought the Christian faith to Japan 50 years earlier. However, in 1588 the Japanese emperor ordered all Christians out of Japan. Some stayed behind, in disguise, to minister to the community that needed them. Among these were Paul and two other Jesuit priests, six Franciscan priests, and 17 other people. They were carpenters, cooks, translators and catechists. Three were altar boys.

Some of the Christians were tortured and marched captive through towns as a warning to anyone else who might think of disobeying the emperor. Then all were placed on crosses. They had their sides pierced with swords. St. Paul Miki and his companions were the first Christian martyrs of the Far East.

More than 200 years later, Christian missionaries were allowed to return to Japan. To their surprise they found that thousands of people living around Nagasaki were secret Christians. They had learned the faith from their ancestors, who remembered the martyrs.

Optional memorial of
St. Jerome Emiliani
religious founder (1481 – 1537)

Jerome Emiliani didn't start out very saintly. Perhaps this was because he lived in rough times. Famine, plague and war were everywhere around him.

Jerome's father died when Jerome was very young. At the age of 15, he ran away from his mother and became a soldier for the city-state of Venice. Like most professional soldiers of his time, Jerome was tough and lived a rowdy personal life. He became the commander of a fortress near the town of Treviso. When the town fell to enemies, he was taken prisoner.

In the dungeon, Jerome started to pray. Then, it seems miraculously, he escaped. Filled with joy, he hung his chains at the altar of the church in Treviso. He promised to devote his life to the service of God.

Soon Jerome returned to Venice, where his military toughness served him well. He took on the most difficult job he could find: caring for incurable patients in the hospitals. Realizing that there were now a great number of orphans in the city, he rented a house for them. He gave them food and clothing, and he taught them about Christ.

In 1531, Jerome became ill with plague. When he recovered, he wanted to do even more to serve the needy than he had before. He established three more orphanages where the children were provided with job training. He worked side by side with the peasants in the farm fields, and he talked to them about the goodness of God. He also created a shelter where prostitutes could find a safe way of life. Helping women was an unusual idea in those days.

Jerome started a religious order for other men who felt called to serve the special needs of people in that time of terrible diseases. They were called the Society of the Servants of the Poor. They still serve orphanages and schools in Italy.

Jerome cared for the poor and the sick all his life. He died of a fever he caught while caring for victims of an epidemic. He was 55 years old.

Byzantine calendar

St. Zechariah

prophet (sixth century BCE)

Zechariah's mission was to encourage the Jews who returned to Jerusalem after their exile in Babylon. He was one of several prophets who were active at that time.

Zechariah's prophecies (recorded in the first eight chapters of the Book of Zechariah) were spoken after the building of the new Temple was begun. The unforgettable images from his visions were meant to energize the Israelites to complete their task. Centuries later those images would also inspire Christian writers, especially the author of the Book of Revelation. One such image describes a new Jerusalem with only God for its walls. The city would have no enemies, unlike the Jerusalem of the past, which had been destroyed by Gentiles.

The later chapters of the Book of Zechariah record the wisdom of another prophet, who spoke 150 to 200 years after Zechariah. Sometimes this person is called Second Zechariah.

Second Zechariah speaks of a great leader to come who will bring peace to all nations — but who will be a humble shepherd. He will not ride a horse, as warriors do. Instead, he will ride a lowly donkey.

A few centuries later, Jesus would call himself the good shepherd, and he would ride into Jerusalem on a donkey. By this action he was letting everyone know that he was not a proud and powerful leader. He was the humble and peaceable shepherd of the Book of Zechariah.

Memorial of

St. Scholastica

religious (c. 480 – c. 543)

When Scholastica was alive, the Roman Empire was falling apart. But Scholastica and her brother Benedict (July 11) spent their lives showing others how to live as Christians in a chaotic world. They did such a good job that even in the chaotic world of today people are still living by the ways they taught.

Benedict founded the abbey of Monte Cassino in Italy, where he wrote a rule of life for monks. The rule taught people how to treat each other with gentleness and respect, as he and Scholastica had always treated each other. Scholastica decided to become the first woman to live under the rule. She established a convent, Plombariola, about five miles south of Benedict's abbey.

Scholastica and Benedict allowed themselves one day a year to talk about God together. They would meet at a little house halfway between the convent and the abbey.

At one such meeting, Scholastica sensed that this would be their last visit. When Benedict got up to leave, she prayed for rain. Immediately such a downpour began that they had to stay up all night waiting for the sky to clear. They talked all the while about God, to Scholastica's delight. Three days later she died.

Scholastica and Benedict are buried together at Monte Cassino.

11

Optional memorial of
Our Lady of Lourdes

On February 11, 1858, 14-year-old Bernadette Soubirous was gathering wood with two other girls at a small rock cave, near the town of Lourdes, in the Pyrenees Mountains of southern France. Suddenly she saw what she described as "a girl in white, no taller than I, and beautiful."

The young woman spoke to Bernadette in the dialect used in her little village. She addressed Bernadette with great courtesy. This made a tremendous impression on Bernadette, who was a below-average student and the daughter of poor parents. She was not used to being treated with such respect.

Bernadette saw the vision 18 times. When she asked the woman who she was, she responded, "I am the Immaculate Conception," using a term Bernadette had never heard. During one of the later appearances the woman in the vision told Bernadette to dig for water with her hands. When the girl did so, she uncovered a spring. The spring still flows, at the rate of 27,000 gallons daily. Many people have come to Lourdes in the years since the appearances to bathe in the spring and to pray for healing from all kinds of diseases.

Bernadette never wanted the fame that the appearances brought her. She retired to a convent where she spent her days living as simply and as humbly as possible. She was very ill throughout her short life, and she died in 1879 at the age of 35. She was declared a saint in 1933. The French and the Canadians remember St. Bernadette Soubirous on April 16.

12

Anniversary of the birth of
Abraham Lincoln
(1809–1865)

All American presidents face challenges. But few have dealt with greater difficulties and shown more courage than Abraham Lincoln.

Lincoln was born in a log cabin in Kentucky. He worked hard from the time he was very small. He helped his father clear the land, plant crops, and build a cabin in Indiana. Because his work was needed on the farm, he was not able to go to school very often. In his spare time, he read every book he could find.

Later he moved to Illinois and studied law. He won election to the Illinois legislature and soon became a member of the United States Congress.

Slavery was an important issue in those years. It was still legal in the South, but many northerners, including Lincoln, were against it. Lincoln was outspoken on the subject. He said slavery was "a cancer," and many people agreed with him.

In 1861 Lincoln was elected president of the United States. The southern states were so unhappy about Lincoln's election that they broke off from the United States and formed their own nation, causing the Civil War. During the war Lincoln issued the Emancipation Proclamation, a statement that freed the slaves. (Slavery was ended completely by the 13th Amendment, which was passed in 1865 while Andrew Johnson was president.)

The war lasted four years. Over 600,000 people died, and parts of the country lay in waste. In 1864 Lincoln was reelected, and he hoped to "bind up the nation's wounds." But on April 14, 1865, he was shot by an assassin

Today is Lincoln's birthday. On this day many people visit his tomb in Springfield, Illinois. Lincoln is also remembered today at Cooper Union in New York City, where he gave a famous speech before he was nominated for president. He is remembered on Presidents' Day as well.

Memorial of
Ss. Cyril and Methodius
Cyril, religious, missionary (826 – 869), and Methodius, bishop, missionary (c. 815 – 884)

Cyril and Methodius were brothers. Born in Thessalonika, Greece, they were the sons of a senator. As young men, both held important posts. Cyril taught philosophy at the University of Constantinople. Methodius was a governor. But both felt a hunger for a life of prayer, so they retired to a monastery.

Soon afterward they were asked to bring the Christian faith to the Khazars, a tribe of people in what is now southern Russia. Before beginning their mission, the brothers learned the Khazar language. Their hard work and study helped them to bring many people to Christianity.

Then they traveled west to Moravia (now in the Czech Republic). Again their ability to speak the native language, Slavonic, helped them to win many new Christians. Up to this time Slavonic

had no written characters, so nothing could be recorded in that language. Cyril and Methodius used Greek letters to invent an alphabet for the Slavic people. (The "Cyrillic" alphabet, a later version of their invention, is still used in Russia and several other countries.)

Now the people could write down their stories and poetry for the first time. Cyril and Methodius began to translate the Bible and liturgical books into Slavonic.

The brothers traveled to Rome because they were having trouble with certain bishops, who complained about the use of the "barbaric" Slavonic language. However, the pope blessed the work of Cyril and Methodius. During their stay in Rome, Cyril died. Methodius was made a bishop and was sent back to Moravia, which became his diocese.

Unfortunately, out of spite, the hostile bishops imprisoned him for two years. He used that time to continue the translation of scripture that he and Cyril had begun. He died a few years later.

Eleven centuries have passed since that time. Ss. Cyril and Methodius are especially honored by Central and Eastern Europeans. The bright and energetic brothers represent common ground between the Catholic and Orthodox churches. With St. Benedict (July 11) they are co-patron saints of the continent of Europe.

Roman martyrology
St. Valentine
bishop, martyr (died c. 269)

There probably were two Valentines, both martyred around the year 269. One of them may have been the bishop of Terni, Italy. In those days of persecution, Christians met secretly and hid their faith to protect their lives. Bishops were unable to hide and were often the first Christians in their communities to be tortured and killed. Often a bishop died in the hope that other Christians would not be hunted out.

The other Valentine was a priest and physician in Rome. A legend says that he sent letters of love and encouragement to the people of his community who lived in fear of persecution. From that legend the practice of sending valentines on his feast day may have begun.

But there is another explanation for the custom of sending valentines. In the Middle Ages people believed that on February 14, the day St. Valentine died, birds began choosing their mates for the springtime. So this day came to be thought of as the perfect day to choose a sweetheart.

17

Optional memorial of the
Seven Founders
of the Order of Servites
religious (thirteenth century)

More is not always better. In about the year 1226, the city of Florence in Italy was a prosperous center of trade and culture. But the booming times had a down side. The noble families fought among themselves for political power. Religious faith was all but forgotten. People were distracted from spirituality by their wealth and the busyness of city life.

At this unlikely time and place, seven men of noble birth began meeting frequently to pray. None of them had taken part in the feuds that rocked the city. Over time they became close friends. Eventually they decided to devote their lives to reflection and prayer.

The men moved into a house just outside of Florence. But so many visitors from the city came

to see them that they didn't have time to pray. They built a retreat in a wild and isolated spot on a mountainside 11 miles from Florence. There they lived as simply as possible.

Several years later, they adopted the title "Servants of Mary," the Servites. They began to admit newcomers, and the order grew rapidly. Only one of the original seven, Brother Alexis, lived to see its approval by the pope. By that time Servite houses for women had been established, too. The order soon spread all the way to Crete and even India. Some Servites live contemplative lives, focusing on prayer, work and silence. Others teach or work in parishes or missions.

The seven founders who had worked and prayed together for so many years were all buried in the same tomb.

18

Anniversary of the death of
Martin Luther
(1483 – 1546)

Martin Luther lived in a time when greed was an especially serious problem. In attempting to fight the injustice, he found himself the leader of the Protestant Reformation.

Martin was born in 1483 in Eisleben in Saxony (in what is now part of Germany). His father wanted him to study law. Instead, Martin became a monk. He studied scripture at the newly founded University of Wittenberg. On a trip to Rome during his studies, Martin visited the ancient shrines of Christianity. He was shocked by the corrupt priests and monks who made a profit at those holy places. Many had become wealthy by pretending to sell God's blessings.

In 1517, Martin wrote out his concerns about what was wrong in the church. On the eve of All Saints' Day he posted them on the door of All Saints Church in Wittenberg so that other people could discuss them. Over the next few years the discussions grew angry. Almost everything about the church came into question. Reconciliation seemed unlikely.

Eventually, like many other people during those years, Martin was excommunicated — banned — by the Church of Rome. His writings were supposed to be burned, but copies were made on the newly invented printing press and distributed throughout Europe. Martin's German translation of the Bible and his other works became available to many.

Martin taught at the University of Wittenberg until he died at the age of 62. His students spread his message throughout Germany, Scandinavia, eastern Europe and beyond.

Martin Luther never intended to divide the church, but that is what happened. The efforts to correct abuses split the church into many factions. These divisions have remained, but today, many of the churches have finally begun to work and even to pray together.

Anniversary of the death of
Frederick Douglass
(c. 1817–1895)

American slave owners thought that educated slaves were dangerous. So one of the many freedoms slaves were denied was the right to learn to read. However, a slave from Maryland named Frederick Douglass somehow did learn to read and write. We are fortunate to have his powerful firsthand record of what slaves went through.

Frederick was sent away from his family to work in Baltimore at the age of ten. (This was typical for a slave child.) His new owner's wife noticed that he was bright and eager to learn. She taught him some basic reading skills. When her husband found out, however, he stopped the lessons. Frederick struggled to continue the process alone. For hours each night he studied the only books he owned, a Bible and a hymnal.

During the next several years Frederick suffered brutal treatment. He felt discouraged at the thought of a lifetime of slavery ahead of him. At the age of 21, he managed to escape to New York by disguising himself as a sailor. Though he found prejudice in the North as well, Frederick was happy to be free. He and his wife Anna worked hard to make a life for themselves.

Frederick was asked to speak about his life to people who opposed slavery. The crowds who came to hear him were spellbound at the story he told. No slave had ever described the experience in a public way. In making his story known, Frederick took the risk of being captured and returned to his owner. Finally, for safety's sake he traveled to England for two years. While there, he received donations of money to buy his freedom.

Frederick became known as an "abolitionist," a person who works to abolish slavery. He began a newspaper to guide slaves to freedom. He also published the story of his life. During the Civil War, Frederick used his influence in the African American community to recruit soldiers for the Union army.

After the war, Frederick Douglass held several important positions in the federal government. His home, called Cedar Hill, is now a national shrine located in Washington, D. C.

February

Optional memorial of

St. Peter Damian

bishop, religious, doctor of the church
(1007 – 1072)

"That which does not kill me makes me strong."
The life of Peter Damian proves the truth of this
old saying.

Peter was a survivor. Born into an already large
family in Ravenna, Italy, Peter was seen by his
family as just an extra mouth to feed.

When his parents died, Peter found himself in
the household of an older brother, who underfed
him and treated him as a slave. Like the prodigal
son in the Gospel of Luke, Peter was forced to
tend pigs. Finally another brother provided him
with the money to go away to school.

Despite his lack of early training, Peter was
a fine student. By the time he was 25 years old he
had become a famous professor. He taught at the
universities at Parma and Ravenna. Perhaps
because he knew what it was like to go hungry,
Peter invited poor people to dine with him almost
every evening. He served the meal himself.

Peter wanted to pray and study scripture, so he
became a monk. Soon he was appointed head of
his community, and he remained in that position
for 30 years.

Eventually Peter was named bishop of Ostia
and a cardinal of the church. He fought hard
against abuses of power by the clergy, such as paying bribes to obtain important jobs in the church.
He encouraged monks to live a simple life of
prayer. He was asked many times by popes to
assist other monasteries, especially when they had
arguments or scandals. Seven popes considered
Peter their trusted advisor.

On the way home from one of his papal missions, Peter caught a fever and became very ill. He
died a peaceful death while the monks around him
sang Morning Prayer.

Feast of

The Chair of Peter

apostle

In pagan times in Rome today was "Ancestors'
Day." People remembered the dead, especially
their parents. The Christians of Rome began to
celebrate this day in memory of St. Peter, their
"founding father," their first bishop. Peter had
come to Rome because Rome was the center of
the empire and a center of the new Christian faith.

Why is today's feast called the *Chair* of St. Peter?
Every bishop has a chair from which he presides
and preaches. In Rome, in the basilica of St. Peter,
an ancient wooden chair is preserved because it
is thought to have been St. Peter's. The Latin word
for a bishop's chair is *cathedra*. From this word
comes our word "cathedral," which is the home
church of the bishop in each diocese.

Today's feast of the Chair of Peter honors the
unity of the church. Peter's chair has served as a
symbol of his role as pastor of the whole church.
This role has given popes great influence to speak
for human needs and to condemn injustice.

Anniversary of the birth of

George Washington

(1732 – 1799)

All George Washington ever really wanted to do was work on his farm in Virginia. However, he had to leave that work to lead the 13 colonies to independence against tremendous odds. Later, as president, he guided the new republic through its first years.

George Washington's father, a farmer in Virginia, died when George was very young. When George was just 20, his older brother also died. George took his brother's place as head of the army in Virginia. He showed courage during the French and Indian War. In one battle he rescued an English general who lay wounded in the midst of the fighting.

When the colonists decided to fight for their independence, George Washington was the obvious choice for a leader. He encouraged his troops in all their hardships. They endured because they trusted him, and they won the war.

After the Constitution was written, George Washington was unanimously elected the first president. He served for eight years. Then he went home to Mount Vernon and worked on his farm.

The people of the United States remember Washington on Presidents' Day.

Memorial of

St. Polycarp

bishop, martyr (died c. 155)

Polycarp knew people who had known Jesus. That made him a "second generation Christian." We know the names of very few people of this generation. (Two others are Justin, who is remembered on June 1, and Ignatius of Antioch, remembered on October 17, who met and talked with Polycarp.) The apostle John appointed Polycarp bishop of the city of Smyrna (now Izmir in Turkey). This link with Jesus made Polycarp precious to people.

During his long service as bishop of Smyrna, Polycarp faced many challenges. Christians were a minority there. Most of the people of Smyrna enthusiastically worshiped not only the Roman gods but the living emperor as well. Polycarp also faced difficulties from within the faith. A parade of false teachers appeared, one after the other. Polycarp bravely spoke against them to protect his people from confusion.

Around the year 155, a great pagan festival was held in Smyrna. The Romans were hunting for known Christians who could be sacrificed. Polycarp was a very old man, and his friends insisted that he hide. When Roman police found his hiding place, he offered them a meal. While they ate, Polycarp prayed for all Christians throughout the world.

Polycarp was taken to the Smyrna stadium. The festival crowds gathered the wood for his execution by fire. But, according to an ancient story, the flames would not burn him, so he was stabbed to death. Polycarp showed so much courage when he died that the emperor's police burned his body so that Christians would not try to worship it.

Polycarp's burnt bones are entombed with honor in the church of St. Ambrose in Rome. The name Polycarp means "many fruits." In northern lands, the sap begins to rise in trees around this time, which means the spring is almost here.

March

March is the month of the vernal equinox, when daytime grows equal to nighttime and spring begins in the Northern Hemisphere. The lengthening days warm the air and help create the March winds. A few days in March are as cold as deep winter, a few are as warm as springtime, and many of the days are stormy. No wonder March is named after Mars, the Roman god of war. The struggle against winter is a strong sign of the season of Lent. Summer and winter seem to battle through this month.

The first Friday in March
World Day of Prayer

Imagine the entire globe encircled by Christians with their arms outstretched. In a sense, that's what happens today. On this day each year Christian people from many traditions and in more than 170 countries join in a great "circle of prayer." It is held at the beginning of March, so in most years it falls during Lent.

The idea for the World Day of Prayer came from Church Women United, a group that works for peace and justice. Each year a prayer service for the event is written by women from a different part of the globe. It deals with an issue such as homelessness, the environment, or children in poverty. The service includes scripture readings, poetry, dramatic readings, music and a sermon. Study materials help people to reflect on what they will hear and how they can respond.

Some American churches hold a supper on the eve of the service, and many take up a collection to support food drives and other service projects around the world.

1

Roman martyrology
St. David
abbot (c. 520–c. 589)

People who turn up wearing green leeks or a daffodil today are probably Welsh. Leeks and daffodils on the first of March are used to celebrate today's remembrance of David, patron saint of Wales.

David started out as a hermit. He lived a very simple life of prayer. He ate only bread, water and vegetables, such as the leeks that grew wild in Wales. (Leeks are like large green onions.)

When people learned of David's holiness, they came to him for guidance. Eventually, other young Welshmen joined with David in more than a dozen monasteries he founded. Like him, they lived a stern life. They even pulled plows themselves instead of using oxen. They hoped that they'd become as prayerful as David. He was considered such a good teacher that in time he was made bishop.

A legend about David says that he assisted his homeland when the Saxons invaded Wales. David told each Welsh warrior to wear a leek in his hat so they would know friends from foes. The Welsh won the battle and the leek has been the emblem of Wales ever since.

People from Wales have settled all over the world. Because many men had worked as miners in Wales, large colonies of Welsh can be found in the mining areas of Pennsylvania, Ohio, Wisconsin and Tennessee. The Welsh are noted for their love of song and poetry and for their many beautiful hymn tunes.

In this country, the daffodil often replaces the leek as the symbol of St. David's Day, and it is still worn with pride.

2

Anniversary of the death of

John Wesley

(1703 – 1791)

John Wesley and his brother Charles (1707 – 1788) were the sons of an English minister. While students at Oxford University the two brothers gathered a group of their Protestant friends. They prayed together, visited prisons and performed other kinds of Christian service. Other students gave these serious Christians several nicknames. The one that stuck was "Methodist." It described the Wesleys' method of regular prayer, Bible discussion and spiritual reading.

One evening at a prayer meeting, John Wesley suddenly felt sure of Christ's love for him. Later he wrote in his journal, "I felt my heart strangely warmed." This experience gave John's preaching new energy. He began to travel through the English countryside on horseback and foot. He preached to huge crowds of people in their fields and factories, homes and streets.

In those early years of the Industrial Revolution, people worked in the factories under terrible conditions. Millions of these working poor knew little about the gospel, even though they lived in a Christian country. John assured them that their hearts could be renewed just as his had been. He also offered uneducated men and women opportunities to preach. This was unheard of in those times.

John's brother Charles also boosted the appeal of the new movement. Knowing that the people loved to sing, he wrote the words and music for hundreds of hymns. Most everyone today knows some of his songs, such as "Hark, the herald angels sing" and "Jesus Christ is ris'n today."

For 50 years the brothers led the Methodist Revival. They worked for the end of slavery, better conditions for workers, and a free education for every child.

3

In the U. S. A., optional memorial of

St. Katharine Drexel

religious founder (1858 – 1955)

Katharine Drexel was from a wealthy and well-known Philadelphia family. Her parents were good to the poor. Her father made large donations to charity and her mother helped poor families to pay their rent every month. As a child, Katharine reflected on this. She wanted to help the poor when she grew up but wasn't sure how to do so.

Katharine and her family traveled all over the United States and Europe. On one unforgettable trip, the Drexels traveled to the state of Washington on a private train. Katharine was shocked by the poverty she saw on Indian reservations there. Later, while visiting Rome, the family spoke with Pope Leo XIII. Katharine begged him to send missionaries to help neglected Native American communities like the ones she had seen. To her shock, he said, "My child, why don't you become a missionary yourself?"

Eventually Katharine Drexel did just that. Then, as always, talented and committed workers were more urgently needed than donations. In 1891, with 13 other women, she founded the Sisters of the Blessed Sacrament. They worked to provide for the needy, and over time Katharine donated 12 million dollars of the fortune she had inherited.

Katharine and her sisters first opened a boarding school for Pueblo Indian students in Santa Fe, New Mexico. In time they founded missions for

Indians in 16 states. They began a secondary school for African American students in New Orleans. This school was the forerunner of Xavier University. (Other universities in the South were not open to black students in those days because of segregation laws.)

In the years after the First World War, when African American people moved from the South to work in northern cities, the sisters also started schools in Chicago, Boston and New York City.

It wouldn't have been easy to recognize Reverend Mother Katharine as the same person who had once toured the West on a private train. As she traveled across the country spending her fortune on new schools, she tried to live as simply as she could. Her clothing was threadbare. She bought the least expensive railroad tickets and carried her lunch in a brown paper bag.

Katharine Drexel died in 1955 at the age of 96. People of all races from across the United States journeyed to Philadelphia to attend her funeral.

4

Optional memorial of
St. Casimir
prince (1458–1483)

Casimir's father was the king of Poland. Like most kings, he fought wars to expand his power. His son Casimir was expected to fight for treasure and the family's honor, but Casimir found a different mission. He fought for what he thought was right. Casimir had a tutor who guided his natural concern for others and his talent for leadership.

While his father was away in Lithuania for two years, Casimir ruled the kingdom with great skill. Throughout his life he dedicated himself totally to serving poor people. He gave away all he owned.

He considered himself "father, son and brother" to widows, orphans and all oppressed people.

Casimir died of tuberculosis when he was only 26. For the greatness he showed during his short life, he is honored as a patron saint of Poland and of Lithuania.

7

Optional memorial of
Ss. Perpetua and Felicity
martyrs (died c. 203)

Perpetua and Felicity were two of a small group of Christians who were arrested in Carthage in northern Africa. They encouraged each other and prayed together in prison. All the prisoners were then martyred in the amphitheater.

In that part of the Roman Empire, the authorities were no longer trying to eliminate all the Christians. But every so often, a few Christians were killed to discourage anyone else from becoming Christian.

Perpetua, who was only 22, was probably arrested because her family was wealthy. However, her mother and brothers — who were also Christians — were spared. Her father was a pagan and begged her to deny Christianity, but she explained to him that she couldn't tell a lie and renounce her faith. Perpetua's name means "eternal."

Felicity, whose name means "happy," was the wife of a slave, and she may have been from Perpetua's household. She was pregnant at the time they were arrested, and she gave birth to her baby during their imprisonment.

Both women were treated cruelly in prison, but they showed so much courage and patience through their hardships that the jailer, Pudens, became a Christian, too.

8

Optional memorial of

St. John of God

religious founder (1495 – 1550)

No one is quite sure any longer what happened to John of God as an eight-year-old boy. He may have run away from his home in Portugal; he may have been kidnapped. What is certain is that soon after that he found himself homeless in Spain.

John served in the army, then became a shepherd. When John turned 40, he became anxious about what might be left of his life. He wanted his remaining years to have meaning. He went back to Portugal to find his parents, only to learn that both had died. He felt sad and guilty. He thought back on his life as a soldier and decided that he had brought harm to people instead of goodness.

John opened a house in Granada. He invited in anyone who had nowhere else to go. His guests were beggars, prisoners just released from jail, prostitutes, the poor. He came to be a familiar sight in Granada, carrying home a cripple he had found on the street. Years of soldiering had taught him how to care for wounds. Now he used that knowledge to nurse the sick.

John begged strangers for money to feed his friends. Volunteers, including some of the needy people John had rescued, joined him in his work. They became a religious order, the Brothers Hospitallers, still serving the sick to this day.

At age 55, John got sick after he jumped in a river to save a drowning man. His illness grew worse, but he would not rest in the Lord until the archbishop of Granada promised to watch over all John's house guests. Then John died peacefully.

International Women's Day

Although this holiday originated in the United States, it is not well-known here. It is celebrated in many other countries of the world. Even small countries such as Mauritania and the Cape Verde Islands hold a national holiday today in honor of the working women of their land. On this day in China and countries of the former Soviet Union, working women receive gifts or flowers.

A hundred years ago, workers who made clothing in factories had no one to speak for them or to support their rights. In New York City, women worked 59 hours a week for a paycheck of nine dollars. They were fined half a day's wages if they came to work even a few minutes late or if they made a mistake in their sewing.

In the summer of 1909, many women in New York City began to strike — they walked off their jobs and refused to return until their concerns were heard by the owners of the companies. Workers who took this courageous step were sometimes beaten by police.

In November, workers from many different companies met and decided to call a general strike against all the companies that were treating workers unjustly. In time 30,000 people joined them and the strike spread to Philadelphia.

The workers continued to strike through the next few months. Many people who weren't garment workers supported them, and in time the companies gave in on some points. They lowered the number of hours in the workweek to 52, and they agreed to treat employees more fairly and give them better working conditions.

A few years later, an international women's conference established this day to remember the garment workers' victory. The day now has special meaning for women in developing nations.

March

9

Optional memorial of
St. Frances of Rome
married woman, religious founder (1384–1440)

As a young woman, Frances had a very comfortable life. Her husband Lorenzo, the son of Roman nobles, prized her beauty and her goodness, and they had several children whom they dearly loved. The family lived in a castle with cooks, maids and a gardener. But there was one thing that prevented her life from being complete: Frances wanted with all her heart to serve the poor.

Most of the noble people Frances knew would have thought this a senseless desire, but her sister-in-law Vannozza shared her secret dream. Dressed in their plainest clothes, the two young women would take baskets of food to the poor of the city.

Lorenzo supported Frances's unusual service to others. He donated money from his family's riches for the work. Frances was so respected in Rome that many other rich women decided to serve with her.

But Frances's life suddenly changed. Rome was split by civil war. Lorenzo and their son Battista were taken prisoner. Soldiers burned and looted the castle.

Frances, Vannozza and the children continued to live in a part of the castle that remained standing. There they cared for the many refugees wandering the city. When money ran out, they sold their jewels for food and medicine. After that, they begged in the streets.

Three years later, Frances's children Evangelista and Agnes died from plague. Even in her grief, Frances cared for others. After a time Lorenzo and Battista were allowed to return from exile, but Lorenzo's health had been ruined, and he died three years later.

In the last years of her life Frances lived with the order of women she had founded to care for the sick. She is still beloved in her city, and each year on her feast day, her family palace is opened to the public. Romans come in crowds to remember and honor her.

Roman and Byzantine martyrologies
Forty Holy Martyrs
(died 320)

During the season of Lent, Eastern Christians celebrate the feast of the Forty Holy Martyrs. These saints were Christian soldiers of various races from the city of Sebaste in Armenia. They refused to obey the demand of the emperor Licinius that they abandon their religion, so they were sentenced to death by freezing. Forced to lie on a frozen pond, they encouraged each other during their ordeal.

One soldier lost heart and ran for a warm bath that the emperor had prepared to tempt them. A pagan soldier, inspired by the courage of the other 39, joined the martyrs. So their number remained complete.

This feast tells us something about Lent itself. During the 40 days of this season, we try to die to whatever is not life-giving in us. On this March day it is a custom to search for the returning birds and to listen for their songs. The deadly power of cold winter will not last forever. The Easter victory of Christ is coming soon.

10

Anniversary of the death of

Harriet Tubman
(c. 1820–1918)

Before the Civil War, many thousands of Africans were kidnapped and brought to the United States. They were enslaved and used by Southern farmers to harvest tobacco and cotton crops. Slaves who could somehow escape to northern states, where slavery was illegal, could live in relative safety as free people.

But escaping was difficult and dangerous. Slave owners trained hunting dogs to track runaways, who were punished brutally when they were caught. A large number of Northerners and Southerners who thought slavery was wrong banded together secretly to help runaway slaves reach freedom. Their escape routes came to be called the "Underground Railroad."

During these times, Harriet Tubman was born into slavery in Maryland. Like most slave children, Harriet dressed in a sack with holes cut out for her arms and head. She went shoeless all year round. She was underfed and was beaten severely for mistakes. She received no schooling.

Harriet grew up strong from years of farm work, such as plowing fields and driving oxen. This made her a valuable slave. She worried that her owner might sell her as he had already sold her two older sisters. Then she would be chained to other slaves and taken even farther south.

One evening Harriet learned that her fears were about to come true. She decided to escape to the North before morning, although she had little money and had never traveled anywhere alone. She couldn't say goodbye to those she loved, so she walked through the plantation where she lived, singing lines from a hymn, "Goodbye, I'll see you in the kingdom."

Following the North Star, wading through streams to disguise her trail, Harriet searched out black and white "conductors" on the Underground Railroad. They gave her directions, food and disguises. Showing great ingenuity and courage, she found her way to Philadelphia, where slavery was outlawed. She found a job, worked hard and saved money. But she could not be content until she shared her freedom with her family. Though it would be dangerous, she decided to make her way back to get them, saying, "I can't die but once."

Harriet rescued her three brothers, who also had been sold. Later she drove her aged parents north in a cart she had built herself. Altogether, Harriet made 19 trips south and rescued more than 300 slaves. Each trip was more dangerous than the last because her name became known to slave owners. A $40,000 reward was offered for her capture. That was an enormous sum of money in those days.

Harriet acted as scout, nurse and spy during the Civil War. Afterward, she opened a home for elderly people. She cared for her parents and spoke out for the rights of women and of black people. She was known to African Americans as "Moses" because she delivered so many people from slavery.

13

Anniversary of the death of

Susan B. Anthony
(1820–1906)

Susan Brownell Anthony was born in South Adams, Massachusetts. Her father was known for speaking out against slavery. Susan received an excellent education, which was very unusual for a girl in those days.

March

As a young woman Susan worked hard for social change. She started a group called a "temperance society" to protest the selling of liquor. She worked for the freeing of slaves and for improvements in the education of children.

In time, she decided that none of her ideas would become reality unless women were granted more rights. In most states women could not vote or own property, and married women who worked had to give their wages to their husbands. So Susan worked for the passing of laws that would help women, including one that allowed women who worked to keep their earnings.

Susan worked especially hard to change the Constitution of the United States so that all women in America would have "suffrage," which is the right to vote. She published a newspaper called *Revolution* so that more women would understand her ideas. In 1869 Susan and some of her friends began the National Women's Suffrage Association.

Susan B. Anthony lived and worked until the age of 86. Fourteen years after she died, the 19th amendment to the Constitution gave women in the United States the right to vote. Some states and many schools celebrate Susan B. Anthony's birthday on February 15. Other states honor her on August 26, the day the 19th amendment became law.

15
The Ides of March

This day has been noted in history since 44 BCE, the year the Roman leader Julius Caesar was assassinated on this date. This event was so unsettling for Rome that a law was passed making the Ides of March an official unlucky day! Its bad reputation was sealed in the sixteenth century when William Shakespeare wrote the play *Julius Caesar*. "Beware the Ides of March" is one of its most famous lines.

Before Julius Caesar's time, each month lasted from one new moon to the next new moon, about 29½ days. So half the months of the year had 29 days and the other half had 30.

The Romans named days to mark the phases of the moon. The *kalends* was the first day of a month, at the new moon. (We get the word "calendar" from this word.) The *ides* marked the middle of the month, when the moon was full.

Julius Caesar changed the calendar to one very much like the one we use now. (See January 7.) Months no longer began with every new moon, and the ides of a month didn't always come at the time of the full moon, although people kept using the old words kalends and ides for the beginning and middle of months.

16
Roman martyrology
St. Abraham
patriarch (c. nineteenth century BCE)

Abraham is honored by Jews, Christians and Muslims as their father in faith. Abraham understood his friendship with God to be a covenant, a sacred trust on both sides. He passed that understanding along to his descendants.

Abraham's story begins in the eleventh chapter of the Book of Genesis. He first appears as Abram, a prosperous herdsman living in the city of Ur of Chaldea (near the tip of the Persian Gulf). There he married Sarah (August 19), and they moved to Haran in Mesopotamia.

However, Abram was willing to leave his secure life when God promised him a new land. With only God's word as his guide, he led his family to Canaan, which would one day be known as the land of Israel. Then God made another remarkable promise: Abram's descendants would be as many as the stars in the sky, and through them all the nations of the earth would be blessed. Although Sarah and Abraham were old, Sarah gave birth to a son, and they named him Isaac.

The greatest test of Abraham's faith is told in chapter 22 of Genesis. God asked Abraham to sacrifice Isaac. In sorrow, Abraham again made a journey of faith, this time to a place called Moriah where he would offer up his son to God. (Traditions say that Moriah is a hill in the holy city of Jerusalem, and that Solomon's temple was built on this hill.)

Abraham prepared to kill his son, but at the last moment an angel held Abraham's hand. God assured him that such a sacrifice would not be required. Abraham's trust and obedience were enough of a sacrifice.

When Abraham died he was buried next to his beloved wife Sarah in the land promised to them by God.

17

Optional memorial of

St. Patrick
bishop, missionary (c. 389 – 461)

When Patrick was 16, his father's farm in Britain was invaded. The raiders carried Patrick off with his father's servants to be slaves in Ireland.

Patrick spent the next six years tending sheep. As a slave, he suffered greatly from loneliness. But in his isolation he found a deep sense of God's love for him. He began to pray.

Finally Patrick was able to escape. He made his way home to Britain. He became a monk and studied so that he could return to Ireland as a missionary. By the year 433, he had also become a bishop. Patrick went back to Ireland and traveled throughout the land. He preached to the Irish in their own language, which he had learned during his years of slavery. By the time Patrick died 25 years later, most of the Irish people were baptized.

Monasteries in Ireland became centers of learning. Missionaries sent from Ireland later played a large part in bringing Christianity back to Europe after European cities were destroyed by invading tribes.

St. Patrick's Day always comes during Lent, when the church is getting catechumens ready for baptism at Easter. Patrick used the three-leafed shamrock to try to explain to catechumens the mystery of the Holy Trinity.

Irish people the world over celebrate today by wearing green. In Ireland, most Catholics attend Mass. In the United States, there are parades and many celebrations.

18

Optional memorial of

St. Cyril of Jerusalem
bishop, doctor of the church (c. 315 – 386)

Cyril was born near Jerusalem around the year 315. He studied the scriptures and the great teachers of the early church. Then he was ordained a priest. Cyril's bishop knew that he was an excellent teacher, so he placed Cyril in charge of instructing catechumens. Because many people wanted to become Christian, and there weren't enough believers to prepare them, Cyril designed a program to teach catechumens in groups.

Cyril became bishop of Jerusalem about the year 350. At this time the Arian heresy — the belief that Christ was a man who gradually became God — was causing division among Christians. The emperor believed in this false teaching. Even Acacius, the bishop of the city of Caesarea, had fallen into this mistaken belief.

Acacius wanted to be named the bishop of Jerusalem, so he accused Cyril of misusing church funds. Cyril was driven out of Jerusalem, and he escaped to Tarsus. By the time he was able to come back home, Jerusalem had fallen into a terrible condition. Cyril tried to help the people, but Acacius demanded that the emperor exile him. Cyril was forced out again and could not return until the emperor died. Of his 35 years as the rightful bishop of Jerusalem, 16 were spent in exile. However, he was never bitter about his difficulties. He remained kindhearted all his life.

Cyril was able to spend the last eight years of his life quietly working with the people of his diocese. He left behind him a peaceful Christian community that loved the liturgy and that ministered to the poor. For his clear teaching about the divinity of Christ, Cyril is called a "doctor," which means a "wise teacher."

19

Solemnity of

St. Joseph

husband of the Virgin Mary (first century)

Matthew's gospel describes Joseph as "a just man." In Bible times, the most beautiful compliment one person could give another was to call him or her a *tzaddik,* a person of justice and virtue.

Mary and Joseph were engaged to be married. Joseph found out that Mary was pregnant, and he knew that he was not the father of the baby. But an angel appeared to Joseph in a dream. The angel said, "Do not be afraid to take Mary as your wife. The child is from the Holy Spirit." The angel told Joseph to name the baby "Jesus," which means "God saves."

After Jesus was born, Joseph had another dream. He was warned of King Herod's plan to kill Jesus. That very night Joseph and Mary and Jesus fled to Egypt to hide from Herod's soldiers.

People in many countries honor St. Joseph. His day always falls in Lent, and he is considered the patron saint of the poor. Many Sicilian people combine all three lenten disciplines — prayer, fasting and almsgiving — by inviting the poor to a special banquet called a "St. Joseph's table." Lenten dishes such as meatless pastas are served, along with wine and fruit. Italian and sometimes Polish parishes in the United States sponsor St. Joseph's tables. The custom includes prayers and songs for Joseph and for Lent.

In Spain, the city of Valencia hosts fireworks and parades to celebrate the week between St. Joseph's Day and Annunciation Day, March 25. The streets are decorated with papier-mache figures of Joseph and Mary and other saints.

Joseph is a patron saint of Mexico, Canada, Bohemia (in the Czech Republic) and Belgium, too. He has become known as the patron saint of the church, of fathers, of a happy death and of prayer.

20/21
Vernal equinox

On two days of the year, one at the beginning of spring and one at the beginning of fall, day and night are each exactly 12 hours long. That's what the word "equinox" means. The word "vernal" means "spring."

Today marks the first day of spring in the Northern Hemisphere. From now until the autumnal equinox, days will be longer than nights.

The most important date of the Christian year, the date of Easter, is determined by the vernal equinox. For most Protestant and Roman Catholic Christians, Easter Sunday is the first Sunday after the first full moon after the equinox. That can fall any time between March 22 and April 25.

The vernal equinox occurs during Lent. In fact, the word "Lent" is related to the word "lengthen" because during Lent the days lengthen and the nights get shorter. The word Lent also is an old word for springtime.

Optional memorial of
St. Turibio de Mogrovejo
bishop (1536–1606)

Even though he's not well-known in the United States, St. Turibio was one of the first canonized saints of the Western Hemisphere.

Turibio had carved out a brilliant career for himself in his homeland of Spain. He was a teacher of law at the great university at Salamanca. He was also respected as the chief judge of the church court. Imagine his shock when he learned that he had been named bishop of Lima, Peru. He wasn't even a priest!

Turibio protested the appointment, but the decision was final. At the age of 43 he was ordained a priest, consecrated bishop, and sent across the Atlantic. Turibio had been chosen because conditions in Peru were very grave. The Spanish conquerors were so eager to make themselves rich that they had forced the Peruvian people into slavery to work in gold mines.

Turibio wanted to understand the needs of his people. In a journey that took seven years, he traveled the 18,000 miles of his diocese. Sometimes he had a mule to ride, but often he went on foot, traveling alone. He braved storms, wild animals, jungles and mountains. He began to speak out boldly against the unjust actions of the Spanish. They resisted him in every way they could.

All his life Turibio studied native languages so that he could teach the people and understand their situations. He baptized and confirmed a great number of people. Among them were Rose of Lima (August 23) and possibly also Martin de Porres (November 3). He supported the building of churches, hospitals, schools and even roads.

Altogether Turibio crossed the vast diocese three times. He was traveling when he became fatally ill at age 68. He asked to be carried into the nearest town so that he could receive the eucharist. He gave away everything he owned to the poor before he died.

March

24

Anniversary of the death of
Oscar Arnulfo Romero
(1917–1980)

"Be a patriot; kill a priest." In the troubled Latin American country of El Salvador, handbills bearing this violent slogan were once seen everywhere. In spite of the danger, Archbishop Oscar Romero kept speaking out for justice. His boldness eventually cost him his life.

Oscar Romero was born in a small town in a remote part of El Salvador, which is a tiny country in Central America. Oscar's family was neither rich nor poor. This was unusual in El Salvador, where there are almost no middle-income people. A few rich, powerful people rule the many poor.

Oscar was apprenticed to a carpenter at age 13, but he wanted to be a priest, so a year later he entered the seminary. Oscar was bright, and he was placed in church jobs that would train him to become a bishop. When he was appointed archbishop of San Salvador, he was welcomed by the rich ruling families of the country. Although they were guilty of violence against the poor, they thought Oscar would not make any trouble for them. He was known to be shy and conservative.

But after a short time as a bishop, Oscar could no longer overlook the sufferings of the poor. He said, "They are crushed in their homes, taken prisoner, made to disappear. They go to jail, are judged falsely, and no one pays any attention."

He felt called to be the voice of all the people without a voice. During his sermons in church he spoke against political repression. These sermons were broadcast on radio and thousands of people listened.

Some Salvadoran priests and other church workers were being called traitors for defending the rights of the poor. Some had already been murdered. After three years of constant threats to his life, Oscar was shot to death while celebrating Mass at a hospital chapel. His assassination shocked the world.

The violence in El Salvador was only beginning. Bomb blasts and rifle shots exploded into the huge crowds attending his funeral, killing 40 more people. During the 1980s, many thousands died violently. The people of El Salvador know that their bishop died for the sake of his flock. To this day, they treasure his memory.

25

Solemnity of
The Annunciation of the Lord

According to the first chapter of Luke's gospel, the angel Gabriel came to tell Mary about God's plan of salvation. The angel announced that Mary was chosen to be the mother of Jesus, the Son of God. Mary freely answered, "Here I am, the servant of the Lord." Despite her puzzlement over the angel's mysterious words, she trusted in God's goodness.

At Easter we take joy in the willingness of Jesus to be our Savior by his death and burial and rising. Today God begins that work by becoming flesh in Mary's womb. This mystery is expressed in the Angelus prayer, which some people recite at the beginning, middle and end of each day. Here are its final words:

> Lord, fill our hearts with your grace:
> once, through the message of an angel,
> you revealed to us the incarnation
>   of your Son;
> now, through his suffering and death,
> lead us to the glory of his resurrection.

Artists often show Mary in a garden when Gabriel appeared to her. They want to remind us of the garden of Eden, where Adam and Eve said "no" to God. Here, today, in a new garden, Mary said "yes."

In ancient times, scholars worked out all the feasts of the year mathematically. They decided that March 25 is a remarkable day. They calculated that this is the day Jesus died on the cross. Perhaps too the Jews' exodus from Egypt and even the creation of the world began on this day. And if all those things occurred on this one wonderful day, then surely this must be the best day to begin each new year.

For several hundred years, beginning in the twelfth century, March 25 was the official New Year's Day in many Christian countries. This matches the practice of several other cultures and countries, such as Iran, which still begin the year at the vernal equinox.

The Annunciation of the Lord is celebrated with symbols of the Holy Spirit, such as wind and fire. Christians in Greece fly kites on this holiday. Jamaicans have sailboat races. Scandinavian and French people make yeast-raised waffles and serve them with whipped cream. It is a day to search for signs of the newly arrived springtime.

April

The word April means "to open." This is the time of year that leaf and flower buds open. In most northern countries, this is a month of transformation. The day is now longer than the night. Even if the nights are still chilly, the daytime sun is strong and growing stronger. The earth itself seems to take part in the Passover of the Lord.

1
All Fools' Day

The first of April probably became All Fools' Day in 1564. That was the year the French began to use the new Gregorian calendar. A few centuries before that, Christians had moved the start of the year from January 1 to March 25, Annunciation Day. Everyone celebrated the New Year for eight days. On April 1, the festival ended with parties where gifts were exchanged.

In 1564, the first of January once again became the first day of the year, but some people loved the old custom. They didn't give up their New Year's parties on April 1. They were called "April fools."

Nowadays in France an April fool is called a *poisson d'avril,* an "April fish." Young fish that appear in streams around this time of year are more easily caught than older, cagier fish. French shops sell chocolates shaped like fish for the occasion. People try to pin paper fish on each other's backs as a joke.

In some places in England, an April fool is called a "noddy." In Scotland on this day, don't let anyone send you out searching for hen's teeth or pigeon milk, or you'll be called a "gowk" — a cuckoo!

Optional memorial of
St. Francis of Paola
hermit (1416–1507)

From the time he was very young, Francis of Paola had a gift for prayer. He modeled himself after his namesake, St. Francis of Assisi. At age

15, his parents allowed him to retreat to a little spot of land on their property in Paola, a small town in southern Italy. Later he moved to an even quieter place, a seacoast cave.

Francis's goodness soon became known throughout the area. By the time he was 20, two other men asked to join him in his very strict way of life. As more disciples came, he formed them into a Franciscan community and called them the Hermits of St. Francis of Assisi.

These men were called "Minims" because they wanted to be thought of as the least of God's servants. When they began to build a monastery and a church, everyone who lived nearby — even the rich nobles — cheerfully carried stones to help with the building.

When King Louis XI of France was deathly sick, he asked the pope to send Francis to his side to cure him. When Francis got there, the king offered him money in exchange for a miracle. Francis sharply pointed out that only God can heal. Then he consoled the king and helped him to prepare for a holy death.

The two kings who succeeded Louis admired Francis. They wouldn't allow him to return to Italy. Instead, they kept him in France so they could ask his advice.

Francis spent the last 25 years of his life in France. Being unable to go home made him sad. However, the advice he gave to the French kings during that time restored peace between France and its neighbors, Great Britain and Spain.

At age 91, Francis spent three months preparing for death. Then, on Holy Thursday, he called his community to his side. He encouraged them to continue their work in the humble spirit of Christ, who on this night washed the feet of his disciples. On Good Friday, while the Passion according to St. John was being chanted in the church, Francis died in peace.

Optional memorial of
St. Isidore of Seville
bishop, doctor of the church (c. 560–636)

Isidore's brother, Leander, was the bishop of Seville. After the death of their parents, Leander became Isidore's teacher. He was much older than Isidore, and very strict. Isidore often felt discouraged. But he learned so much that he was later known as the "Schoolmaster."

When Leander died, Isidore became bishop. Over the 37 years of his office, Isidore worked with the Visigoth people who had invaded Spain.

Isidore valued education. He designed a plan to place a cathedral school in every diocese of Spain. These schools were very unusual in those days. The instructors taught law, medicine and every other branch of knowledge.

Isidore wrote the first encyclopedia. He tried to include everything known at that time. He also wrote a history of Spain.

Isidore was a humble man. Poor people came to his house in great numbers. When he knew he was dying, he gave away everything he had not already shared. He asked two brother bishops to help him clothe himself in sackcloth and ashes, which was the clothing sinners and criminals wore. That is how he prepared himself to die.

5

Optional memorial of

St. Vincent Ferrer

presbyter, religious, missionary (c. 1350–1419)

Vincent Ferrer was a Spanish Dominican priest, born in the city of Valencia. He was one of the greatest preachers of his time. With singleminded determination he made preaching journeys through Spain, France, the Netherlands and Switzerland, drawing large crowds.

Unfortunately, Vincent was also known for his attacks against the Jewish people and for trying to convert Jews to Christianity against their will.

There are other saints guilty of this terrible sin, just as there are saints who supported slavery and saints who treated women badly. Saints are human beings and therefore are sinners. In the gospels Jesus reminds us that he came for sinners, and that even the angels rejoice whenever a sinner repents.

Vincent continued to preach, working until just before he died at the age of 70.

7

Optional memorial of

St. John Baptist de la Salle

presbyter, religious founder (1651–1719)

In the days of King Louis XIV of France, the country had only two classes of people: the very poor and the very rich. In time, these unjust conditions would lead to the French Revolution. But John Baptist de la Salle did something revolutionary of his own. Born to a rich and well-known family, he spent his life teaching the poor.

John was born in the city of Rheims. As a youth he was intelligent, handsome and a smooth talker. He became a priest and studied to receive a doctorate in theology. With so much education, he expected to hold a powerful position in the church.

John's ambitions took an unexpected turn while he was serving as a priest at the cathedral in Rheims. There he met Adrian Nyel. In those days, only the rich could afford to send their children to school. Adrian had a dream of educating poor children, and he wanted John to help him.

John did not enjoy going into the slums, but Adrian convinced him to help begin a school for poor boys. John began training teachers. He taught them how to plan lessons and keep order in classrooms.

Soon his community of teachers became the "Brothers of the Christian Schools." They were the first religious group whose special mission was to teach the poor. The brothers taught their students how to live in the world as Christians.

Back in those days, classes were taught in Latin. If you didn't understand Latin, you couldn't learn. The brothers began to teach in French so ordinary students could understand. John realized that this work was a call from God. He resigned from his post at the cathedral and gave away his share of the family fortune to the victims of a famine. John opened the first teachers' college, schools for poor children in Paris and other French cities, and industrial schools for boys.

Not everyone understood John's bold actions. His wealthy family opposed his choices. Schoolmasters disapproved of his teaching methods. Some of his schools were raided by the police and closed down.

John Baptist de la Salle died on Good Friday at the age of 68. He is a patron saint of teachers.

April

9

Anniversary of the death of
Dietrich Bonhoeffer
(1906–1945)

Dietrich Bonhoeffer began his life in a world very different from the one in which he died. He was born into a prosperous Lutheran family in Breslau, Germany. His father was a doctor, and most people thought that Dietrich would become a doctor, too. Instead, he decided to become a minister.

Dietrich studied theology at a famous German university. Afterward, he continued his studies in New York City, where he occasionally attended African American churches in Harlem. He was struck by the faith he found there.

Dietrich returned to Germany for ordination in 1931. At this time Adolf Hitler and the Nazi Party were beginning their climb to power.

In a strange way Hitler brought hope to the German people, who were suffering from an economic depression. He blamed Jews and Communists for everything that was wrong in the country.

Hitler did not permit people to speak their minds in universities or newspapers. But Dietrich opposed the Nazis' racist policies from the start and was not afraid to speak out. In 1934, with other concerned clergy, he formed the "Confessing Church," a group of German Protestants who refused to cooperate with the Nazis.

Because of his stand, in 1936 Dietrich was removed from his teaching position. When staying in Germany became too dangerous for him, he went to London for a while. But he turned down a teaching position far away in America where he would have been safe. His conscience would not let him leave his friends behind.

Somehow, even though he was well-known to the Nazi government as a troublemaker, a few of his friends managed to get him a position in the German secret service. Here, within the Nazi war machine itself, a secret plan to assassinate Hitler was underway. However, the Nazi police found out about the plan.

In April of 1943, Dietrich was arrested for crimes against the state. He spent many months in prison in Berlin. During this time he wrote letters and reflections. In the closing days of the war, he was taken to various concentration camps. Finally he was hanged. The prison doctor, who witnessed the execution, said later that Dietrich knelt peacefully in prayer just before he died.

Dietrich's writings were nearly all unpublished until after his death. Now, people of all Christian churches study them. They challenge the church to preach the gospel even in difficult times.

11

Memorial of
St. Stanislaus
bishop, martyr (1030–1079)

Stanislaus Szczepanowski (shchep-an-OV-skee) was the son of noble parents in Poland. He decided early in life that he wanted to be a priest. He was sent to the best schools, even as far away as Paris. Later, as a young preacher back in Kracow, on Sunday mornings he drew crowds from all over the city.

In 1072 Stanislaus was chosen to be bishop of Kracow. The people of the city were overjoyed. They loved their new bishop. They felt free to ask him for advice, shelter, food or whatever they needed. He kept open house for the poor.

The king of Poland, Boleslaus II, was called "the cruel." He led his country into unjust wars. He cheated the poor. Of all the people of Poland, only Stanislaus spoke out. Everyone else was afraid. Stanislaus said that if a king was unjust, he had no right to be a king. He also said that an unjust king could not be a member of the church.

King Boleslaus attempted to destroy the bishop's reputation by spreading rumors about him. But the people did not believe the lies. Finally, King Boleslaus brought his guards to a church where Stanislaus was celebrating Mass. He ordered them to kill Stanislaus. When the guards wouldn't obey him, Boleslaus took a sword and did it himself.

After some time, the king was forced out of Poland. According to a legend, he repented of the wrongs he had done and spent his last years in a monastery in Hungary.

13

Optional memorial
St. Martin I
pope, martyr (died 655)

We Christians believe that Jesus Christ is fully God and also fully human. When Martin was pope, many people were teaching that Jesus was not really a human being. Martin spoke out clearly against this mistaken idea. He said that it was a heresy, a false teaching. That put him on a collision course with Emperor Constans II, who believed the heresy.

The emperor tried to set the bishops against Martin. When that plan didn't work, Constans sent a servant to have Martin killed. But this plan also failed. Finally Constans sent his troops to Rome, where they found Martin sick in bed.

Martin was taken to Constantinople and accused of being a traitor because he would not honor the false teaching about Jesus. As punishment, Martin was dragged through the streets with a chain around his neck. Then he was put in a jail cell with murderers.

Martin was sentenced to death, but after several months he was instead sent to a faraway prison, where he died from starvation. Martin was the last pope to die a martyr.

Optional memorial of
St. Anselm
bishop, doctor of the church (c. 1033 – 1109)

Anselm's father was rich and stubborn. He wanted Anselm to spend his life looking after the family estates in the Piedmont, a region in northwestern Italy. However, Anselm wanted to be a monk.

When he was 22 years old, Anselm entered the Benedictine Abbey at Bec in Normandy, a region of France. Only three years after his ordination, he was elected prior. He treated the monks in his care with great kindness.

Anselm became known in England, and in 1093 he was named Archbishop of Canterbury. It was a difficult position for a man who was already 60 years old and in poor health.

The king of England, William Rufus, wanted to control Anselm's decisions. Though Anselm was a gentle and humble man, he would not yield an inch to the king. The other bishops were afraid, so Anselm was forced to stand alone. Though he longed for the peace and quiet of his monastery, he fought endless legal battles and was even sent into exile for a while.

Anselm spoke out against injustices. He said that slavery was wrong. Through his efforts, a law was passed making the sale of human beings illegal in England. He cared for the poor people in his diocese. He also wrote hundreds of letters giving spiritual direction to people who asked him for guidance.

When William Rufus died, Henry I became king. At first he struggled with Anselm, just as Rufus had. But in time Henry came to respect Anselm so much that when the king traveled he left the bishop in charge of the country.

Anselm found time to write books and essays about the Christian life. Because his work was so rich in meaning, he has been given the title of "doctor (teacher) of the church."

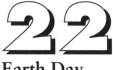

Earth Day

Perhaps the most important thing the astronauts on the first trip to the moon did was bring back photos of Earth. Until that time, most people probably thought of their planet as a larger version of a globe, with every country a different color edged by visible borders.

In the historic 1969 photos we earthlings saw a very different picture. The earth was mostly vast blue ocean misted with clouds. No borders between nations could be seen on the land masses. Citizens of Earth were reminded that we all share the same home.

Just at the time the photographs appeared in magazines, scientists found out that almost every creature in Lake Erie had been killed by pollution. This discovery made many people aware of the dangers we humans cause ourselves and the creatures who share our planet, by the ways we treat our air, farmland and water. The first Earth Day was held in 1970, and people came together all over the United States to show their concern.

Since then new laws and a new organization, the Environmental Protection Agency, have been created in the United States. Lake Erie has been cleaned up. Some dangerous pesticides have been banned from use for growing fruits and vegetables. Air pollution from lead, a serious problem not long ago, has all but disappeared. That's the good news.

But we've found new reasons for concern, too. Around the world, millions of square miles of tropical rain forest are being burned. Pollution from factories and automobiles is killing northern forests. Pollution also may be causing holes to open up in the protective ozone layer of the earth's atmosphere.

The problem is global. Air pollution created in the United States doesn't stop at the borders. It drifts into Canada. It travels to Europe. Eventually it circles the world. We need to act as united citizens of the planet to protect the environment. In 1992, 178 world leaders met in the city of Rio de Janeiro in Brazil to discuss environmental concerns. This meeting was called the Earth Summit. This was the largest gathering of leaders ever held. It reflected growing hope that people everywhere might begin to work together.

During this Easter Season, we Christians celebrate a reverence for all life. At the first reading of the Easter Vigil, we hear how God created the earth and called it good. Today we pray that our children's children will still be able to describe it that way.

Optional memorial of
St. George
martyr (died c. 303)

Born in Cappadocia in Asia Minor (in what is now Turkey), George may have been a soldier in the Roman army. He died a martyr's death, probably at Lydda in Palestine. He was much admired by the other Christians of his time.

There are many myths about George. The best-known tale tells of a dragon that was terrorizing a town because it wanted meat. When the townspeople ran out of animals to feed it, it demanded to be fed children. The king's brave daughter dressed herself in a wedding gown and went to the dragon's cave to offer herself as its dinner. But George killed the dragon before it could harm her. Then he married the princess and together they barbecued the dragon to serve at their wedding feast.

In the Middle Ages, theater guilds put on plays about the lives of the saints. The life of St. George became a favorite. The play had a happy ending, even for the dragon, who came back to life. The princess would lead it through the streets with a ribbon tied around its neck, and everyone followed behind singing "alleluia."

People loved the play because they knew it was really about the good news of Easter. St. George represents Christ. The princess is the Church, Christ's bride. Whenever we are willing to lay down our lives for one another, death itself dies.

In Greece, where today is a holy day, George is called the "Great Martyr." George is a patron saint not only of Greece but also of England, Portugal, and the Italian cities of Venice and Genoa.

George's name, in Greek, means "earth-worker." (The "geo" in "George," "geology" and "geography" comes from the word *ge,* "earth.") George is the patron saint of farmers, fruit tree growers, gardeners and anyone who works with the soil. George is also the patron saint of spring. In Eastern Europe, farmers and their families walk in procession through the fields today, singing hymns and welcoming the springtime.

Optional memorial of
St. Fidelis of Sigmaringen
presbyter, religious, martyr (1577 – 1622)

Sigmaringen is a town in southern Germany. Fidelis started life there, but he later traveled all over central Europe. As a young man he studied law. Then he spent six years tutoring a group of wealthy young students. Fidelis's kindness toward the poor impressed the students. They never forgot how in cold weather he would give beggars the clothes off his back. He was known as "the poor man's lawyer" because he took the cases of people who had no one else to fight for them.

Fidelis gave half his money to the poor and the rest to student scholarships. He became a Capuchin friar and soon was chosen to be a leader. He spent a lot of time in prayer and gladly did the lowliest work. When an epidemic broke out, Fidelis turned his home into a hospital.

He was well-known as a teacher and spiritual director. With eight other Capuchin priests, he was sent to Switzerland to preach. It was a dangerous assignment. Catholics and Protestants were arguing with each other about religion, and often the disagreements got violent. In 1622, Fidelis was killed by an angry crowd.

April

25

Feast of
St. Mark
evangelist (first century)

The Gospel of Mark records a strange detail not told in the other three gospels. In the garden of Gethsemane, when the crowd arrested Jesus, an unnamed young man followed at a distance. The crowd tried to catch the man, but all they could grab was his clothing. He ran away naked. Some people think the young man was Mark.

Mark was not an apostle. He was probably a member of one of the first Christian communities. His mother's house in Jerusalem is mentioned in the Acts of the Apostles as a center where Christians gathered.

Mark was baptized by Peter. Then they both moved to Rome, where Mark served as Peter's secretary. Mark also traveled with Paul and Barnabas on their first missionary journey. Later, during Paul's two prison terms in Rome, Mark helped him to continue his work.

Mark's gospel is simple and direct. It challenges the reader to share in Jesus' sufferings. It is filled with details that help us to understand the human side of Jesus.

Mark's symbol is a winged lion. The lion is a desert animal, and Mark's gospel begins with the story of John the Baptist in the desert.

Traditions say that Mark went to Alexandria in Egypt. He worked there for ten years before he was martyred. The city of Venice in Italy has Mark for its patron saint. His bones are said to rest in the great cathedral there.

The old Roman Catholic calendar
Rogation Day
See also page 21.

The word "rogation" comes from the Latin word *rogare,* "to ask." The bishops of a country set aside rogation days when there are troubles, such as war or drought. We ask God for peace, for health, for better times. And we make our prayer as a people who are united.

There have also been annual rogation days at planting time. Spring is a life-or-death season. Crops are planted, farm animals are born, and orchards begin to produce fruit. The unpredictable weather of this time of year can affect these life-giving processes, so a day of prayer is fitting. We thank God for the gift of life. We ask for the fruitfulness of the earth.

28

Optional memorial of
St. Peter Chanel
presbyter, religious, missionary, martyr (1803–1841)

As a young boy in France, Peter Chanel (shuh-NELL) herded sheep. The local parish priest noticed his intelligence and love of God. He encouraged Peter's parents to allow the boy to be educated, which was an unusual thing for a farm boy in those days.

Peter did well in school, and then he became a priest. He was sent to a run-down area where most people weren't interested in church. By tending the sick of the district with great care, Peter drew many people back to the parish.

Peter had always wanted to do mission work. Finally, in 1836, Peter was sent with a small group of other priests to the island of Futuna in the New Hebrides Islands of the Pacific Ocean. It was an area where people knew nothing of Christianity.

Gradually, Peter and the other missionaries learned the language used on the island. They taught by the example of their kindness. Peter used his skills at healing the sick to win the confidence of the islanders, although only a few were baptized.

The leader of the people on Futuna became angry when his son asked to be baptized. The leader sent his soldiers to murder Peter. Within a few months after Peter Chanel's death, the whole population of Futuna became Christian. Peter Chanel was the first Christian martyr of the Pacific islands.

Memorial of
St. Catherine of Siena
doctor of the church (1347–1380)

Catherine of Siena could barely read, but by the time she died she had written 400 letters and a book. She has been honored with the title "doctor (teacher) of the church."

Catherine of Siena was the 23rd child in her family. In those times, girls were told by their parents whom they would marry and where they would live. But Catherine convinced her parents that she must not marry. She willingly took on the duties of a maid within her own home. She became a member of the Third Order of St. Dominic. While still living at home, she prayed, cared for the sick and visited people in prisons.

Although she was young, she developed a reputation for being wise. Priests, politicians and nobles came to her for guidance. She called them all her

family and built them into a group of spiritual and social workers who influenced the whole region.

Italy was loaded with quarreling families. The church itself was badly divided. More than one person claimed to be pope. Catherine and her spiritual companions worked to restore peace.

Catherine spent two years in Rome working to make peace in the church. The stressful situation affected her health. She suffered two strokes and died.

Catherine's deepest love was for reflective prayer. Yet she also achieved much good in the world. In her brief lifetime of 33 years, she counseled popes, healed divisions within her country, and shaped the church of her time.

Optional memorial of
St. Pius V
religious, pope (1504–1572)

Early in the sixteenth century, Martin Luther (February 18) had raised serious concerns about wrongs within the church. Many people agreed with Luther, and the Protestant Reformation began. Gradually the leaders of the Roman church came to realize that the concerns raised by Luther and other reformers had to be dealt with. The Council of Trent was called to design a plan for reform in the Catholic church.

In 1563 the Council ended after 18 years of work. Two years later, a former shepherd boy from the Piedmont region of Italy was elected pope. He chose the name Pius. It would be his task to put the reforms recommended by the Council into practice.

Pius was a gifted man who came to the papacy from the Dominican Order. He was not gentle or flexible. In fact, he was stubborn, but he was known for his humility. In processions through the streets of Rome, Pius walked barefoot with no hat. He often fasted. He built hospitals, and he personally tended the sick. He spent many hours in prayer.

Pius insisted that church finances be accounted for and that clergy lead simple lives. He began seminaries to train priests properly. He established the Confraternity of Christian Doctrine to teach the faith to young people. Pius died after only six years in office.

Roman martyrology
St. Walpurgis's Night
(c. 710 – c. 779)

According to the Roman martyrology, April 30 is St. Walpurgis's Day. She was an English nun who founded religious houses in Germany. She studied medicine and was known for her ability to cure diseases. She died about the year 779. In the Middle Ages, many people came to visit her tomb. Because her feast day was April 30, Walpurgis's name was attached to a great annual celebration.

The year at that time was divided into two seasons, the warm season and the cold. The day after April 30, May Day, was the start of the warm season. November 1, All Saints' Day, was the start of the cold. People thought that at midnight on the eves of these two days, the two seasons met together. A bit of eternity could seep through the crack between them. And alongside eternity might come a few of God's creatures that live in eternity — such as good and evil spirits.

In country villages of Austria, on this night people still stick brooms, rakes and spades upside down into the ground. This is supposed to snag any ghosts or witches that happen to fly by.

In some rural areas, there are ceremonies on Walpurgis's night to mark the change from winter into summer. Young people circle orchards and fields. They do this during the night, using a special rhythmic dance step. Herdsmen build two fires close together and drive their cattle between them. Then the herds are taken out to pasture for the new season.

In some parts of Sweden, bonfires are still lighted tonight. Once they were intended to ward off ghosts, but now they have become a custom to welcome spring.

May

The fifth month is named after the goddess Maia. She is the oldest of the Pleiades (PLEE-ih-dees), the seven sisters. According to legend, the Pleiades were placed in the sky to shine as a beautiful cluster of tiny stars.

The word *mai* is also a northern European word that means fresh green growth. In England, hawthorn blossoms are called "may." Originally, maypoles were small trees that had the lower branches chopped off. They were hung with ribbons and gifts and given to newlyweds as a wish for a life filled with blessings. In some places they were set up in the centers of towns to celebrate Easter or May Day or Midsummer Day, June 24. Many central European towns continue to keep this custom.

The second Sunday in May
Mother's Day

In the Middle Ages, many people had to travel far from home to earn a living. They became servants where work was available, or they learned a trade from someone who was willing to teach them.

These people were given a special holiday every year. It came on the Fourth Sunday of Lent, on Laetare ("rejoice") Sunday (see page 15). In the liturgy on this day, the city of Jerusalem is called our mother. We rejoice because when Easter arrives we will be reunited with mother Jerusalem.

Laetare Sunday came to be called Mothering Sunday. On this day people would go home to see their mothers. Many family reunions were held. People were even excused from the lenten fast on that day.

The Mother's Day we have in May was started in the early twentieth century by an American woman named Anna Jarvis. After her mother died, she suggested that a memorial service be held in church to honor all mothers. The first such service was held in a Philadelphia church in 1908. Those who attended were asked to wear white carnations in memory of their mothers.

People were so taken with the observance of such a day that in 1914 Congress proclaimed the second Sunday in May as Mother's Day. Other countries adopted the idea. In England they restored the old custom of Mothering Sunday in Lent.

A mother provides life and nourishment. On this day we remember all who are examples of a mother's love.

The Monday on or before May 24
Victoria Day (Canada)

This Canadian national holiday is a remembrance of the birthday of the queen who ruled the longest of any British monarch. Queen Victoria's reign lasted 60 years. Her subjects in Canada and other countries became so used to celebrating her birthday that they continued the custom even after she died. They began to use this day to tell about the deeds of British heroes.

Victoria's actual date of birth is May 24, 1819. In 1952, the celebration was moved to the Monday on or before that date.

In Canada, the birthday of Queen Elizabeth II is also observed on Victoria Day, although her actual birth date is April 21.

The last Monday in May
Memorial Day (U. S. A.)

In 1868, a national day was held to remember the dead of the Civil War and to pray for reconciliation. The idea had come from Southern women who visited battlefields in late spring to decorate the graves. Some people still call Memorial Day by its original name, "Decoration Day."

Memorial Day now honors all United States citizens who died in war. Every city and town has its war dead. Often they are remembered with a parade to a cemetery or war memorial. With bouquets strewn over the waters, coastal cities honor those who died at sea.

Gettysburg, Pennsylvania, is the site of a Civil War battle where many thousands died. Today schoolchildren in that town will decorate the tombs of soldiers who could not be identified after their deaths. A service will be held at the Vietnam War Memorial in Washington, D. C.

In recent years Congress has proclaimed this as a day when the nation should strive for peace. As we honor those who have died, we look forward to the day when we will be willing to settle our disagreements without war.

As Christians, we also pray today for all the innocent victims of war. Across the world, millions of people are homeless because their countries are ravaged by fighting. Those people are called refugees. Many of them are orphaned children. Some are hungry. All are suffering.

May

A day of sorrow and mourning is hard to keep. We probably would rather celebrate the beginning of summer. But Memorial Day can bring with it much needed sorrow and forgiveness and peacemaking.

1

Byzantine calendar
St. Jeremiah
prophet (c. 650 – c. 580 BCE)

Jeremiah gave his work everything he had. Born into a priestly family, he knew even at a very young age that he was called to be a prophet. From the time he was 18 until his death some 50 years later, Jeremiah spoke out to the people of Judah.

It wasn't an easy task. He understood that doom lay in store for the entire country unless the people changed their lives. When he tried to convince them of this, he was punished and mocked. Because of his prophecies Jeremiah was publicly flogged, thrown in prison on more than one occasion, locked into stocks, and even tossed into a cistern filled with mud.

The Book of Jeremiah records his times of deep discouragement. But Jeremiah never lost faith in God. He taught about God's special care for the *anawim*, the poor and lowly people of the earth.

May Day

In Southampton, England, a choir of schoolboys will greet the sun on May Day morning by "singing in the May." In other parts of Britain, people in small villages used to rise before dawn to "bring in the May." Going out to the countryside, they gathered hawthorn blossoms and other flowers.

As the sun rose, they decked doors and windows with the blooms. People of every social class, even kings and queens, joined together in this joyful work.

In northern France, people gather fragrant lilies of the valley today. In Belgium, parades and street fairs are held. In Austria and Switzerland, this is a time to pray for good crops.

In centuries past, just about every European village built its own maypole in the town square. Dancing around the maypole is a May Day tradition still observed in some towns in the United States. Dancers hold streamers that hang from the top of a wreath on the pole. As they circle around the pole they weave the ribbons into patterns under, over and around the maypole. When they change directions, the streamers untangle again and blow free in a great jumble.

Ancient Celts and Romans held spring festivals on the first of May. The custom of crowning a May queen was borrowed from the Roman festival of Flora, the goddess of spring. To counteract those leftover pagan ways, the church began to celebrate May as the month of Mary, the mother of God. One reason we honor Mary in Eastertime is that she is an image of the church. We remember how, after Jesus ascended into heaven, Mary gathered with the disciples in the Upper Room to await the coming of the Holy Spirit. This month, in many parishes, she is crowned *regina caeli,* the queen of heaven.

In many countries May Day is Labor Day, a day to honor workers. The memorial of St. Joseph the Worker may be kept today in celebration of Labor Day.

2

Memorial of

St. Athanasius

bishop, doctor of the church (c. 295 – 373)

Athanasius was born in Alexandria, Egypt. His parents were Christians, and they were wealthy enough to provide their son with the finest education available. After his schooling Athanasius went into the desert to study with Abbot Anthony (January 17). When he returned to Alexandria he became a deacon, was chosen secretary to the bishop, and wrote his first famous work.

Not long afterward, Arius, who was also a deacon, began to teach that Jesus had not always been the Son of God. Rather, he was a human being who later became the Son of God. This false idea was believed by many Christians.

Athanasius attended the famous Council of Nicaea, where a version of the Nicene Creed was born. This clear statement of what Christians believe contradicted Arius's false teaching, and it is still recited every Sunday in churches around the world.

Shortly after the council, Athanasius was named bishop. He wasn't even 30 years old. He traveled through his huge diocese, teaching, preaching, and caring for people. Soon Arius and his friends started spreading lies about Athanasius and Athanasius was exiled from his diocese.

This began a long period of suffering for Athanasius. Of his nearly 50 years as bishop, more than 20 were spent in exile. Five separate times he was sent away from the diocese he longed to serve. He was forced to defy four different emperors, and so he lived in constant danger of death. Yet he was always kindly, humble and faithful to the needs of his people.

Athanasius used his time in exile to write great teachings about Christ and the scriptures. During the last seven years of his life — which were spent in peaceful service — Athanasius wrote the life of St. Anthony. This helped people to learn about the way of life of the first Christian monks.

Because of his teachings, Athanasius bears the title "doctor (teacher) of the church." An important Eastertime saint, his name means "deathless."

3

Feast of

Ss. Philip and James

apostles (first century)

"Come and see." This famous invitation from scripture was extended by Philip. Later he would become one of the Twelve, but at this point he had just decided to follow Jesus. Immediately he invited his friend Nathanael to "Come and see."

Philip's invitation to his friend was good practice for the apostolic work he would do after the descent of the Holy Spirit on Pentecost. Tradition says that he preached in Asia Minor. He died a martyr's death.

Today we also celebrate the apostle James, son of Alphaeus. He was one of the Twelve Apostles. He is called "James the Less" because another member of the Twelve also was called James (see July 25). This other James is called "James the Greater."

The feasts of the two apostles, Philip and James, have been celebrated together since the sixth century. That was when, with great pomp and ceremony, their relics were brought to rest in the Church of the Twelve Apostles in Rome.

May

St. Irene
martyr (first century)

Irene is remembered on the calendar of the Byzantine church. Legends about her say that she was a princess and was baptized by St. Timothy (see January 26). She brought her parents to Christianity. Later she was beheaded by order of the procurator of the city of Ephesus (a city in Turkey).

Her bones were brought to Constantinople. Three churches there were dedicated to her. Her name means "peace" in Greek, and many women throughout the centuries have been baptized with the name Irene. During Eastertime, her name reminds us of the peace of the risen Christ.

Because John's gospel was written in Greek, "irene" is the risen Christ's greeting to the disciples. Like St. George, St. Irene bears the title "great martyr" in Greek.

Byzantine calendar

St. Job
(parable)

Why do bad things happen to good people? At some point in their lives, everyone longs to understand this mystery. The Book of Job puts the question to God. Its reflections provide hope for anyone who is suffering.

The story of Job was based on an old folk tale. Job, the story relates, had a beautiful family and great prosperity. A good man, he felt blessed by God. But then hard times befell him. His children were killed, all his wealth was taken from him, and he was stricken with a horrible skin disease.

What made all this even more difficult was that people of Job's time believed that the good were rewarded and the wicked punished during their lives. Suffering was considered to be a punishment for sin.

Though he was angry, confused and depressed by his suffering, Job continued to turn to God. In the process he learned that prosperity is not a reward for good behavior. Nor is suffering a punishment. God's plan is a mystery beyond our the power to understand. And yet, somehow, God's mystery is spread before us as a gift. God's mystery surrounds us. Trust is the only fitting response to joy and pleasure, to pain and sadness.

In some of the most beautiful writing in the scriptures, God reminds Job of the splendors of creation. Perhaps Job suddenly sees himself, even with his sufferings (or maybe even because of his sufferings), as part of God's wonderful works. Job is filled with awe and thanksgiving and praise.

Anniversary of the death of
Henry David Thoreau
(1817–1862)

Henry David Thoreau was born in the small village of Concord, Massachusetts. He learned from nature even as a boy, observing the woods and fields near his home. At 16 he began studying at Harvard. An excellent student, he tackled tough subjects like Greek, Latin, and the English classics. He taught school for a while, but soon gave that up. He took long walks and recorded in his journals everything he saw and heard.

Thoreau especially liked to wander the shores of Walden Pond. In his late 20s he built a little hut there. He wanted to see how simply he could live. Thoreau believed that most people wasted their lives wrapped up in cares about money.

Thoreau spent two years at Walden Pond. Later his experiences were published in a book called *Walden.*

Thoreau often talked with his friends about justice. He believed the United States was waging an unjust war against Mexico. He also knew that slavery, still legal in many states, was wrong. Because he thought his government was acting unjustly, he once refused to pay a tax. He was briefly sent to jail. Later he wrote a famous essay called "Civil Disobedience" about this experience.

After leaving Walden Pond, Thoreau traveled a bit and wrote several more books. He died on this day at the age of 45. He had kept his journals faithfully every night from the time he was 20 until his death. What we still have of them fills more than 14 volumes. For generations they have provided Americans with a sense of the beauty and possibilities of our country.

Byzantine calendar
St. Isaiah
prophet (eighth century BCE)

In the midst of quiet prayer, Isaiah was suddenly wide awake. He saw the glory of God, so dazzling that he feared he would die. An angel cleansed his lips with a burning coal. He felt no pain. Then Isaiah heard himself volunteering to speak for God to the people of Judah. (This event is described in the sixth chapter of the Book of Isaiah.)

Isaiah lived at a time of tremendous national crisis. After the death of King Solomon, Israel split into two parts. The northern kingdom was sacked by the Assyrians. Only the southern kingdom, Judah, was left. Isaiah feared for Judah and its beloved city of Jerusalem. He thought that if the people refused to follow God, Judah too might be overrun.

Isaiah was a member of the royal court and a trusted adviser to its kings. He spoke out against the rich and powerful people in Judah who were unfaithful to God. In his 40 years as a counselor, he urged the kings of Judah to depend only on God and to avoid alliances with powerful pagan nations, such as Assyria and Egypt.

Isaiah and his disciples after him wrote the Book of Isaiah. It describes a time to come when people will beat their swords into plowshares and peace will reign in the world. This promise has been carved on the great wall facing the United Nations headquarters in New York. It still expresses the hope of humankind.

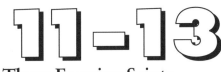

Three Freezing Saints
Ss. Mamertus, Pancras and Servatus

They're also known as the Ice Saints, the Frost Saints and even the Three Severe Lords. Beware them all!

The people of the wine-growing regions of Central Europe keep watch on the nights of May 11, 12 and 13 for evidence that the Three Freezing Saints are lurking in their vineyards. The owners of walnut and apple orchards also keep a wary eye open, as do gardeners and farmers.

A frost this time of the year will destroy crops. A heavy frost may even kill fruit trees and grape vines. The memorial days of St. Mamertus (died c. 475), St. Pancras (died c. 304) and St. Servatus (died 384) fall in mid-May, when frost is most

May

feared. So these three saints were associated with cold weather.

Actually, these are saints of the early church (see May 12, St. Pancras). Archbishop Mamertus began the custom of the three rogation days (page 21) before Ascension as times of prayer for farmers and their needs. Perhaps that is why people imagined that once a year these saints returned to earth to play pranks on farmers—like freezing the grapevines. And so people hoped that the three saints (or at least their feast days) would go away and take any cold weather with them.

After the days of the Three Freezing Saints are over, gardeners and farmers can breathe easier. According to folk custom, it's now safe to plant the tender crops, such as maize, pumpkins and tomatoes. Settled weather may be here at last.

12

Optional memorial of

Ss. Nereus and Achilleus
martyrs (first or second century)

Nereus and Achilleus were Roman soldiers, perhaps in the late first or early second century. They helped to persecute Christians until they themselves came to believe in Christ. Then they resigned the army and left Rome to live as Christians. Later they were captured and put to death. They were among the first Christian martyrs to be honored as saints by the members of their own community.

Pope Damasus I (December 11) served the church in the fourth century, just after the Roman persecutions ended. He praised the martyrs Nereus and Achilleus in the inscription he wrote for their tomb. He said they "threw away their shields, their armor and their bloodstained javelins" because of their love for Christ.

Optional memorial of

St. Pancras
martyr (died c. 304)

As the Roman Empire was decaying, a brutal soldier named Diocletian rose up through the ranks, killing his rivals until he became emperor. Determined to restore Rome to its former glory, he had himself declared a god. Romans were no longer citizens but only subjects of the emperor-god. In this atmosphere, Christians were a threat to the empire.

Diocletian began the last and most thorough attempt to stamp out the new religion. Many Christians lost their lives during these years.

Pancras was martyred in Rome, probably during the persecutions of Diocletian. He was only about 14 years old when he was beheaded. His story inspired Christians of all ages for many years. In Rome, a church was built to honor Pancras. Later, many churches were named for him in France, Italy, England and Spain. Some of these churches are called St. Pancratius, another form of his name. Because he was so young when he died, he is a patron saint of children.

13

Roman martyrology

St. Julian of Norwich
recluse (c. 1342 – c. 1423)

In today's world there is no such thing as an "anchorite," but there probably ought to be. Anchorites were a kind of counselor. They would live in a little apartment called an anchorhold, which was attached to a parish church. Anchorites would promise to stay in the anchorhold for the rest of their lives. They spent their time in prayer, spiritual reading and giving guidance to people who asked for help. Some anchorites, such as Julian of Norwich, became so well-known for their wisdom that people seeking God would travel long distances for their advice.

Julian lived her life quietly. The precise dates of her birth and death are unknown. We don't even know her real name, because when anchorites became part of a parish church, they took that church's name for their own. Julian served at St. Julian's Church in the town of Norwich, England.

When Julian was 30 years old she became very ill. Her parish priest and her mother thought she was going to die. During the illness Julian had a vision of the passion and death of Jesus. When the vision was over she recovered from her illness. This vision gave tremendous new meaning to the rest of her life. She shared this new sense of meaning with the many people she counseled in later years.

Julian was a person with a deep faith in the goodness of humankind (although she was fully aware of how hard-hearted people can be). She was also very bright. Her writings reflect on the deepest questions of the Christian faith. She used simple, practical examples to help readers understand her profound thoughts. As an example, she called Jesus her loving mother, a mother whose child knows where to turn for help and encouragement.

Julian's reflections are so brilliant that she is considered the first great woman writer of the English language. She ends her reflections with their most important point. Jesus, she says, is about love. Jesus is love. Jesus showed us love for the sake of love.

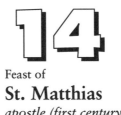

Feast of
St. Matthias
apostle (first century)

The first chapter of the Acts of the Apostles describes the scene just after the ascension of Jesus. The Eleven had returned to Jerusalem to wait for the descent of the Holy Spirit, as Jesus had instructed. Peaceful and filled with hope, they were now very different from the fearful and isolated people they had been after Jesus' death on the cross. Peter took his place as their leader.

Peter called the Eleven to an important task. They needed to select a twelfth disciple to replace Judas, who had hung himself after he betrayed Jesus. Like the twelve tribes of Israel, the Twelve symbolized the complete family of God. So it was important that their number remain complete. The person chosen had to be someone who had witnessed firsthand all that Jesus had done. Two highly respected candidates came forward. After prayer, they drew lots, and Matthias was chosen.

No further mention of Matthias is made in the scriptures. Legends about his later missionary work are confused, but he may have worked in Greece. Christians in Ethiopia have a tradition that Matthias was the first to bring them the good news of the gospel. He was martyred for his faith. When his bones were moved to Treyes, France, during the Middle Ages, it became a place that pilgrims loved to visit.

15

In the U. S. A., optional memorial of
St. Isidore the Farmer
married man (c. 1070 – 1130)

Isidore the Farmer was not educated, but he has something important to teach people living today. He had a deep connection with the earth God gave us. All his life, from the time he was very young, he worked as a farm laborer. He prayed joyfully all day while he worked at plowing, planting and harvesting.

Isidore lived near Madrid in Spain. His name in Spanish is Ysidro. He was married to Maria Torribia. The two had one son, who died at a young age. They were poor, but despite these sorrows, Isidore lived a rich life. He was noted for visiting churches on his days off and for providing food for those even poorer than himself.

Maria and Isidore also were known for their kindness to animals. All through their lives they had a special concern that animals be treated with compassion, whether they were the beasts that pulled the plow or the birds that twittered in the fields. Isidore is the patron saint of Madrid. Maria is also known as Santa Maria de la Cabeza. They are patrons of farmers and of farm communities.

The Catholic Rural Life Conference requested that St. Isidore's Day be celebrated in mid-May in the United States, during the seedtime of the year and during Eastertime, too. Perhaps a blessing over our own gardens and vegetable plots would be appropriate today in memory of Maria and Isidore.

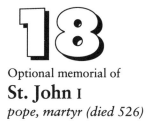

18

Optional memorial of
St. John I
pope, martyr (died 526)

John was born in Tuscany, a section of Italy. He became known as a gifted scholar. In 523, as an elderly man, he was elected pope. Immediately he was caught in the middle in a fight between two rulers.

The ruler of Italy, Theodoric, believed the false teaching of Arian Christians. Justin I, the emperor in Constantinople, was persecuting Arians. Suspecting that the emperor might decide to invade Italy, Theodoric asked Pope John to go to Constantinople. He wanted John to convince Justin to stop persecuting Arians.

This was a difficult situation for John. After all, John did not believe in what the Arians believed, but he also did not think that Christians should persecute each other. If he sided with Theodoric, the other bishops in the world would misunderstand his motives. But if he sided with Justin, Theodoric would want revenge. So, for the sake of peace, Pope John left Rome and went to Constantinople.

John's trip turned out to be magnificent. During his stay he celebrated Christmas and Easter liturgies in the great churches there. He also had some success in convincing Justin to back down.

However, when John returned to Rome, Theodoric threw him into prison. He had decided that John was conspiring against him with Justin. It was John's success that grated on the nerves of the suspicious king. John was in poor health. After only a few days in prison he died of mistreatment. John was a martyr for the unity of the church.

20

Optional memorial of

St. Bernardine of Siena

presbyter, religious, missionary (1380–1444)

When Bernardine was 20, the plague struck his city of Siena, Italy. As many as two dozen people a day were dying from the disease. Everyone else was terrified of catching plague, so hospital patients were left to die alone and untended.

Bernardine not only agreed to run a hospital, but he also brought 12 friends with him. For four months they worked day and night to bring cleanliness and order. They cared for the sick and consoled them. Afterward, Bernardine was worn out and became ill himself. He never completely recovered his health.

Soon after that, Bernardine joined a Franciscan friary. So many friends and relatives came to see him that he moved to a much quieter place with a more severe lifestyle. For the next 12 years, he spent his time praying and preparing for whatever God might want him to do.

In 1417 Bernardine began preaching. Before his life was over, he would travel on foot throughout Italy. He drew tremendous crowds at each stop. In one city, Perugia, he was able to work out a peaceful end to civil war. He is still honored there.

Bernardine loved preaching so much that he turned down three offers to be named a city's bishop. But he did say yes when asked to serve in a leadership post within the Franciscan community. In that job he improved the education for all the friars in his care. But he missed preaching, so for the last two years of his life, although he was in poor health, he went back to the strenuous life of a traveling preacher.

21

Anniversary of the death of

Jane Addams

(1860–1935)

During the late nineteenth and early twentieth centuries, immigrants poured into the United States from all over Europe. They came to large cities at the rate of 1000 per week. They took the roughest jobs in factories and slaughterhouses because that was the only work they could get. They lived in dirty, crowded neighborhoods with no running water. Into such a neighborhood came Jane Addams.

Jane was born in Freeport, Illinois, where her father was a state senator. From childhood she wanted to do something to help people. As a young woman she visited Europe, where she learned several languages. When she returned home, she decided to use her knowledge of languages to help immigrants.

In Chicago, Jane rented a large house in the middle of an immigrant neighborhood. She called it Hull House. She started daycare for the children of women trying to work and raise families alone. She began sewing classes. Dances and parties were held for adults. Children learned games and put on plays.

Children were Jane's special concern. Because children had no place to play except the dirty streets, she got herself appointed garbage commissioner in order to make sure the garbage collectors did their job. She also built the first playground in Chicago. At that time children as young as six were working at dangerous jobs in factories and were unable to go to school. So Jane got a law passed against child labor.

In 1914, when war broke out in Europe, Jane visited the countries involved to beg for peace.

She knew that people from many nations could live together in harmony. They were doing so in her neighborhood.

From everywhere people came to Chicago to study Hull House as it grew. In 1931, Jane Addams won the Nobel Peace Prize. This award is given to a person who helps people live together in peace and freedom. Four years later, at the age of 75, she died. By then her creative answers to the problems of city life were being carried out all over the world.

Optional memorial of

St. Bede the Venerable

presbyter, doctor of the church (c. 672 – 735)

Bede went to live with the Benedictine monks when he was eight years old. He spent just about his whole life at the abbey of Jarrow in England. But from these quiet surroundings he made an impact on his world. How did he manage this? In his own words, "I ever took delight in learning and teaching and writing."

Bede's interests covered everything. He wrote about why the Red Sea is red and where rainbows come from. Music, arithmetic, medicine, science were all examined in his work. He educated over 600 other monks in these subjects. Bede wrote scripture commentaries, too. Because of his book about the history of the church in England, he is considered the first English historian. Yet he was a simple and faith-filled person who lived by the rule of his community and spent a lot of time in prayer and song.

Bede worked and prayed until his death. In his old age he completed a translation of the Gospel of John. He said that he didn't fear death, "for we have a loving Lord." He died on Ascension Day. When news of his death got around, Boniface (June 5) said that a "candle of the church, lit by the Holy Spirit, is now extinguished."

The word "venerable" means holy or worthy. To this day Bede is called by that title, which was given to him while he was still alive. His tombstone says, "Here in the grave are the bones of the venerable Bede."

Optional memorial of

St. Gregory VII

pope (c. 1020 – 1085)

On becoming pope, a person receives a new name. Pope Gregory VII was first known as Hildebrand. He became an important leader, and to this day both his names are remembered.

Hildebrand was born in Tuscany, a region of Italy. His parents were not wealthy, but he did receive a fine education. Then he became a monk in the order founded by St. Benedict. He was so gifted that he soon became a counselor to popes. In 1073 he himself was elected to the office. Immediately he began making changes. His Benedictine training had given him important values in a time when the church needed them.

He knew that his task would not be easy. One of his first actions was to replace every high church official who had paid a bribe to get a position. This courageous stand made him hated by many people. He also spoke out against a group that was causing civil war in Rome. They were so angry that they had him arrested as he celebrated the Christmas Midnight Mass. But the next day, the people of Rome rose up in protest and rescued him from jail.

In those days kings thought they should have the right to choose their own bishops. Of course, a bishop selected in such a way probably would care more about doing the king's bidding than about serving the people. When Gregory began to correct this, he found himself arguing with Emperor Henry IV of Germany.

Henry refused to obey Pope Gregory. In time Gregory cut the emperor off from membership in the church. The people of Germany no longer considered Henry their leader. He was forced to back down. But in the long run it became clear that he had no intention of changing. He grew stronger and later began an attack against Rome that lasted for three years. Gregory was an old man by that time. He was forced to escape into exile, where he died.

Gregory loved justice and struggled for what was right. He wisely understood that bishops must be free from the control of governments.

Optional memorial of
St. Mary Magdalene de Pazzi
(1566–1607)

When you live in the same house with someone else, it's pretty difficult to fool them into thinking you have no faults. People very rarely think of the folks who are close to them as heroes. They do so even less frequently when those people are their parents or bosses. But the young women who were supervised by Sister Mary Magdalene called her "the mother of charity." They thought her goodness was the heart of their convent.

Her real name was Catherine de Pazzi and she was born in Florence to a wealthy and powerful family. She had a gift for prayer from early childhood, and she entered a Carmelite convent at age 16. In those days, people took a new name when they entered the convent. She chose the name Mary Magdalene.

It was probably her deep spiritual life that made her so kind-hearted. She was chosen to be mistress of the novices (the beginners) in her convent because she understood them. Then she became a teacher of the younger nuns.

For the last three years of her life she was bedridden. She died when she was only 41. Her last request was that the other sisters in her convent promise to trust Christ, to encourage each other, and always to give witness to the good news.

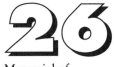

Memorial of
St. Philip Neri
presbyter, religious founder (1515–1595)

As a young man Philip Neri came to Rome, where he went out to the squares, shops and banks. There he challenged the other young men he met, asking them when they meant to begin doing good. Many of them, rich and poor alike, soon joined him. They volunteered in the hospitals of the city to care for patients. They did the dirtiest jobs. In the afternoon, they met with Philip for prayer, song and study at a place called the Oratory.

Philip was good at guiding those who wanted to grow in their prayer. Pilgrims who came to Rome to visit its holy places attended his teachings in such great numbers that a large room had to be built to hold them all. People in trouble felt calmed just by being in the same room with him.

People came to him for spiritual direction. Some of them also became famous saints, including Ignatius of Loyola (July 31), Francis de Sales (January 24) and Camillus de Lellis (July 14).

Yet Philip never took himself seriously. He wore old clothes and once shaved off half his beard just because people were saying how saintly he looked. When the pope wanted to honor Philip by appointing him a cardinal, the pope hung a cardinal's hat on Philip's door. A cardinal's hat is flat, so Philip tossed it in the air like a frisbee.

One of the people Philip guided, Francis de Sales, said that "a sad saint would be a sorry saint." Philip's joy was convincing to so many people that he would come to be called the second apostle to Rome. By the time he died at age 80, the whole city had been transformed by the spirit of the Oratory.

Optional memorial of
St. Augustine of Canterbury
bishop, religious, missionary (died c. 605)

Augustine was an Italian monk who was living a quiet life as the head of a group of monks in Rome. All that changed when his friend, Pope Gregory (September 3), decided that Augustine was just the person to take leadership of the Christian faith in Britain.

Augustine and his missionary team of 30 monks started from Rome on their journey. When they got as far as Provence, in southern France, they heard some frightening tales. Britain, they were told, was still a place of uncivilized tribes. The monks convinced Augustine to tell Gregory the trip was a bad idea. But Gregory said he wished he could join them himself, and he was sure that the time was right.

It turned out that Gregory was correct. After several years, King Ethelbert of Kent in England was baptized. His people followed his example. Before long the English people would themselves be sending out missionaries.

Augustine worked among the English for eight years before he died. He is honored as the apostle of England.

Roman martyrology
St. Joan of Arc
(1412–1431)

When Joan of Arc was born, the French and the English had been fighting for almost 100 years, and the English were winning.

Joan's family were French farmers. As a girl, she helped to spin wool and tend sheep. Because there was no school in her village, she never learned to read and write.

At about the age of 12, Joan began to hear the voices of saints. They told her things she could hardly believe. They said she would save France. Joan had no idea how to do the things the voices were telling her.

At about age 17, Joan persuaded the captain of a French fort to take her to Charles. Charles was the son of the dead king of France, but he was afraid to claim his crown. She convinced him to let her fight for his cause. Soon she rallied the French troops at the city of Orleans, which was under attack. She led the troops to free the city.

No one had ever heard of anything like this before — here was a young girl leading armies! Under her leadership, the French army defeated the English in four other battles. Six months later the English withdrew. With Joan's encouragement, Charles was crowned king of France.

About a year later Joan was captured by the English. They threw her into prison and tried her for witchcraft. Then they burned her at the stake in the marketplace of Rouen. When she died she was not yet 20 years old.

31

Feast of
The Visit of the Virgin Mary to Elizabeth

Our mission on earth is to bear Christ to others. The first chapter of the gospel of Luke describes a missionary journey. Mary, pregnant with Jesus, visits her cousin Elizabeth, who is pregnant with John the Baptist.

Mary has just learned amazing news. Angel Gabriel has told her that she will bear a child by the power of the Holy Spirit. This child will be called the Son of God. The angel has said that Elizabeth also is pregnant. This is wonderful, because Elizabeth and her husband Zechariah are an elderly couple who have wanted a child all their lives.

Luke says that, in response to this news, Mary sets out "with haste." Elizabeth and Zechariah live a distance away. Mary chooses to make this journey because she is concerned for her cousin. She also wants to share her joy with someone who will understand. Her own pregnancy is still a secret.

Elizabeth greets her cousin with words that will be repeated by generations of Christians at prayer: "Blessed are you among women, and blessed is the fruit of your womb."

In paintings of the Visit of Mary and Elizabeth, the two women are shown embracing. Elizabeth in her old age and Mary in all her youthfulness together hold fast to each other. Mary sings a song that begins with the words "My soul magnifies the Lord. . . ." This song weaves together the words of the prophets to proclaim God's goodness and care for the poor. *Magnificat* is the first word of this song in Latin.

The visit of the cousins is also the first meeting of their unborn children. Elizabeth tells Mary that, at the sound of her voice, "the child within my womb leaped for joy." Luke reminds us of the words of the Bible's Song of Songs, "The voice of my beloved! Look, he comes, leaping upon the mountains, bounding over the hills."

We celebrated the Annunciation in March. Now it is the end of May. In the Song of Songs we read, "The winter is past. The rain is over and gone. The flowers appear on the earth; the time of singing has come." Soon John will be born, and spring will have passed over into summer.

June

The sixth month is named after Juno, the Roman goddess of hearth and home.

Juno's month was lucky for weddings. In years past among Christians, weddings were rarely held during the paschal seasons of Lent, the Triduum and Eastertime, which ends on Pentecost. After Pentecost the time of summer weddings began.

In the Northern Hemisphere, June is the month of the summer solstice. The church keeps many solemnities this month. Perhaps the reason is the good weather, because June is often the best month of the year for outdoor processions, street fairs and other festivities.

The third Sunday in June
Father's Day

Sonora Louise Smart Dodd of Spokane thought that her father, William Smart, had done a remarkable thing. A veteran of the Civil War, he had raised his six children alone on the family farm in Washington after his wife died in childbirth.

When Mrs. Dodd suggested a day for fathers in 1909, she meant it to be a church service.

June

Mother's Day (page 72), which had just come into wide practice, was originally a church service too. Public interest in establishing Father's Day was strong at once in both the United States and Canada. Father's Day became an official national day in 1966.

1

Memorial of
St. Justin
martyr (c. 100–165)

Justin was born in Palestine around the beginning of the second century. His pagan parents gave him the best education available. He became a professor of philosophy. In his work, Justin dealt with educated people. Among his friends, Christians were thought of as uncivilized. Other philosophers had studied the new religion and had decided it was ridiculous. Who could believe that God would come to die for love of humankind?

There existed at the time all sorts of rumors about Christians. People said that their gatherings were just an excuse to get drunk. But Justin saw some of the Christians martyred. He decided their courage was so great that "it was impossible that they should be living in evil."

Finally, when Justin was about 30 years old, someone told him that the only place he would find real truth was in the writings of the Jews and Christians. From then on it became his life's work to explain Christianity to the educated people of his world. To do this better, he opened a school of Christian studies in Rome. There he taught, wrote, and debated with other philosophers.

Justin wrote letters to explain the new faith to the emperor and other officials. To dispel the rumors about Christian liturgies, he described what really went on. The letters of Justin are treasured records of how Christians worshiped in those times.

Because of his work, Justin was very visible as a Christian. He was put on trial with several of his pupils. Justin was convicted of being a traitor and he was beheaded.

2

Optional memorial of
Ss. Marcellinus and Peter
martyrs (died 304)

Diocletian was a military dictator. Like most dictators, he was put into power by the army. Rome had been a place where citizens enjoyed many rights, but now the emperor vested all power in himself.

Diocletian decided that Christians were a threat to him and that all Christian churches and holy books should be destroyed. Many people were killed because they protested. He also ordered that all Christian pastors be imprisoned. Soon the jails were packed. He offered to free anyone who would sacrifice to the pagan gods. All others were tortured and put to death. The killings took place all over the empire.

During this persecution, Marcellinus and Peter were beheaded. Other than that, almost all we know is that Marcellinus was a priest and Peter was an exorcist. In those days, any illness or emotional problem was thought to be the result of an evil spirit. Exorcists helped people pray for freedom from evil.

In the years after Peter and Marcellinus died, they were held in high respect by the Christians in

Rome, where they are buried. They are still honored today. Their names are included in one of the eucharistic prayers of the Mass.

Memorial of
St. Charles Lwanga and companions

Charles Lwanga, catechist, martyr,
and his companions, martyrs (died c. 1885)

Today there are more than six million Christians in the African country of Uganda. The seeds of this African faith were sown in the blood of St. Charles Lwanga and his 21 companions.

Charles and his friends were part of a group of Catholic and Anglican Christians martyred only a century ago in Uganda. A small Christian community had developed when missionaries worked there starting in 1879. The new Christians included members of the royal court.

Then a new king, Mwanga, came to power. He vowed to eliminate all "those who pray." He killed two members of his own court because of their new beliefs. He thought this would discourage others from wanting to become Christians. But to his shock, more and more of his pages — young people being trained in royal service — became catechumens preparing to be baptized.

Finally all the pages were called together. The Christians were asked to step forward. Then they were marched to a place of execution some miles away. They were placed on a huge funeral pyre.

Charles Lwanga and his friends were the first martyrs of equatorial Africa. As the palace guard Bruno Serunkuma was led away to die with the others, he told his brother, "A fountain fed from many springs will never dry up. When we are gone, others will rise in our place."

Anniversary of the death of
Pope John XXIII
(1881 – 1963)

When Cardinal Angelo Giuseppe Roncalli was elected pope in 1958, the first people to be taken by surprise were the papal tailors. They had prepared white cassocks for the cardinals who were most likely to be chosen pope. That way, the new pope could put on papal robes and then bless the people of Rome as soon as his name was announced. But short, stubby Cardinal Roncalli's name hadn't been on their list. So he stepped out onto the balcony in a white cassock that didn't fit. He had a good laugh about this.

Pope John was one of ten children of a peasant farmer near Bergamo in Italy. The family was poor. He would walk to school barefoot and carry his shoes so he wouldn't wear out the leather.

After serving a term as a medical chaplain during World War I, Angelo Giuseppe Roncalli was assigned to the church diplomatic corps. His army experience taught him about the horrors of war, and his diplomatic missions sent him to countries where there was misunderstanding between Orthodox and Catholic Christians. This work filled him with the hope that someday the churches might be reunited.

In 1953, Angelo was named a cardinal and became the bishop of Venice. He enjoyed his role as the city's pastor and expected to remain there his whole life. However, five years later, when Pope Pius XII died, Angelo was chosen to replace him. Angelo was probably elected because he was nearly 78 years old and was not expected to make sweeping changes. But if a quiet, conservative pope was what some of the cardinals had in mind when they cast their votes, they were about to be surprised.

Angelo, now Pope John, served as pope for only five years before he died of cancer. But in that time he accomplished much. He gathered the Second

Vatican Council to examine the church's role in modern life. He reached out to the leaders of other Christian churches and called for reconciliation. He spoke boldly against the arms race and challenged the superpowers of the world to give up their stockpiles of nuclear weapons.

Amid this hectic schedule, John found time to pay surprise visits to hospitals, orphanages and jails around the city. He enjoyed talking with people so much that he often took walks through Rome disguised in a priest's cassock. He was much loved. When he died, the whole world grieved.

Memorial of

St. Boniface

bishop, religious, missionary, martyr (c. 672–754)

Boniface was born in England during a frightening time. People didn't leave their houses any more than they had to. They were afraid of the Vandals, warrior tribes who were raiding villages.

Boniface became a Benedictine monk at an early age. Later, he became a priest. He felt called by God to preach the gospel to the Vandals. At about age 46, he set off for Germany, where many of the warriors had settled.

What he found there concerned him greatly. Some people had heard the Christian message, but their Christianity was mixed with paganism. He realized that people needed education in their faith. Fortunately, many Benedictine nuns and monks from England were willing to follow Boniface and to help him teach people. He set up prayer-houses, churches and seminaries. He held councils to help the bishops there feel more connected with the church far away in Rome. He was named the leading bishop of Germany.

By the time Boniface was 73, he had accomplished a tremendous amount. But his missionary spirit wouldn't let him rest. He set off for Holland. Many people wanted to be baptized after Boniface and his team of missionaries began teaching there. On the eve of Pentecost, Boniface was preparing for the baptisms. Suddenly he and 53 companions were seized and murdered by bandits.

Boniface is the patron saint of the German people. Because of the legend about his using an evergreen tree as a symbol of God's faithfulness, Boniface is credited with beginning the custom of the Christmas tree.

Optional memorial of

St. Norbert

bishop, religious founder (c. 1080–1134)

Norbert's parents were German nobles. As a young man, Norbert held office in the emperor's court, where he lived a life of luxury and high status. He was horseback riding one day when a thunderstorm came up and he was struck by lightning. He lay on the ground unconscious for almost an hour. When he came to, he must have remembered the story about the apostle Paul being thrown to the ground, because his first words were the same. "Lord," he said, "what would you have me do?" The answer seemed to be, "Turn from evil and do good. Seek peace and pursue it."

Norbert's life took an about-face. He went home to fast, to pray and to examine his life. Soon he sold everything he owned and gave the money to the poor. He wanted to warn people about the dangers and responsibilities of wealth and power, so he began to live on a very small income as a wandering preacher. Most people thought he had lost his mind. But others wanted to follow him. He began an order of white-robed priests who followed his strict way of life.

Norbert's monasteries were built in remote places. Usually he provided a hospice for travelers and sick people nearby. Later Norbert took on another challenge. He became archbishop of Magdeburg, where the local churches had many problems. He was able to bring about a number of needed reforms.

Norbert is the patron saint of Bohemia, which is part of the Czech Republic.

Optional memorial of

St. Ephrem

deacon, doctor of the church (c. 306 – 373)

Ephrem is honored as one of the great saints of the Syrian church. He was a monk who possessed many different gifts. He was famous for his preaching. He taught at a school for theologians in the city of Edessa, in what is now Turkey. His writings about the scriptures were so useful that they were translated into other languages during his lifetime.

Ephrem also wrote many hymns. Today, 16 centuries later, some of them are still in use, especially among Orthodox Christians. He also wrote poetry. Because of his musical talents, he was called "the Harp of the Holy Spirit."

Ephrem never looked for credit for his achievements. To keep his life simple and dedicated to prayer, he chose to live in a cave. He ate only barley bread and vegetables. He used his imagination to find ways to help others, and he treated people with compassion.

One year, almost no rain fell and all the crops died. Rich people could afford to import food from other countries, but the poor starved. The rich refused to donate to the hungry. They said they knew of no one who could be trusted to get money and food to people who needed it. So Ephrem (who was trusted by everyone) volunteered. He set up an effective way to get supplies to the needy. Shortly afterward, worn out by that effort, he died.

11

Memorial of

St. Barnabas

apostle (first century)

One of the earliest disciples of the new Christian faith was a Jew from the island of Cyprus named Joseph. As the book of Acts explains, Joseph was so generous and filled with faith that the apostles gave him a new name. They called him Barnabas, which means "the son of encouragement."

In those days, most Christians were Jewish. They thought it was a mistake to talk about Jesus to people who were not Jewish. The Jewish Christians in Jerusalem decided to send someone to find out what was happening in Antioch, where many people who weren't Jewish were interested in the faith. For this important task they chose Barnabas.

Barnabas reported back that he thought the Christians in Antioch were filled with the Holy Spirit. He realized that many more people would be open to hearing Christ's message if someone with a powerful faith were there to help him preach. So he convinced Paul to come with him to Antioch. They stayed for a year and drew so many new Christians that Antioch became the second capital of the Christian faith.

Paul and Barnabas then traveled to other towns. Some leaders were afraid to trust Paul because earlier in his life he had persecuted Christians. But Barnabas lived up to his name and encouraged Paul to preach. Barnabas also encouraged the other Christian leaders to accept Paul into the community. He reminded them of Jesus' call to bring salvation "to the ends of the earth."

Barnabas himself obeyed that call so faithfully that, even though he was not one of the Twelve, the Book of Acts honors him with the title of apostle.

Memorial of
St. Anthony of Padua
presbyter, religious, doctor of the church (1195 – 1231)

Anthony made such an impression on Padua in Italy that he is still admired there 700 years later. He is a much loved saint throughout the church.

Anthony was actually from Portugal, not Italy. His parents were nobles, and he could have chosen to live in luxury. But Anthony decided to devote his life to prayer and study. He became an Augustinian priest. He was a brilliant student who came to know the Bible inside out.

Ten years later Anthony learned about a new order, the Franciscans, who did missionary work. He wanted with all his heart to join them, and soon he was able to arrange it. Francis of Assisi (October 4), who had founded the Franciscans, was still alive. His spirit of poverty and love fired Anthony's heart.

Anthony traveled to Morocco to preach the gospel. But severe illness sent him sailing for home. His ship blew off course and he landed in Italy instead. By chance, Francis had called the friars together there at this very time, so Anthony attended their meeting. Soon afterward the other friars heard Anthony preach. They realized he had a great gift. The wayward ship had steered him to what would become his life's work — preaching throughout Italy and France.

When Anthony preached, no church could hold the crowds that came to hear him. He spoke in the marketplaces and town squares. Because of what he said, parents and children made peace with each other. People gave back things they had stolen. People who had told lies admitted them publicly and corrected them. Maybe that is why Anthony is known as the patron saint of lost items. He worked to find lost people.

His words were especially powerful because everyone knew that Anthony practiced what he preached. He was a humble person who chose to live in poverty. So many people experienced the love of God through his work that he became known as a "wonder worker."

Anthony spent the last three years of his life in Padua. He died when he was only 36 years old.

Byzantine calendar
St. Elisha
prophet (ninth century BCE)

The First Book of Kings tells the story of the friendship between the two prophets Elisha and Elijah. Elijah warned the people of Israel against idol worship. Most refused to listen to him, and he was worn out from his work. He needed a helper.

Elijah found Elisha plowing a field and he threw his cloak over him. This was his way of letting the young man know that he had been chosen to continue Elijah's work.

Elijah and Elisha were two of many great prophets of Israel. All would share the task of protecting poor and oppressed people from injustice. Many of the later prophets wrote down their visions. Elisha, like Elijah his teacher, was more a man of action. The two were said to have worked many wonders.

Their deeds are recorded in the First and Second Books of Kings. They are fascinating stories. Sometimes there are surprise endings.

The stories seem to tell us that heaven's justice turns things upside down and inside out. Something that first seems like a blessing turns out to cause trouble. And some troubles turn into blessings.

Byzantine calendar

St. Amos
prophet (eighth century BCE)

Amos was an unlikely prophet. A shepherd from a small village in the south, he found himself confronting the rich and sophisticated city dwellers of the north.

The king in Amos's time was Jeroboam II, a military leader who won important victories. The fighting was not good for the people of Israel, though. Many of them lost their land. Some were sold into slavery, while others grew richer and richer. The poor couldn't get a fair hearing in the courts because the judges were unjust. This was not God's will for Israel. The Law of Moses, given by God, had kept everyone neither too rich nor too poor.

Dressed in his rough shepherd's clothing, Amos appeared at the shrine where Jeroboam's victory celebration had just ended. He roared out his stern message: Worship alone means nothing. Mistreating the poor would bring God's judgment, but God's mercy would be there for those who changed their ways.

Amos's new career was short-lived. With the help of the king, the priest of the shrine sent Amos packing. He returned to Judah and stayed there. No one changed their ways or their worship as a result of what he said. But the parts of his message that were written down in the Book of Amos have challenged people ever since. Amos is called the prophet of social justice.

Optional memorial of

St. Romuald
abbot, religious founder (c. 950–1027)

Romuald was a reckless young man of 20 when he saw his father murder a relative in a duel that had started as an argument about money. He ran in horror to a monastery to pray for his father. He planned to stay for only 40 days, but soon he realized that he was called to make his whole life a life of prayer. In later years Romuald's father realized the wrong he had done. He too entered a monastery to commit his life to prayer.

Romuald spent three years at the monastery. Then he became a hermit and founded monasteries around Italy. The most famous of them was at a place called Camaldoli, a wild desert spot. The monks who came there to learn Romuald's ways of prayer lived in little rooms called hermitages, which were built around a church.

Romuald loved deep communication with God so much that he once spent seven years in complete silence. Because people felt that Romuald was holy and wise, they came from all over to seek his guidance.

June

21

Memorial of
St. Aloysius Gonzaga
religious (1568–1591)

As the oldest son of the Marquis of Castiglione in Lombardy, Italy, Aloysius Gonzaga stood to inherit great wealth. So from earliest childhood he was trained in the manners of a Renaissance prince. He was sent to be a page in the Medici court in Florence when he was only eight years old.

But there was something else about Aloysius that was special. From about the age of seven he had an unusual sense of closeness to God. Sometimes these two currents in Aloysius's life fought each other. He became aware of this conflict in his early teen years when he was sent to the royal court of Spain. It was a materialistic and immoral place. He needed self-discipline and courage to live as a Christian in these surroundings.

In 1584, Aloysius returned to Italy. He sensed that his society could not be reformed from within. The only way to survive was to get out completely. He decided to release all his property rights to his younger brother and to become a Jesuit. He knew the Jesuits would treat him like everyone else, not like royalty. Also, he would be expected to take a vow of poverty.

In 1591, an epidemic hit Rome. Victims died in agony in the streets of the city. The priests of Aloysius's order opened a hospital. Aloysius, who was 23, volunteered to serve the sick. On his back he carried the dying into the hospital. He washed them, made their beds, and cheered them. Then he caught the disease himself. Three months later he died.

His integrity and toughness have made him the patron saint of young people. He is also the patron of people dying from AIDS.

Summer solstice

On this day the sun is at its highest in the Northern Hemisphere. It's the official beginning of summer and an ancient day of celebration. In places north of the Arctic Circle, called "the land of the midnight sun," the sun never sets during the days near the summer solstice. In most of northern Europe, although the sun does set for a while each day, these are called "the days that never end" because dawn begins before the evening twilight has faded. The sky is never completely dark.

Many ancient peoples made today one of their great feasts. People lit huge bonfires during these shortest nights of the year to announce the official change of seasons. Some sort of protection at this time of year seemed especially important because spirits were thought to wander about during festival times.

As European nations became Christian, the solstice traditions became associated with the birth of St. John the Baptist (June 24), called Midsummer Day because it is midway between the vernal and autumnal equinoxes.

22

Optional memorial of
St. Paulinus of Nola
bishop (c. 354–431)

Paulinus was born near Bordeaux, in what is now France. For generations, his family had been Roman senators, prefects and consuls. He inherited a lot of property in various parts of the Roman Empire. Because of his wealth, he received a fine education. He became a lawyer, writer, governor and poet. He traveled, making friends in Italy, Gaul and Spain. Then he married Therasia, a wealthy Spanish woman.

In the year 389, Paulinus and Therasia became Christians. Together they sold their estates and gave the money to the poor. Paulinus's friend Jerome (September 30) said that "east and west were filled with their gifts." Paulinus was so admired that in time he was named the bishop of Nola, a town near Naples in Italy.

Bishop Paulinus came to be a friend not only of Jerome but also of Augustine (August 28) and Ambrose (December 7).

Paulinus and Therasia settled in a building outside the walls of the city. They opened their home to anyone who needed a place to stay. They shared their love, generosity, and knowledge of Christ with everyone they could find.

Optional memorial of
Ss. John Fisher and Thomas More
John Fisher, bishop, martyr (1469–1535), and Thomas More, married man, martyr (1478–1535)

Both of these great English saints laid down their lives to be faithful to their consciences. For serving God with all their hearts, both were judged guilty of treason.

John Fisher was born in Yorkshire. He studied at Cambridge and rose to the highest position of leadership of that great university. He led the school to new discoveries in the sciences and helped the nation to understand the importance of a university. He was so respected by other scholars that they named him chancellor for life, a rare honor. He tutored the young King Henry VIII. For years afterward Henry thought of John as a second father. After many years at Cambridge John unexpectedly was appointed bishop of Rochester. He held that post for 30 years.

In those days bishops could become very rich, but John lived simply. He rode throughout the diocese to minister to his people. He spent many hours at the bedsides of the dying.

Henry's fondness for John vanished when the elderly bishop refused to cooperate with the king's plan to abandon his wife and marry another woman. John believed in persuading rather than judging others. However, he felt a need to speak out against this injustice. As a result, he was thrown into prison and was released only after the pope in Rome protested his treatment.

Four years later Henry decided to separate the church in England from the church of Rome. Most of the other bishops of the country, and many other officials, signed an oath in support of Henry's action. For the sake of his people, John refused. He was imprisoned again in the Tower of London. He was 65 years old and already suffering with a fatal disease.

Thomas More was born in London. He served as page to the archbishop, who was so impressed with the boy that he sent Thomas to Oxford University when he was only 14. Thomas was elected to parliament as a young lawyer still in his 20s. Like his close friend John Fisher, he had served as tutor to Henry.

A charming and witty man, Thomas had friends all over Europe. His home in London became known as a center of laughter, learning and good conversation. He provided a fine education for his daughters in a time when women were thought to be not worth educating. He wrote poetry and history. His book *Utopia* is still read today. It describes Thomas's dream of an ideal society.

In 1529 Henry appointed Thomas chancellor, which made him the second most powerful person in England. But when Henry demanded he sign the oath, Thomas (like John) refused. Soon he was fired from his high post and imprisoned in the Tower of London.

June

Henry didn't want to kill Thomas or John; he just wanted to force them to do his will. So he made life as miserable as possible for them.

It was deathly cold in the Tower during the winter. John, who had often chosen to fast throughout his life, pleaded for more food, warm clothing and the consolation of a chaplain's visit. Thomas was denied books, visits from friends, and at the end even pens and paper. He spent more than a year in prison before being sentenced to death. With charcoal he scratched out a note to his daughter in a final attempt to cheer her as he went to be executed: "Pray for me, as I shall for you, that we may merrily meet in heaven."

Both saints were beheaded within a two-week period. John was too weak to walk to the scaffold, so the executioners carried him. Thomas' last words describe John as well as himself: "I die the king's good servant, but God's first."

Midsummer Eve

For centuries, Midsummer was one of the most important festivals of the year. And why not? The return of summer is a good reason for rejoicing. It is said that anyone who goes out tonight in search of mystery will not be disappointed.

Tonight is the eve of the Birth of St. John the Baptist — the summer nativity. John's two great emblems, fire and water, unite in the celebrations.

In many places, St. John's fires sparkle on the mountains and hilltops tonight. In Montreal, Canada, where the French settled, a communion of bonfires is lighted tonight along both sides of the St. Lawrence River. In France, the fishermen of Brittany light every ship in the fleet with a fire set on the mast. In other parts of France, everyone

in town, even newborn babies, must contribute at least a twig for the bonfire. On the coast of Denmark people light fires along the shore and then go out in boats to view them. In some places, people gather around their bonfires to sing hymns and say a prayer in honor of St. John. Later, fires in homes are lighted from the communal bonfire.

Irish farmers toss burning sticks from the bonfire into their gardens. In Norway, farmers jump over the flames with the merry wish that their grain might grow as high as they jump. In many countries, lovers leap over the fire holding hands.

In San Juan, Puerto Rico, which is named after St. John, people will take a dip in the Caribbean Sea between midnight and dawn to honor John the Baptist. Bonfires along the beaches will light their way.

24

Solemnity of
The Birth of John the Baptist: Midsummer Day

During the great cycle of the Christian year, there are three festivals in celebration of a person's birth. We celebrate the births of John the Baptist, of Mary, and of Jesus. These are the holy ones who were filled with the Spirit even before their birth.

Keep in mind that, in the liturgy of the church, a "nativity" is not a birthday. Birthdays are anniversaries of a birth. Instead, a nativity is the birth itself. Today is not John the Baptist's birthday. Today John is born. That's what we sing in the liturgy today.

Rejoicing at John's birth is a commandment of the gospel. Even the angel Gabriel tells us to rejoice (Luke 1:14). The Gospel of John records that Jesus himself praises John the Baptist.

The feast of John's birth was established very early in the church's history, at about the same time as the feast of Christmas. Luke tells us that the angel Gabriel announced the conception of Jesus six months after announcing the conception of John. So the date of this feast is six months before Christmas.

The old customs that centered around the summer solstice became ways to honor John. In Europe and other parts of the world, some people stay up all the night to burn St. John's fires. And the celebration goes on all day as well.

In Poland, wreaths lit with candles — which look like Advent wreaths — are tossed into streams to float downriver. In Morocco, the Muslim people light fires to celebrate John's birth. The Muslim holy book, the Koran, calls John a great prophet.

In Sweden, doors, autos and even buses are decorated with green birch twigs. In midafternoon, a maypole (*mai* means "greenery") is decorated with wreaths and then hoisted up amid shouts of joy. In Lithuania a cheese sweetened with honey is prepared to look round like the sun. The honey is a reminder of one of the foods John ate in the desert.

27

Optional memorial of
St. Cyril of Alexandria
bishop, doctor of the church (c. 376 – 444)

Alexandria was a thriving Egyptian port that for centuries had been a center of learning and trade. In the year 412, Cyril was chosen to be its bishop. The position brought him tremendous political power and personal wealth. He was not always wise in the way he used these gifts, and so his life was very stormy.

Cyril and another bishop, Nestorius, had a disagreement about Jesus. Nestorius couldn't believe that God would be willing to become a helpless human infant. So he taught that Mary was the mother only of Christ the human. He said Christ's divine nature was given to him later. Cyril disagreed. He condemned Nestorius's teaching and sent him into exile. Over the centuries, it has become clear that Cyril's understanding of Jesus was correct.

Some good came out of his dispute with Nestorius. Christians were reassured of the total love and humility of Jesus, who was willing to become completely human. Just to make sure everyone understood that point, Cyril called Mary *Theotokos*. This Greek word means "the bearer of God."

Memorial of
St. Irenaeus
bishop, martyr (died c. 203)

Irenaeus was born in Smyrna, a port in what is now Turkey. One of his teachers was the bishop of Smyrna, Polycarp (February 23). Polycarp's teacher had been John the apostle, whose teacher was Christ. So Irenaeus's early training gave him a solid foundation for his later work.

Irenaeus traveled to Lyons in Gaul (now France) as a young man. He became the assistant of Pothinus, the elderly bishop of Lyons. The city's leaders were murdering Christians. When Bishop Pothinus was martyred, Irenaeus was named to take his place.

The new bishop had a challenging task. Lyons was a rapidly growing city. Of course, any place where the Christian faith was found also found many false and confusing teachings being spread. Some people even wrote their own gospels. This confused many people.

Irenaeus was bright and had a clear understanding of what the apostles and Christian teachers had taught. He wrote five volumes in which he showed that what the false teachers were saying did not match Christ's words and actions. He wasn't interested in proving his opponents wrong; his hope was to win them over by providing greater understanding.

Solemnity of

Ss. Peter and Paul

apostles (first century)

In the fourth century on this day, Roman Christians would follow the bishop in procession as he celebrated the liturgy first at the church of St. Peter (which was built over the saint's burial place) and then at the church of St. Paul outside the Walls.

Rome isn't the only city that celebrates this great day. Today's celebration is kept by all the liturgical churches all over the world. Eastern churches even have a period of fasting to prepare for this feast.

Peter and Paul came from thoroughly different backgrounds and had different gifts, but they had one great bond: Both were called forth by Jesus' love.

Jesus gave Peter his name — which means "rock" — at their first meeting. Jesus had chosen him to be the rock on which the new church would be built. According to the gospels, Peter often showed an understanding of Christ, but when Jesus was arrested and crucified, Peter denied Christ

three times and hid in fear. When Jesus was risen from the dead, he told Peter, "Feed my lambs."

Peter was recognized by the other disciples as their leader. He called the apostles to select a replacement for Judas. On Pentecost morning, he preached a bold sermon. He performed the first miracle of healing in the name of Jesus. In a dream, he came to understand that the gospel message was for everyone on earth, not only the Jews like himself. Finally, he made his way to Rome, the center of the empire.

Peter was probably imprisoned three or four times before being martyred around the year 64 during the persecutions of the emperor Nero. According to legend, he asked to be crucified upside down, since he did not feel worthy to die in the same way Jesus died.

Early in his life, Paul persecuted Christians with determination. But then he had a vision of Jesus, which left him with a complete change of heart. When Paul began preaching Christ, the Christians naturally were afraid of him. But over the next 30 years, Paul was able to convince them of his sincerity.

Paul was well-equipped to be a missionary. He had a bright mind and a good education. He was familiar with the scriptures because he had studied to be a rabbi.

Paul made four missionary journeys, crisscrossing the Mediterranean Sea. It's difficult to imagine what a challenge travel was in those days. Traveling by ship back then was something like traveling by space shuttle is today — it was expensive, dangerous and highly unusual. Paul was even shipwrecked. The exciting story is told in chapter 27 of the Acts of the Apostles.

Wherever Paul went, he left behind small Christian communities. Paul preached to all classes of people. We know a lot about the person Paul was from his letters to the various people and communities he cared about. His letters are the first

Christian writings. They were written even before the gospels.

Like Peter, Paul was martyred by Nero, perhaps around the year 67. Unlike Peter, Paul was a Roman citizen. This gave him the right to a trial and, when he was convicted, to a quick execution.

There is a legend that the city of Rome was founded by the brothers Romulus and Remus, who were raised by wolves. Peter and Paul came to be called the new founders of Rome. Their solemnity is a grand holiday in the city, a day on which Rome celebrates itself and all its treasures. Tomorrow's memorial continues the celebration.

Optional memorial of the
First Martyrs
of the Church of Rome
(died 64)

The Roman emperor Nero came to power as a teenager in the year 54. It was during his reign that the living emperor was first declared to be a god. Nero has sometimes been portrayed comically as a madman who saved his tears in little glass bottles so that future generations could worship them. However, he was a crafty tyrant, a ruler who cared nothing about the people he ruled.

In the year 64, a tremendous fire burned for over a week in the city of Rome. It destroyed two-thirds of the city, including some of Rome's great treasures and fine buildings, but mainly it wiped out the section of the city where poor people lived, leaving the survivors homeless and injured. By "coincidence," this fire cleared a section of land where Nero wanted to build a new palace. Many people of the city were angry and frightened when they realized what had really

happened. Nero needed to turn the spotlight away from himself. He decided that Christians were a convenient target.

There were many rumors about Christians, because their services were open only to the baptized. People had heard that they were cannibals who ate the body and drank the blood of their savior. Also, the Christians weren't very patriotic. In those days people would pledge allegiance to Rome by burning a bit of incense in front of a statue of a god. But Christians refused to do this, and their refusal made them stick out, like someone who doesn't stand up in a ballpark when the national anthem is sung.

Up until this time Nero had been indifferent to Christians, but now he began the first Roman persecution. Christians were found guilty of "hatred of the human race." In all, probably a few thousand people were martyred during his reign, including Peter and Paul. The killing would last, on and off, for another 250 years.

July

The seventh month is named after Julius Caesar. He was a Roman general and politician who was assassinated in the year 44 BCE, on the Ides of March, March 15.

Julius Caesar had ordered that the calendar be reformed. The Roman mathematicians came up with a calendar that is almost identical to the one we use today. It is called the Julian calendar (see January 7) in honor of Julius Caesar.

July

1

In the U. S. A., optional memorial of
Bl. Junípero Serra
presbyter, religious, missionary (1713 – 1784)

Junípero Serra was born on the island of Majorca off the coast of Spain. He joined the Franciscans and soon became a professor. But he wanted to work in the Franciscan missions in Mexico.

Junípero sailed for the Americas at age 35. He taught in Mexico City. After six months, he volunteered to serve at the remote mountain missions of Sierra Gorda. He was the first missionary there to learn the local language. During his eight-year stay he saw to the building of several churches, which are still in use. The native people who became Christians were taught to care for cattle, grow crops and work various trades. During this time Junípero defended the Indians in a disagreement over property rights.

In 1768, the Spanish decided to explore "Upper California" (now the state of California). Junípero, by now 55 years old, traveled along. His dream was to begin a string of missions, each a day's walk from the last, all the way up the Pacific coast. During the next 15 years he organized nine missions, including San Diego, San Francisco, Carmel and Santa Clara. Each became a trading center and then a city. Junípero traveled constantly between the missions, although he was plagued with health problems. He died at age 70.

In 1988, Junípero was beatified. Because of the harsh treatment received by Native Americans from the military forces of Spain and even from the missionaries, many historians and Native American groups oppose his canonization.

Byzantine calendar
St. Aaron
first high priest, prophet (c. thirteenth century BCE)

Aaron's story is found in the books of Exodus, Numbers and Leviticus.

The Israelites had been living in terrible times of slavery in Egypt. God called a faithful servant, Moses, to confront Pharaoh and to lead the slaves into freedom. Moses begged that someone else be chosen for this work. He thought of himself as "slow of speech and slow of tongue."

God replied that Moses's half-brother Aaron would speak for him. Aaron became Moses's assistant. They began a long journey of adventure, suffering, disobedience and growth as they guided the people to the Promised Land of Canaan.

Canada Day

It used to be said that the sun never set on the British Empire because Britain held lands all over the world. Even after the United States fought for its independence, the sun still shone on British soil in North America for nearly 100 years. Then, on July 1, 1867, the provinces of New Brunswick, Nova Scotia, Ontario and Quebec joined together to form their own government. Now the country of Canada has ten provinces and two territories.

Canada Day (also called Dominion Day) will be celebrated all over the vast nation today. A jazz festival in Montreal, a gold panning competition in the Rocky Mountains and even a rubber duck race on the Yukon River will be held, along with fireworks, parades and family reunions.

Since 1959, Windsor, Ontario and Detroit, Michigan have celebrated their countries' independence days with the International Freedom Festival. It's held on the days between Canada Day and July 4. The Detroit River, which separates the cities, is the site of a spectacular fireworks display.

3

Feast of

St. Thomas

apostle (first century)

Thomas was probably born in Galilee. The gospels don't say what he did for a living or how Jesus invited him to become a disciple. Glimpses of Thomas in the Gospel of John show a man who liked to believe the worst so that he would never be disappointed.

One example of this occurred after Jesus' friend Lazarus died. Jesus decided to go into Judea, even though the authorities there were threatening to arrest him. This frightened the apostles. Possibly their lives would be in danger, too. But Thomas said to the others, "Let us also go, that we may die with him."

The Gospel of John doesn't explain why Thomas was the only disciple not there when the risen Christ first appeared to the others. Later, when they told him what had happened, Thomas said he would never believe their story unless he saw and touched Jesus' wounds. A week later, Jesus graciously offered Thomas peace. He made it clear that he knew and understood Thomas's doubt. Thomas responded, "My Lord and my God!"

There are various ideas about where Thomas preached after the descent of the Holy Spirit. One tradition says that he did his mission work in India. To this day a group of people living along the Malabar Coast call themselves "Christians of St. Thomas." Records show that this community is very old. They claim that their ancestors were baptized by St. Thomas himself.

4

Optional memorial of

St. Elizabeth of Portugal

married woman, queen (1271 – 1336)

Elizabeth of Portugal was known all her life as a woman with a remarkable gift for peacemaking. At the age of 12, she was married to the king of Portugal. That background provided her with chances to use her special gifts all through her life.

As queen, Elizabeth lovingly raised two children. She also worked with the poor and sick. She visited hospitals, cared for lepers, and provided a place for pilgrims and strangers to stay. When there was famine in Lisbon, she provided for the hungry. She also donated dowry money for poor girls so they would be able to marry. She built hospitals, orphanages and even the first school to teach farming methods. Although surrounded by the luxury of the court, she never forgot that most people in her country lived in poverty and need.

Elizabeth assisted her husband, her brother and other relatives in working out their differences with other leaders. She saw how the common people she loved suffered from their leaders' quarrels. Innocent people died on the battlefields, and, while the kings were away fighting, evil people made themselves rich by taking land and property from good citizens.

In 1324, the king became fatally ill. When he died, Elizabeth left the palace. She moved to a small house to devote herself to prayer. On a final journey to bring about peace between two warring members of her family, she died of the hardships of her travels.

July

Independence Day (U. S. A.)

Imagine flying over the United States in a small private plane at twilight tonight. You could watch fireworks going off beneath you in all directions, as every town celebrates the birthday of the nation. They celebrate because, on this day in 1776, the Declaration of Independence was announced publicly.

The Declaration was basically a list of the reasons why the 13 colonies had broken ties with their mother country, Great Britain. It was written by a committee headed by Thomas Jefferson. It stated that all people have a right to life, liberty and the pursuit of happiness. By the time the Declaration was produced, the Revolutionary War had already been going on for some months. It would take eight years for the colonists to win the independence they prized so greatly.

Traditional celebrations for Independence Day include torchlight parades, bell ringing, picnics, family reunions, band concerts, and, of course, fireworks. It's a time for fun and a time for reflection, too. People give thanks today for a beautiful country and for a system of government that is admired all over the world.

Even in the United States, the poor and some minority citizens are often robbed of their basic rights. Frederick Douglass (February 20), the great anti-slavery writer, was once asked to give a speech on the Fourth of July. Pointing out that many African Americans were still held as slaves, he told those who had asked him to speak, "The blessings for which you on this day rejoice are not held in common."

Our bright celebrations this day are done in the hope that one day all will be free, that one day the earth itself will shine with liberty.

Optional memorial of
St. Anthony Mary Zaccaria
presbyter, religious founder (1502 – 1539)

There are two ways to bring change to a society. One is to go outside of the system; the other is to work within it. When things get so bad that massive change is needed, both kinds of action are usually necessary before things can improve.

The sixteenth century was a time when the church needed massive change. Some reformers, like Martin Luther, became so discouraged that they left the church. Others, like Anthony Mary Zaccaria, worked from within to correct the wrongs they found.

Anthony was born in Cremona in northern Italy. He studied medicine at the University of Padua, then came home to set up his practice. He was a fine physician. But more and more he became aware that people also needed a spiritual doctor.

Anthony lived in a time of wars and epidemic diseases. To make things worse, many religious leaders had abandoned their responsibilities and were living in luxury. People had no one to guide them. Anthony realized this and he decided to provide the kind of help people would need to live as Christians.

With two other young priests he founded a new religious order called the Barnabites. Instead of spending their lives in a monastery to pray and study, its priests went out to teach the poor and to help victims of the plague. The Barnabites soon brought a new Christian spirit to the city of Milan.

Anthony died while still in his 30s. The order he founded was one of several new orders designed to serve the needs of a new time.

6

Optional memorial of

St. Maria Goretti

martyr (1890 – 1902)

Not too many people in history have lived to see their child declared a saint. But in 1950, a simple Italian woman named Assunta Goretti joined throngs of other people in the plaza outside St. Peter's as the pope canonized her daughter, Maria.

Maria Goretti died very young — she was not even 12 years old. The people of Italy were so moved when they learned the story of her life and death that they put out a loud call for her to be honored in this way.

Maria's mother and father were farm laborers, but they couldn't raise enough food in their home village to feed their four children. When Maria was about eight years old they were forced to move to a very unhealthy area — a marshland where the mosquitoes carried malaria. There they became tenant farmers in partnership with a widower, Giovanni Serenelli, and his son Alessandro. The two families shared living quarters that had once been an old dairy barn.

About a year after their move, Maria's father died and Maria's mother was exhausted, discouraged and worried. Maria encouraged her mother, tended her sisters and brothers, and was noted by all the neighbors for her cheerfulness.

Alessandro, who was about nine years older than Maria, was an angry youth who had grown up without a mother. He was usually very silent, but when Maria was 11 he made sexual advances to her. She refused him. He threatened to kill her if she told anyone. She remained silent and was careful not to be alone in the house with him.

One day Alessandro made an excuse to come back to the house when he knew Maria would be there alone. When she refused him again, he pulled out a knife and stabbed Maria repeatedly. She lived for 24 hours. During that time she forgave Alessandro and prayed for him.

Alessandro was tried and sentenced to 30 years in prison. Over time he changed completely as the result of Maria's forgiveness. When he was released, he went straight to Assunta and asked her forgiveness for taking the life of her daughter. He, too, attended the canonization of Maria Goretti.

Anniversary of the death of

John Hus

(c. 1369 – 1415)

John was a priest from Bohemia (in the modern-day Czech Republic). Bohemia had many poor people who were angry at the church, which was rich and powerful. Noble-born priests and bishops often lived like princes. This was not the kind of example people needed from their spiritual leaders. John Hus became an official of the University of Prague, and in this position he spoke boldly against such wrongs. He suggested ways that the church could serve the people more effectively.

In those times the Bible and the Mass were written and spoken in Latin. Only educated people could understand them. John said that the Bible and the Mass should be translated into languages all the people could understand. He also believed that people should be able to receive the eucharist under the forms of both bread and wine.

At first John received encouragement from the University, the king and the archbishop of Prague. But as he became more outspoken they withdrew their support. Finally, in 1411 or 1412, the pope declared that John could no longer be a member of the church. John asked for support from the Council of Constance, a church group that was meeting at the time to deal with such issues. He was guaranteed safe passage to come and state his views before the Council, but that promise was broken. Less than a month after he got there, he was condemned to death and burned at the stake.

Memorial of
St. Benedict
abbot, religious founder (c. 480 – 550)

In some ways, the sixth century was a lot like the twentieth. People were afraid of strangers. The rich didn't speak to the poor. People within the same social class competed with one another for status by showing off their wealth and possessions. Benedict taught people a way to use prayer and Christlike attitudes to get over their fear and mistrust of each other.

Benedict was born to a noble family of northern Italy. The Roman Empire was breaking apart. Invading tribes from beyond its borders had been taking over the land and looting cities. Many people lived with no thought of the future.

In those years people who wanted to be close to God often gave up on society altogether. They would find an isolated place and spend the rest of their lives there. So for several years Benedict became a hermit. He lived in a cave on a high cliff that was almost impossible to get to. Over time people heard about Benedict and many came to join him.

Around the year 530, Benedict founded a monastery called Monte Cassino. Everyone in the community lived under one roof. To help them, Benedict wrote a common-sense guide called the Rule of Life. It divided the day into times of prayer, study, work and rest. St. Scholastica (February 11), Benedict's sister, settled nearby and formed the first community of women to use Benedict's rule.

In these communities, everyone worked and no one kept personal possessions. This helped to prevent envy and pride. Benedict encouraged a spirit of generous forgiveness. This generosity was extended to strangers and the needy. Every visitor to the abbey was treated like Christ. No one was ever turned away. Hospitality is still a trademark of Benedictine communities around the world.

Benedict spent his life leading his monks, counseling visitors to the abbey and caring for the sick who lived nearby. When he died, he was buried with Scholastica at Monte Cassino.

Benedictine monks and nuns would later be given credit for preserving European civilization during the Middle Ages. Because of this, Benedict has been named the patron saint of Europe.

Byzantine calendar
St. Olga
married woman, duchess (c. 879 – 969)

Today Orthodox Christians honor Princess Olga of Kiev (a city in Ukraine). Vladimir (July 15) was her grandson. The two saints brought Christianity to the Ukrainian people.

Olga was a shrewd and clever peasant woman. In her early life she used violence to protect her power. When her husband Prince Igor was assassinated, she punished the murderers with an agonizing death and killed thousands of their followers.

But then in 958 she became a Christian and changed dramatically. She was baptized and took the name Helen.

Olga grew to be a wise ruler who gave generously to the poor. She built churches and wayside shrines to introduce her people to the new faith. She even sent to Germany for missionaries.

13

Optional memorial of

St. Henry

married man, emperor (972–1024)

Henry's father and mother were the duke and duchess of Bavaria. When he became emperor of Germany in 1002, Henry prayed for humility. His prayers must have been answered because he lived his whole life surrounded by wealth and honors without becoming self-centered. Henry took his job seriously and worked hard. Because of that, he was able to establish peace and order in an empire that had been neglected before he came into power.

In time Henry was crowned Holy Roman Emperor. He ruled a large portion of Europe and traveled constantly, staying at monasteries that he helped to fund. The monasteries were an important way to provide for the local people, because the monks went out to the neighborhoods to tend the sick and needy. Each time Henry entered a new city he spent the first evening of his visit in a prayer vigil.

Like all rulers, Henry made some unwise decisions. For instance, Henry equipped his bishops with land and power as if they were kings. Over time both the church and the state suffered as a result. The confusion of roles became one cause of the Protestant Reformation.

Henry and his wife Cunigunde, who also has been named a saint, are buried in the cathedral of Bamberg, which they helped to build.

Byzantine calendar

St. Ezra

(fourth or fifth century BCE)

Ezra was a scribe—one of a group of Jews whose work was to understand the Law of Moses. He realized that people were living immoral lives because they were so discouraged. They needed God's Law at the center of their hearts.

The Law had been recorded in what are now the first five books of the Hebrew Bible. It included guidelines for everything from the highest moral values, such as the Ten Commandments, to basic aspects of everyday life, such as diet and cleanliness.

However, people didn't know the Law. Ezra changed that. He collected all the books of scripture and called everyone together so that he could read and explain the Law to them. They cried for joy when they heard it.

After this, synagogues were built in every town so that each community could hear the Law and sing psalms together every week. Hearing and keeping the Law helped the Jews to become one people.

14

In the U. S. A., memorial of

Bl. Kateri Tekakwitha

(1656–1680)

Kateri Tekakwitha is a classic example of the student who taught her teachers. The French who explored the Mohawk nation where she lived thought that her people were uncivilized. Yet in her short life Kateri lived out a strong example of the Christian way of life. Soon after her death Europeans were making pilgrimages to her tomb, hoping to learn from her example.

Kateri was born in what is now upstate New York. Her father was chief of the Turtle clan of Mohawks. Her mother, an Algonquin, was a Christian. When Kateri was four, her family was killed by smallpox. The deadly disease left Kateri, the only survivor, with a scarred face and weakened eyesight. Her name, Tekakwitha, means "one who feels her way along." She was taken to live with her uncle, who became the new chief.

Kateri was respected in her community for her many skills. She was especially talented at sewing beautiful beadwork. When she was 11 years old, some "blackrobes" visited her uncle's lodge at Kanawake on the Mohawk River. ("Blackrobe" was the Indian name for a Jesuit missionary.) Their stories of Jesus reminded her of the stories her mother had told her long before.

By the time she was 17, the age when Mohawk girls marry, Kateri had decided to become a Christian. She knew this decision would not be well understood by her relatives. People who called themselves Christian had burned Native American villages and had spread diseases like the smallpox that had killed Kateri's family.

Kateri was baptized on Easter Sunday of 1676. She was named for the martyr St. Catherine of Alexandria. Her uncle, who was fond of her, supported her decision, but her aunts were very angry. She fled to a Christian settlement near Montreal. There she spent the last few years of her life.

At the settlement, Kateri continued to do beadwork and other tasks. She cared for the children of the community, tended the sick, and spent many hours in prayer. Her health began to fail, though, and by the winter of her 24th year, Kateri was so weak that she had to be carried to church on a sled. Soon she was unable to leave home at all. She had the children of the settlement gather in her cabin so that she could tell them Mohawk legends and stories from scripture.

When she knew she was dying, she promised a friend, "I will love you in heaven." Her funeral was held on Holy Thursday, amid the mourning of her community.

In 1980 Kateri Tekakwitha was beatified. That means she was given the title "blessed," and is considered very close to being canonized a saint. She is the first Native American and the first American layperson to be so honored. At the beatification ceremony, 500 Native Americans from 33 different tribes danced at St. Peter's in Rome.

Optional memorial of

St. Camillus de Lellis
presbyter, religious founder (1550 – 1614)

(In the U. S. A., the memorial of Blessed Kateri Tekakwitha takes precedence over this optional memorial.)

The father of Camillus de Lellis was a professional soldier and was away from home for long periods of time. Camillus's mother died very young, so Camillus was on his own a lot. Big and strong at an early age, he grew to be 6'6" tall with a hot temper. At age 17, Camillus was already addicted to gambling.

By the time Camillus was 24, gambling had cost him everything he owned, even his clothing. He went to Rome and worked in a hospital for the incurably ill. He hoped to get treatment for painful sores on his feet and legs. But because of his bad temper and continued gambling, they sent him away before he was completely healed.

After some time he decided to return to the hospital that had sent him away. By this time he developed a spirit of love and compassion. He nursed the sick with so much kindness that after four years he was made director of the hospital.

Camillus educated himself so he could care for the spiritual needs of sick and dying people.

In time he founded a religious order with a commitment to this work. He encouraged them to serve with the very latest information about medicine. They wore a large red cross on their clothing. When ships pulled into harbor carrying plague victims, people from Camillus's order would go on board to tend them. Many new ideas for treating sick and wounded people came from Camillus. He invented field ambulances and military hospitals.

Through it all, Camillus's own health was never good. Finally he resigned as head of the order so that he could devote the little energy he had left to the sick. People who saw him said that Camillus treated each patient as tenderly as if the person were Christ.

Memorial of

St. Bonaventure
bishop, religious, doctor of the church
(1221 – 1274)

Not much is known about Bonaventure's childhood near Viterbo, an Italian town northwest of Rome. At an early age he entered the Franciscan Order, where he could imitate Jesus as Francis of Assisi (October 4) had done. Francis had died in 1226, when Bonaventure was about five years old. Since that time the Franciscans had been struggling to decide how best to follow their founder's example. Many different groups within the order had strong opinions about how things should go.

Bonaventure was appointed the leader of all the Franciscans around the world when he was only 35 years old. In the 18 years that Bonaventure was their leader, he worked hard to bring all the groups into peaceful agreement. He called five general meetings of the order. He also visited the friars. To help them understand Francis better, Bonaventure wrote a biography of the saint.

Everyone who knew Bonaventure seemed to agree that he was a lovable person. He also was considered, with his friend Thomas Aquinas (January 28), to be one of the great thinkers of his time. Despite Bonaventure's own intelligence, he taught that people didn't have to be bright or well-educated to be loved by Jesus.

Byzantine calendar
St. Vladimir
ruler (c. 956 – 1015)

Vladimir was the grand-prince of the city of Kiev. When he was born, his land, Ukraine, was ruled by Vikings. Vladimir's grandmother, Princess Olga (July 11), had been baptized a Christian. She was one of the first people in that region to be baptized. But when Olga's son came to power, he thought if he became a Christian he would be betraying his fellow Viking warriors. So he brought up his son Vladimir as a Viking.

When Vladimir became ruler, he was violent and ruthless, but his people loved him. He hosted spectacular feasts with his nobles. He sacrificed to the pagan gods whenever he won a battle.

But something stirred in Vladimir's heart, perhaps some memories of his Christian grandmother. He began to feel doubtful about the pagan ways. He decided to learn about Christianity and was struck by the beauty of Christian worship. In 988, at the age of 32, Vladimir was baptized.

Over time Vladimir became a humble and devout person. He set about providing his people with education and relief from all their needs. He built schools, churches and even a library. (Books were rare in those days.) He sent missionaries into remote areas. People worshiped in their Slavonic language.

The prince still feasted with his friends. But now he sent messengers out into the city to invite the poor to feast with him. Later he even sent carts of food out into the streets for the sick. When he knew he was dying, he gave away everything he owned to the poor. For the next two centuries, in Vladimir's spirit, the Kiev princes ruled their people wisely and with faith.

In Ukraine, St. Vladimir has the title of an "Equal to the Apostles."

Roman martyrology

St. Swithun

bishop (c. 800–862)

> St. Swithun's Day, if thou dost rain,
> For 40 days it will remain.
> St. Swithun's Day, if thou be fair,
> For 40 days 'twill rain nae mair.

This is a bad time of year for rain. Harvest time is here, and when grain is ripe in the fields, heavy rain can knock it down and make it rot. So it's best to begin the harvest as soon as possible. Yet if the harvest is begun too soon, the grain will not be fully ripe. A way to forecast weather at this time of year is especially valuable.

The St. Swithun's Day rhyme, still said in England, is a prediction that whatever weather happens today will last for more than a month. For many people the rhyme keeps alive the memory of a wonderful man.

Swithun was born in Wessex in England. He was a fine student and was ordained a priest and soon named chaplain to Egbert, king of the West Saxons. Egbert chose Swithun to tutor his son Ethelwulf, who in turn became king. Both kings considered Swithun their trusted advisor because he was prayerful, well-informed and wise.

In time Ethelwulf named Swithun to tutor his son, Alfred the Great, who would become the most famous of all the Saxon kings. Ethulwulf also honored Swithun by naming him bishop of Winchester.

Despite all these honors, Swithun remained a humble man. As bishop he loved to travel around his diocese to meet and work with his people. But so that they would not make a big fuss about his visits, he made his journeys quietly, on foot during the night.

Even when Swithun was dying, he asked to be treated as simply as possible. He asked that his grave be dug at the north end of the churchyard. There, he said, the rain could fall on it and members of his church might sometimes walk on it as they passed by.

16

Optional memorial of

Our Lady of Mount Carmel

Mount Carmel was a holy place hundreds of years before Christ. There the prophet Elijah (July 20) challenged the prophets of the pagan god Baal to a contest where the power of God was shown forth. Later, in the early centuries of Christianity, people who wanted to pray and grow close to God settled on the slopes of Mount Carmel. In time a monastery was built there.

In the year 1251, the prior-general of the Carmelites, Simon Stock, had a vision of Mary the mother of God. Today became the special feast day of the Carmelite Order. In the eighteenth century the feast was extended to the whole church. It is celebrated widely in Italy, where people parade through the streets and carry a statue of Mary. Italian Americans have kept up the custom.

Byzantine calendar
St. Elijah of Tishbe
prophet (9th century BCE)

Queen Jezebel worshiped the pagan god Baal and wanted the whole kingdom of Israel to do the same. The prophets who lived in Israel would never allow the people to fall into such confusion, as Jezebel knew. So she had many of them killed. However, one prophet was so bold that he confronted Jezebel. This was Elijah, whose story is found in the First and Second Books of Kings.

Elijah challenged all the prophets of Baal to a contest. He said that two bulls should be prepared for a sacrifice. One would be dedicated to Baal, the other to God. Whoever was more powerful would accept the sacrifice by consuming it in fire. The contest was held on Mount Carmel.

King Ahab and 450 prophets of Baal were there. The people of Israel gathered around the mountain. The followers of Baal danced around their altar and wailed loudly for hours. But no fire appeared to consume the sacrifice.

Then Elijah ordered that God's altar be drenched with water. He prayed to the Lord, "Let it be known this day that you are the God of Israel and that you have brought your people back to their senses." Suddenly the bull that was offered to God burst into flames. Amazingly, even the water was burned up in the fire.

Jezebel was furious. Elijah fled for his life. He returned to the source of the Jewish faith — to the mountain where Moses had accepted the Law from God. There he cried out his loneliness and discouragement. He listened for God's voice.

God provided Elijah with the strength to go back to his work. So Elijah is known as the father of prophets.

According to the prophet Malachi (January 3), Elijah will return to welcome the Messiah. To this day, during the Jewish Passover (page 199), an extra cup of wine is set at the table of the Seder meal for Elijah. According to legend, he wanders the streets this night correcting wrongs and bringing justice.

Optional memorial of
St. Lawrence of Brindisi
*presbyter, religious, doctor of the church
(1559 – 1619)*

Lawrence of Brindisi was born near Naples in Italy. At the age of 16, he became a Capuchin friar. He was a brilliant student who studied the scriptures in their original ancient languages. This intense Bible study helped him to preach with great power later in his life.

Lawrence was also gifted in dealing with people. His fellow friars thought he was good, simple and wise. They elected him their superior when he was only 31.

Because Lawrence was a talented diplomat, the most powerful rulers of his time asked his advice. Over the course of his life, he served as a peacemaker in disputes between kings. He worked for understanding between Germany, Spain, Bavaria and Savoy. On one such errand of peace he became ill and died near Lisbon in Portugal.

July

22

Memorial of
St. Mary Magdalene
disciple of the Lord (first century)

Mary Magdalene stood at the foot of the cross on which Jesus poured out his blood. She came to his tomb with myrrh to embalm his body. And she was the first witness to the risen Christ. Because of her witness to the resurrection, Mary is sometimes pictured with a bright red Easter egg in her hand.

Mary was from Magdala, a town on the western shore of Lake Galilee. The Gospel of Luke says that Jesus healed her of physical and spiritual illness. Scenes from scripture make clear Mary Magdalene's intense devotion to Jesus. With the new freedom brought by her healing, she became one of a group of women who were Jesus' disciples and who walked with him on his missionary journeys. In doing this, these women went against the customs of the time: Women had never been permitted to study with a rabbi.

Mary continued to stay close to Jesus even when he was crucified. The Gospel of John names her as one of three women who stood by the cross. This took great courage.

Chapter 20 of the Gospel of John tells us that Mary went to Jesus' tomb before dawn on Sunday morning. When she saw that the stone in front of the tomb had been rolled away, she thought the officials had stolen Jesus' body. She ran to tell the disciples. Then she returned to the tomb and wept.

Angels appeared to her; then the risen Christ came and stood beside her. She did not recognize the Lord until she heard her name. Then she was asked to be the messenger of the good news. Mary Magdalene was the first to announce that Jesus Christ had conquered death. This is why Mary is called the "apostle to the apostles."

23

Optional memorial of
St. Bridget
married woman, religious, abbess (c. 1304–1373)

Bridget's father was governor of the largest province in Sweden. He had a deep love of justice, which he passed on to his daughter. Even as a young girl, Bridget also had a gift of prayer. She reflected on the passion of Christ.

For a woman of her times, Bridget received an excellent education. While she was still in her early teens her father arranged a marriage for her. Fortunately, it turned out better than most arranged marriages. She and her husband loved each other and they had eight children.

Bridget enjoyed her life as a wife and mother. She also reached out to the poor and needy, beginning a hospital on her own estate where she personally tended the sick. Many people came to her for help.

Years later, after her husband had died, Bridget gave away all she owned, and she moved to a monastery. It was at this point in her life, strengthened by deep prayer, that she began confronting the wrongs she saw in the world. Fearlessly she wrote letters to popes, cardinals and rulers, telling them to seek justice.

Bridget also was concerned about the court of Sweden, where a privileged few lived in luxury while the rest of the kingdom was unjustly taxed. She traveled there and urged the king, queen, nobles and bishops to change their ways. In 1349, Bridget moved to Rome. She worked with victims of an epidemic. The people of her country grieved to see her go. She had been their "mystic," their window into heaven.

She died in Rome in 1373. Her body was carried in triumph through Europe back to the abbey of Vadstena for burial. For her fearlessness, honesty and tireless energy, Bridget, who is also known as Birgitta, is remembered today as the patron saint of Sweden.

Byzantine calendar

St. Ezekiel

prophet (sixth century BCE)

The Jewish prophets lived a long time ago. Our world is so different from theirs that often we have a difficult time understanding them. Ezekiel probably is the most puzzling of all the prophets. He gave hope to his people at a time when they needed it, and he was a poet as well. His language is often wild and always thrilling to read.

Part of Ezekiel's strangeness may be the result of the difficult life he led. He was a priest until he was taken prisoner and carried off with a large group of other exiles to Babylon. Once there, he was no longer allowed to do his priestly work. But he still cared deeply about his people and his God. So over time he became a prophet.

Ezekiel's job was to turn the hearts of the people back to hope in God. The Book of Ezekiel tells four unforgettable visions. The first vision is of four creatures, each with four faces. Centuries later, Christian artists used these four faces to depict the four gospel writers. Matthew is shown as a human being, Mark as a lion, Luke as an ox and John as an eagle.

Another of Ezekiel's visions was of a field of dead, dry bones that grow flesh and come to life. The people are like dead bones, Ezekiel is saying, and God will bring them to new life by returning them to their homeland. His message reaches out to all people who face an uncertain future.

25

Feast of

St. James

apostle (died 44)

Today Spain celebrates the feast day of its patron, St. James. There he is called *Santiago*. Centuries ago the Spaniards built a shrine in his honor at a place called Compostela. Pilgrims from all over Europe visited it. They wore in their hats the shell of a scallop or cockle.

The shell recalled that, before he was called by Christ, James worked as a fisherman. It also reminded the pilgrims how in later years the apostle James baptized new Christians. Pilgrims wearing the shell were granted hospitality wherever they went. There were so many of them that James is considered the patron saint of pilgrims.

James and his brother John (December 27) were the sons of Zebedee, a fisherman in Galilee. One day Jesus walked along the lake shore. Speaking to the brothers as they mended their nets, he invited them to come with him and learn to fish for human beings.

Two men named James became apostles. Today's James is called "James the Greater," perhaps because we know more about him than about James the Less (May 3). Whatever the reason, the James we remember today seems to have been a person who earned the trust of Jesus. With John and Peter, the gospels mention James as a witness to some of Jesus' miracles, such as the cure of Peter's mother-in-law and the raising of Jairus's daughter. James also was present at the Transfiguration of Jesus (August 6). James was in the garden of Gethsemane on the night of the Last Supper. Oddly, though, the brothers James and John are often shown to be bull-headed. They didn't understand that Jesus' mission was one of humility and forgiveness. At one point Jesus gave the two brothers the nickname "sons of thunder" because they wanted to send lightning down on a town that turned them away.

According to the 12th chapter of the Acts of the Apostles, James was the first of the Twelve to be martyred. Arrested in Jerusalem by order of King Herod Agrippa, James was put to death with a sword.

Memorial of
Ss. Ann and Joachim
parents of the Virgin Mary

Today we celebrate the parents of Mary and the grandparents of Jesus. Nothing is mentioned in the gospels about them, not even their names. Ann and Joachim are the names they were given centuries later by Christians who wanted to honor them.

According to folktales told about them, Ann and Joachim were devout people of good character. Like Mary and Joseph, like Elizabeth and Zechariah, they were *anawim,* the poor of Israel. Legends say that they dedicated their daughter to God, taking her to the Temple in Jerusalem when she was very young. A church in Israel named after St. Ann is believed by some people to be built over the place where Mary was born. Legends also say that, like Elizabeth and Zechariah, Ann and Joachim waited and prayed many years for the birth of a child.

For centuries people in various parts of the world — including France, French Canada, and the cities of Florence, Naples and Innsbruck — have kept a devotion to Ann and Joachim.

Pilgrims, 200,000 of them a year, still come to the town of Beaupré, near Quebec. Today is one special time of pilgrimage. People also visit at Pentecost.

The name Ann is the English form of the Biblical name Hannah, which means "grace." Stories about St. Ann remind us of the elderly prophetess Anna in Luke's story of the Presentation of the infant Jesus in the Temple. They also remind us of Samuel's mother Hannah, who in tears begged God for a child. In some places, parents make a point of naming one of their girls Ann. This day in many parts of Europe is a celebration for all young women — and all grandparents as well.

Memorial of
St. Martha
disciple of the Lord (first century)

Martha, her sister Mary and their brother Lazarus lived in the town of Bethany, near Jerusalem. The Gospel of John records that Jesus loved all three of them. They were important to him. In that time and culture, women were treated as inferior to men. But Jesus treated women as equals. He called Martha, Mary and Lazarus his friends. The gospels tell us that he laughed and cried with them.

Martha's conversations with Jesus show that she was able to say just what she thought without any pious nonsense. When she gave a dinner in Jesus' honor, Martha asked his support in getting her sister Mary to pitch in and help. In reply, Jesus gave both sisters permission to sit at his feet as disciples. Women weren't permitted to study with a rabbi, so Jesus was taking a bold stand in treating his two friends that way.

Even when her brother Lazarus died, Martha did not give up her faith. She told Jesus, "Yes, Lord, I believe that you are the Messiah, the Son of God, the one coming into the world." Jesus wept at the tomb of Lazarus. And then Jesus raised Lazarus from the dead.

Martha developed a reputation over the centuries as the practical and active Christian, so she is often pictured with a cooking ladle or a set of household keys. She is a patron saint of cooks and of hospitality. Today we celebrate that we, like Martha and Mary and Lazarus, can be ourselves with Jesus. We can say what we really think. We can welcome Christ into our homes through hospitality to family, friends and strangers alike.

Optional memorial of
St. Peter Chrysologus
bishop, doctor of the church (406 – c. 450)

The people of the Italian village of Imola, Peter's home town, didn't know him by the name "Chrysologus." He earned that name later, when he was bishop of Ravenna. It means "golden words."

Peter was the young deacon of the diocese of Ravenna when he was chosen bishop in 433. At that time the western part of the Roman Empire was under attack, but Ravenna remained a peaceful city. It was noted, then as now, for its historic buildings and its beautiful mosaics.

Emperor Valentinian III and his mother chose to live there. They respected Peter. He improved the city by encouraging its citizens in their Christian faith. He helped them to let go of their old superstitious customs.

Peter got his nickname because of his fine homilies, of which 175 still exist. They're short because he didn't want to bore anyone.

Memorial of
St. Ignatius of Loyola
presbyter, religious founder (1491 – 1556)

Ignatius was born in the Basque region of Spain. As a boy he had little interest in schooling. He wanted only to be a military officer like his father and grandfather. In 1521, when he was 30 years old, he reached a turning point in his life. While defending the Spanish castle of Pamplona against a French siege, he was struck by a cannonball. Both his legs were injured.

Knowing he would be unable to move around for a long time, Ignatius asked for some entertaining novels about knights and soldiers. But all that could be found for him were books about Christ and the lives of the saints. In reading them, he began to believe that the saints showed greater courage than soldiers.

The next year, when Ignatius had recovered, he visited a nearby shrine. He hung his sword before a statue of Mary, gave away his uniform to a beggar, and promised to dedicate his life to God's service. The former warrior went to school with children for the next two years until he was ready to enter a university.

At the University of Paris, Ignatius was still much older than his classmates. But he met six talented young men who wanted to share his new life of prayer and service. They studied theology, served the poor and gathered often for prayer. To help them, Ignatius wrote his *Spiritual Exercises*, a guidebook for closer union with God, which is still in wide use today. They learned to do all, as Ignatius said, "for the greater glory of God."

Ignatius hoped that these young people would become a kind of army of God's servants. He challenged them to live as the poorest of the poor, teaching children and uneducated adults, working in hospitals and prisons.

As more and more people came to share in this vision, Ignatius showed a gift for organization. He combined this talent with his love of deep prayer. By the time he died, over a thousand people had committed their lives to this new kind of service. They were called the Society of Jesus, or the "Jesuits" for short. Some of them became missionaries. Others began schools.

In inspiring others to work for God all over the world, Ignatius's own youthful love for adventure was satisfied. Today he is considered the patron saint of the Basque people.

August

The eighth month is named after Augustus Caesar, who was emperor at the time of the birth of Jesus. Augustus was the first Roman emperor. In the Northern Hemisphere, this month marks the fullness of summer. The worship of the church during August reflects summer's abundance in celebrating the feast of the Transfiguration of the Lord and the solemnity of the Assumption of the Virgin Mary into Heaven.

1

Memorial of
St. Alphonsus Liguori
bishop, religious founder, doctor of the church
(1696 – 1787)

In modern times we would call Alphonsus Liguori a "child prodigy." He earned his law degree when he was 16 years old. At his graduation ceremony, the audience chuckled when they saw him in his doctoral robes, which were much too big for him. But by the time he was 20, he was already the leading lawyer in his home town of Naples in Italy. He had many highborn friends and a fine social life. He was known for his talent at playing the harpsichord.

Things continued to go well for Alphonsus until he was 27. It was said that he never lost a case. Then one day in court, he made a serious error. His reputation as a lawyer was damaged. At first he felt so ashamed that he refused to eat or to leave his house. But then he realized that God was speaking to him through this blunder, telling him to take himself less seriously and to change his life.

Alphonsus became a preacher, and for the next several years he gave retreats for the poor in the slums of Naples. Although he was a brilliant and sophisticated man, his homilies were written so that the least educated person in the assembly could enjoy and understand them. He spent a lot of time counseling people, and he encouraged them to form small groups for prayer. In time he founded an order of men to work with laborers. The order is called the Redemptorists.

Alphonsus wrote many books and hymns. He worked toward correcting a mistaken idea called "Jansenism." Jansenists thought people were so sinful that almost no one would be saved. Because of this attitude, people thought no one was worthy to receive communion. But Alphonsus said that celebrating the eucharist was a way to *become* holy, not a reward for *being* holy.

The Seven Holy Maccabees and their mother St. Salome
martyrs (died c. 168 BCE)

Maccabee means "hammer." The name was a badge of honor. It was given to a guerrilla leader named Judas who fought for the land of Judah at a time when its people were oppressed. After he died the name was given to his brothers.

A cruel Syrian king, Antiochus Epiphanes, had taken over the land. He was determined to replace the Jewish way of life with Greek ways. He thought that would strengthen his power, because all his subjects in various countries would then have the same customs. One way to weaken the faith of the Jews was to discredit their priests. The Syrians forced them to eat pork and to violate other Jewish laws.

A priest named Mattathias fled to the mountains with his five sons. One of his sons was Judas, "the hammer." They organized a force of loyal Jews against the occupying armies of Antiochus.

The Syrian armies were much larger and better equipped than the Jewish resistance. However, under Judas's leadership the Jews reclaimed the city of Jerusalem. The people scoured their beloved Temple from top to bottom and restored its furnishings, which had been looted by the Syrians. The rededication of the Temple is celebrated each year during the Jewish festival of Hanukkah (see page 197).

Chapter seven of the Second Book of Maccabees relates powerful stories from the time of the evil king Antiochus. According to one of these accounts, a mother and her seven sons were arrested by the Syrians. They accepted torture and death rather than break the Jewish law. Centuries later the Christians would tell this story to strengthen their determination to remain faithful to the Christian way of life. The Christians called the mother and her seven sons "the holy Maccabees." Today became their remembrance day.

Lammas Day

Lammas Day is a grandparent of Thanksgiving. It began centuries ago as a harvest festival in Britain for the newly ripened wheat crop. On this day everyone went to church to give thanks, and they carried with them a freshly baked loaf of bread made from the new wheat. So the day came to be called Loaf-Mass Day. This was shortened into Lammas.

The ancient Celts divided their year into four quarters. Today began the autumn quarter, the opposite corner of the year from Lent. Now the days will quickly grow shorter. This was a favorite time of year because food was often plentiful and the weather mild. It was harvest time.

In times past, the year had several harvest festivals. First came a thanksgiving day for early crops such as peas and spinach, then one for grains, then later one for fruits, then later still a day for autumn vegetables and grapes. Of course, northern lands had different dates for the festivals than southern lands.

Lammas Day happens to fall at about the time the spring wheat crop ripens across the Great Plains of North America. This is the season of "amber waves of grain." It's a spectacular sight when the wind blows.

August

2

Optional memorial of
St. Eusebius of Vercelli
bishop (c. 283–371)

The Arian heresy was a false teaching that caused confusion in the church for two centuries. Arians taught that Jesus was first a human being who gradually became God.

Eusebius was born on the island of Sardinia. He was named the bishop of Vercelli, a town in northern Italy. His diocese covered a vast area where many people practiced pagan customs. He encouraged people to become Christians.

Eusebius was asked by the pope to attend a meeting of bishops called to deal with all the problems caused by the Arian heresy. Emperor Constantius believed in the Arian heresy and he made it clear that he didn't want the bishops to oppose this false teaching. Bishop Eusebius stood up to him. Constantius was enraged, and he had Eusebius sent away to the Middle East, where he was harshly treated by Arian Christians.

Only when Constantius died several years later was Eusebius able to return to his diocese. St. Jerome (September 30) said that when Eusebius came home the whole nation of Italy was able to stop mourning for him. He is considered the patron saint of the subalpine region where Vercelli is located. He is honored there to this day.

4

Memorial of
St. John Mary Vianney
presbyter (1786–1859)

John Vianney and the French Revolution were born at about the same time. In Paris and other French cities, angry mobs slaughtered the powerful and the wealthy. Because in the past the church had often sided with the rich, many priests were also killed. Those that were left were forced to go into hiding. Every so often, a priest came to the farm village of Dardilly, where John lived, to celebrate Mass secretly in a barn.

By the time John was in his teens, Mass could be said in public again. There was still a great shortage of priests, and John wanted to help fill the gap. He was needed on the farm, but finally when he reached age 20 his parents let him go to the seminary.

John had a lot of trouble with his studies. Although he was older than the other students, school had never come easily for him, and he hadn't had much preparation for difficult subjects, such as Latin. After failing his examinations, he was ordained anyway, mostly because he was so prayerful and committed to his ministry. Soon afterward the vicar general told him, "My friend, you have been appointed *curé* of Ars. Ars is a little parish where there is not much love. You must put some into it." (In French *curé* means parish priest.)

John found that the people of his little parish were indifferent to their faith. He prayed for them, preached to them and tended their needs in every way he could think of. He visited every family, began religious education classes for children and adults, and later began schools and an orphanage.

John reached out most powerfully in the sacrament of reconciliation. He understood that people needed a connection with God. He sat in the drafty church and heard confessions for up to 12 hours a day in the winter — up to 16 hours a day in the summer. After 41 years of faithful service, John had made a great difference in the people of the parish. In one of his sermons he said, "You pray. You love. And there you have our happiness on earth."

5

Optional memorial of

The Dedication of the Basilica of St. Mary in Rome

The city of Rome sits on seven hills. Atop the Esquiline Hill is a famous church called St. Mary Major. The word "major" refers to its size — for centuries it was the largest church in the world named in Mary's honor. It is a basilica, a word that means "a building fit for royalty." In the 1600 years since it was first constructed, it's been rebuilt many times. But it still has the flavor of early Christian times.

One rebuilding of St. Mary Major took place soon after the year 431. In that year, Mary was declared by a church council to be the Mother of God. So this basilica was rededicated in her honor at that time.

Each year Christians honor the "birthday" of their parish church on the date it was officially dedicated. The dedication of the basilica of St. Mary is one of the few church "birthdays" that can be celebrated not just in the parish of St. Mary's but in all parishes.

6

Feast of

The Transfiguration of the Lord

At just the time of year when the harvest is abundant, we celebrate a feast of God's glory. The marvelous events of this day are told in the gospels of Matthew (chapter 17), Mark (chapter 9) and Luke (chapter 9).

Peter, James and John were led up to a high mountain by Jesus. Suddenly his face shone as bright as the sun. Moses the Lawgiver (see September 14) and the great prophet Elijah appeared (see July 20). They talked about Jesus' coming death and resurrection. In awe, Peter blurted out a strange suggestion. He wanted to set up booths for Jesus, Moses and Elijah.

A cloud surrounded them. Then the voice of God proclaimed that Jesus is God's son, the Beloved. The three apostles were terrified. They fell down in fear. Then they looked up, but the amazing scene was gone. Jesus was there alone.

What did Peter mean when he asked if he should set up booths? The answer is found in a custom of the Jewish harvest festival of Sukkot (page 196). During Sukkot, booths are set up. They're constructed out of green branches and decorated with fruits and flowers. They symbolize creation. Moses and Elijah and all the ancestors are invited to enter in spirit. If Peter wanted to set up harvest booths, perhaps he wanted all of creation to share in the Transfiguration of Jesus.

In the time of Moses, when the Israelites traveled through the desert on their way to the Promised Land, God traveled with them. God appeared as a cloud within a tent. In the gospel story of the Transfiguration, God again appears as a shining cloud. But instead of filling a tent or a harvest booth, the cloud surrounds Jesus and his disciples. Perhaps the human body is like the tent of God's presence.

The feast of the Transfiguration is a day of rejoicing. In Rome, the grape harvest is blessed. New wine from these grapes is used at Mass. Eastern Christians hold a harvest procession in celebration of the springtime flowers and seeds that have been "transfigured" into summertime fruit and grain. Altars are decorated with fruit and sheaves of wheat. Often there's a summer fair after the services end.

Hiroshima Memorial Day

Hiroshima, Japan, is a thriving city of shipyards and factories. Along one of its seven rivers sits a building once used to display Japanese products. Now, half-destroyed, the building has become known as the Atomic Dome. It serves as an eerie reminder of what happened on this day in 1945. That was when the first atomic bomb ever used on an inhabited area was dropped on Hiroshima.

At that time the city was built mostly of wood. After the explosion, the few structures made of concrete, like the Atomic Dome, stood in a wasteland. No one knew if grass would grow again in Hiroshima or if humans could ever safely live there. Many people were killed outright by the explosion. Many more died slowly because of radiation sickness. A large group of survivors have suffered throughout their lives with health problems. They are called *hibakusha* — explosion-affected people.

The Atomic Dome is now surrounded by a peace park. All day today the park will be filled with people. Services begin at 8:15 in the morning, when survivors and their children will say a silent prayer for peace. Later, all will gather at the Cenotaph, a monument bearing the names of all who died because of the bomb. After dark, children will set paper lanterns afloat in the

Ohta River. Each lantern bears the name of someone who has died. As the children float their lanterns, they will sing "So long as this life lasts, give peace back to us, peace that will never end."

This day is a time for Americans, and all citizens of the world, to join in heartfelt prayer and work for lasting peace. Pope John Paul II said when he visited Hiroshima, "In the past it was possible to destroy a village, a town, a region, even a country. Now the whole planet has come under threat."

7

Optional memorial of
St. Sixtus II and companions
Sixtus, pope, martyr, and his companions, martyrs (died 258)

Sixtus II was consecrated pope in 257. A writer who knew him described him as "a good and peaceable priest." We know he was courageous because he was willing to become pope in a dangerous time. The Roman emperor Valerian had issued a decree that Christians could no longer meet together, so the Christian community began to gather secretly in the burial tunnels called the catacombs. One day as they prayed together, imperial soldiers burst in on them.

Sixtus came forward with four of the deacons who helped him to serve the Christians of the city. They chose not to try to escape, because their community would be punished if they did. All five were beheaded on the spot, in plain sight of the assembly. Two other deacons were caught in another catacomb the same day and also were killed. Four days later, Lawrence (August 10), the last deacon left alive in the city, was martyred.

Optional memorial of

St. Cajetan

presbyter, religious founder (1480 – 1547)

Cajetan was born in the town of Vicenza in Italy. He studied law at the University of Padua and soon moved on to become an advisor to the pope. Cajetan found that he, like Jesus, needed to spend time with people that his friends and family didn't approve of.

While living in Rome he joined a group called an "oratory." Its members prayed together and went out into the city to work with the poor. Over time, this work had a powerful effect on him. At the age of 33 he resigned from his job and gave away his possessions.

Cajetan returned home to Vicenza and he spent the next six years working with the local oratory. It upset Cajetan's family that Cajetan and his friends worked in a hospital for people with deadly illnesses. Many of the patients in their care were feared, much as people with AIDS sometimes are today.

Cajetan later returned to Rome where he organized a new community. They would own no property whatsoever. This would help them to live in humility. Many of Cajetan's ideas would later be borrowed by the Council of Trent, which helped to reform the church.

Memorial of

St. Dominic

presbyter, religious founder (1170 – 1221)

Dominic was born in the Castile region of Spain. His parents were nobles. He became a priest and lived in community for several years, spending his time in study and quiet prayer. His life might have continued that way except for a group called the Albigensians. They taught that the body is evil and only the spirit is good. This mistaken idea was probably popular because the Albigensians fasted and lived in poverty. People found them more trustworthy than luxury-loving Christians.

Dominic asked the pope for permission to begin a new religious order for men and women. It would be called the Order of Preachers, and preaching the truth of the goodness of the body would be its first task.

The priests who joined Dominic could have as many books as they wanted so that they would continue to study and therefore preach clearly. But they would also live lives of Christian charity and poverty. This would help people trust and believe them.

Unlike other religious orders, the Order of Preachers traveled wherever they were needed. Dominic trained his priests to use only kindness and tact, not harsh judgment, when debating. He sent them to great universities. Many of them received doctorates and became famous teachers themselves.

Dominic traveled through Europe to organize the Order of Preachers. He died when he was only about 51 years old. But by that time the order had spread as far as Britain, Poland, Scandinavia and Palestine. Nowadays, the Order of Preachers also is known as the Dominican Order. Like Francis of Assisi (October 4), Dominic helped to revolutionize the thirteenth century.

August

9

Nagasaki Memorial Day

Today marks the second time in history that a nuclear weapon was used in war. The bomb was dropped in 1945 on the city of Nagasaki in Japan. Nagasaki is a port city on the west coast of the island of Kyushu. The first nuclear explosion, three days earlier, destroyed the Japanese city of Hiroshima.

The bomb dropped on Nagasaki destroyed almost two square miles in the heart of the city, where its medical centers were located. So just at the time when there were large numbers of injured people, the doctors and hospitals to care for them were gone.

Each time a nuclear weapon is tested, the citizens of Nagasaki send a letter of protest. In 1980, they issued the Nagasaki Peace Declaration. It points out that the world's nuclear stockpile could now destroy humanity several times over. It asks the nations to pray for peace, to stop the buildup of nuclear weapons, and to end the arms race. It says that "unless this dangerous course is reversed, no true peace or progress will ever be attained on earth."

In 1983 the American Catholic bishops sent out a letter on the nuclear arms race. They used the scriptures, traditional church teachings and the experience of peacemakers in forming their judgments. The result of their work is called *The Challenge of Peace: God's Promise and Our Response.* In this letter the bishops say "Peace, like the kingdom of God itself, is both a divine gift and a human work. We are called to be a church at the service of peace."

10

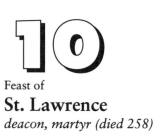

Feast of
St. Lawrence
deacon, martyr (died 258)

The word "deacon" means "servant." The word was first used to describe someone who waited on tables. Stephen (December 26), the first martyr, was a deacon of the church. Christian deacons were men and women who helped the needy. They distributed the community's goods. Because of their work, deacons were especially visible in times of persecution when many other Christians would go into hiding.

Two centuries after the death of Stephen, the emperor Valerian was in power in Rome. He forbid the Christians to assemble. Valerian's henchmen had murdered Pope Sixtus II (August 7). The deacons of the diocese had all been beheaded. Lawrence was the only deacon left alive. Then he too was found and arrested.

Legends about Lawrence say that he spent the last days of his life selling the possessions of the community and giving the money to the poor. When a Roman official demanded that he produce the church's wealth, Lawrence brought blind, lame and needy people to this official. The official was so enraged that he ordered Lawrence roasted to death over a fire. To encourage the poor, who were forced to watch, Lawrence was said to have joked, "Turn me over. I'm done on this side."

When the legends about Lawrence first appeared many years after his death, he became famous. Many churches were named after him, and he has become one of the patron saints of Rome. Outdoor barbecues are a custom to celebrate his feast. That may seem like a grisly way to remember the martyrdom of St. Lawrence. But it is also a way to laugh at Valerian and all dictators.

11

Memorial of
St. Clare
religious founder (1193 – 1253)

It was Palm Sunday in Assisi in Italy. Clare, a beautiful young woman of 18, silently slipped out of her father's palace in the dead of night the only way she could avoid being seen — through a door usually reserved for dead bodies. In a tiny chapel nearby, she met her friend and spiritual guide, Francis. She replaced her jewels and rich clothes with a dress of rough, grey sackcloth tied with a rope. She was determined to trade her old life for a future with "Lady Poverty." As it turned out, that poverty brought her a lifelong friendship with Francis — and with Christ as well.

Clare made this decision after hearing Francis preach and spending time in prayer with him. Like her, he had been born into a wealthy family. But he had given away all he had.

Clare was expected to marry someone of noble birth. When her father heard about her plan to live like Francis, he came with his male relatives to the convent where she was staying. He tried to take her back by force, but when he saw her determination to stay he gave in to her wishes.

Soon Clare's sisters and other young women of Assisi came to join her. They called themselves the Poor Ladies. Francis found a simple house for them next to the chapel of San Damiano on the outskirts of town. They chose Clare to be their abbess.

Clare took an unusual approach to being the head of the convent. She thought of herself as the servant of the other women. She waited on them at meals. When they came in from outside, she knelt joyfully to wash their dirty feet. When they got sick, it was Clare who gently tended them.

Though she never left her convent, her spirit was soon felt all over Europe. Among the women who flocked to join the Poor Ladies were princesses and other nobles. Like Clare, they had lived with wealth and power. They knew these things didn't bring joy.

After Francis's death, Clare lived nearly 30 years longer. Many people thought the Poor Ladies should have farms and vineyards, as other convents had. Three popes tried to give Clare property. Always, though, she won them over to her belief that the Sisters should own nothing. This was Clare's way of protecting the spirit of Francis. In a time when the church and the town of Assisi were wealthy, her choice was a challenge and an example to others.

Clare died on the feast of St. Lawrence. Her order still exists. Now they are called Poor Clares.

12

Perseid meteor shower

Before dawn on the mornings of August 11 and 12 is one of the best times of the year to see meteors. On these days the earth's orbit passes through a collection of tiny pieces of rock that are left over from a comet that passed by centuries ago. This is called the Perseid meteor shower because the meteors seem to radiate from the constellation Perseus. Perseus can be seen in the northern sky, a bit east of the "W" of the constellation Cassiopeia.

This is the best meteor shower of the warm-weather months, with meteors appearing as frequently as one per minute. Because this meteor shower happens so close to the feast of St. Lawrence, it has been called "St. Lawrence's Tears." People have been watching for it every year at this time since the ninth century.

August

13

Optional memorial of
Ss. Pontian and Hippolytus
Pontian, pope, martyr, and Hippolytus, presbyter, martyr (died c. 235)

Hippolytus was a noble Roman Christian of great knowledge. In fact, he wrote some of the finest teachings on scripture in the early church. He was also very strong-willed. Hippolytus didn't approve of Callistus (October 14), an ex-slave and ex-convict who was elected pope in the year 217.

During times of persecution, many Christians were afraid to acknowledge that they were Christian. But when the persecution let up, these people came back to the church and asked for forgiveness. Pope Callistus was always ready to forgive them. But Hippolytus thought that the church would be weakened if it accepted these people.

Hippolytus felt so strongly about this that a group of his admirers named him pope, making him a rival to Callistus. This caused a split within the church. Because of his anger, Hippolytus allowed this confusing state of events to go on for years. Pope Callistus was martyred and Pope Urban was elected; then he too died and Pope Pontian was elected. Throughout this time Hippolytus continued to consider himself the pope.

A new emperor came to power. He arrested Hippolytus and sent him off to slavery in the mines of Sardinia. He also sent Pontian. No one ever came back from the mines. Being sent there was like a sentence of death. Pontian and Hippolytus, two gentle and dignified Christians, were chained to criminals. Somehow, Hippolytus sent word back to Rome saying that he had been wrong all these years and that his followers should now turn to the lawful pope. Pontian forgave him and reconciled him to the church.

Pontian also sent word back to Rome. He resigned his office because it was clear to him that he would never return alive. The two men died within a year of each other. When the persecution ended, their bodies were carried back to Rome with honors. Their memorial reminds us what an important place forgiveness plays in the life of all Christians.

Anniversary of the death of
Florence Nightingale
(1820–1910)

Today everyone knows that a nurse is a person of skill and dedication. But nurses haven't always been valued members of society. Florence Nightingale taught the people of nineteenth-century England that nursing the sick is a valuable service.

Florence Nightingale's parents were very rich. They had several homes, traveled in Europe, and entertained famous people. But Florence called that way of living "a tadpole world of restless activity." She wanted with all her heart to become a nurse. Her mother and sister were shocked. For a young woman from a wealthy family to make her own living was almost unheard of. And in England nurses were untrained.

Florence was 33 when her family allowed her to take a job supervising a small hospital in London. Soon after that, she learned that help was desperately needed in Turkey, where English soldiers were dying in great numbers in the Crimean War. Florence left for Turkey, taking several friends along.

What she found was worse than she had imagined. The hospital had been built over a sewer. There were no windows to let in fresh air. Even worse, because of governmental complications, there were no supplies — no stretchers, no bedsheets, no operating tables. There was no healthy food or clean water, no soap or razors, no clothing for the wounded soldiers to wear, no basins to bathe their wounds. More soldiers were dying from infection than from battlefield injuries.

Florence moved quickly to correct the situation. She used a great deal of her own money to buy supplies and wholesome food. She added another building to the hospital so that the beds didn't have to be jammed together. Soon many soldiers were regaining their health. Florence was as tough as any general in dealing with doctors and hospital officials who resisted changing the system. But at night she moved gently among the beds caring for the soldiers, who called her "the lady with the lamp."

Women all over the world wanted to imitate Florence. They knew that in her dangerous and exciting post she had been a decision-maker with important responsibilities. Florence Nightingale established the first real school of nursing in England. It soon became the model for schools all over Europe and North America.

Memorial of
St. Maximilian Mary Kolbe
presbyter, religious, martyr (1894–1941)

In the Nazi concentration camp called Auschwitz, Maximilian Kolbe was known by the number tattooed on his arm — 16670. During the Second World War, more than four million people died at this camp. Before they were killed, they were stripped of everything they owned, including their names.

Maximilian Kolbe was born near Lodz, Poland. He became a Franciscan priest. He decided that printing religious magazines and newspapers was a good way to spread God's word.

On September 1, 1939, Nazi Germany conquered Poland. The city of Warsaw was packed with refugees. Most of them were Jews, afraid for their lives because they were the targets of Nazi hatred. The friars in Warsaw were able to assist about 3000 of the escaping people with food and other supplies.

Maximilian managed to print and distribute an issue of his magazine *The Knight* that spoke out against the war. Soon afterward, the German secret police came for him. He was taken on a cattle truck to the Auschwitz labor camp, where so many others also would be sent before the war was over.

For prisoners, a dreaded event in the camp was the escape of a fellow inmate. When this happened, ten other prisoners were selected at random to die as punishment. One day during the summer of 1941, a prisoner disappeared. (The guards assumed he had escaped, but later he was found dead on the prison grounds.) One of the ten men chosen to be killed cried out in despair, "I'll never see my wife and children again!"

Maximilian stepped forward and asked to take the condemned man's place. His request was granted. He was herded into an underground cell with the other nine men to be starved to death. Over the next two weeks, all except three of them died. Those remaining, including Maximilian, were killed on August 14, the day before Assumption Day.

August

St. Micah

prophet (eighth century BCE)

The prophet Micah had a heart for the poor. Born in a small village in the hills outside Jerusalem, Micah thought of the simple farmers and shepherds of the countryside as the true people of God. His prophecies were filled with anger that these good people should be cheated by their rich and powerful landlords.

Another prophet, Amos (June 15), had complained about this injustice. Now Micah, who was born 20 miles from Amos's hometown, continued the tradition. His prophecies are recorded in the Book of Micah.

The years before Micah's time had been prosperous ones for some of the Israelites. Powerful people, who lived mostly in the two great cities of Samaria and Jerusalem, had become corrupt and selfish. The religious leaders said what the people wanted to hear. Judges were taking bribes. Everyone involved thought that as long as sacrifices were being offered, God would overlook whatever wrongs they did.

Micah insisted that Israel was the one nation above all that should care for the poor and for those who were treated unjustly. The sixth chapter of the book that bears his name says this pointedly: "And what does the Lord require of you but to do justice, and to love kindness, and to walk humbly with your God?" Micah proclaimed that Jerusalem would be destroyed because of its injustice.

Micah's message was not totally grim. He believed that a faithful few, a "remnant," would continue to remain loyal to God's covenant. He challenged his hearers to renewed justice, kindness and humility. He promised that God's anger would be softened with mercy.

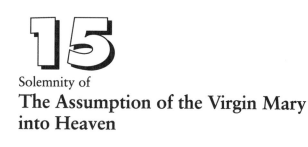

Solemnity of

The Assumption of the Virgin Mary into Heaven

Byzantine Christians keep today as the "Dormition," which means the "falling asleep" of Mary. It is Mary's greatest feast, her Passover. Throughout the evening of August 14 a vigil is kept in mourning for the death of Mary. An icon (a picture) of Mary is decorated with fragrant herbs and fresh flowers. At dawn on August 15, the bells ring out in joy.

After the horrors of the Second World War, after the death camps, after the first use of nuclear weapons, we Christians needed to remind ourselves of the holiness of creation. In 1950, Pope Pius XII declared what Catholics had long believed: After Mary's death, God raised her body. She lives with God for ever. On Assumption Day we rejoice that this broken world will be made new again. The barren, the poor, the unloved and even the dead will be raised into glory.

Assumption Day sometimes is thought of as Mary's "harvesting" into heaven. This is a day to thank God for the bounty of growing things. Many churches gather baskets of garden vegetables, herbs and flowers around a statue of Mary. We remember Mary's song of praise from the Gospel of Luke, "The Lord has lifted up the lowly. The Lord has filled the hungry with good things."

16

Optional memorial of

St. Stephen of Hungary

married man, king (975 – 1038)

Stephen was a Magyar (muh-JAR). The Magyars were a wandering tribe of fierce pagans from western Asia. In the ninth century they settled in central Europe in the land now called Hungary. Stephen's father Géza was their chief. He was baptized with his family when Stephen was ten years old. When Stephen was 22, his father died and Stephen became the new leader. But even at that young age he was well prepared for leadership. He set out to unite Hungary by making it Christian.

Stephen was gentle and compassionate with the poor. He was tireless in his efforts to bring Christian civilization to the land. Most of his people couldn't read, so he built churches that were filled with statues and mosaics. People could study the art to learn the stories of their faith. Stephen established Sunday and religious holidays as days of worship. He also invited teachers from other countries to teach the people to read, to sew, to farm — even to cook.

Under Stephen's leadership the Magyar people were united into a nation. Hungarians became enthusiastic Christians who adapted the Western alphabet and customs. The pope sent Stephen a crown, and it was placed on his head on Christmas Day. This "Crown of St. Stephen" is still treasured in Hungary.

18

In the U. S. A., optional memorial of

St. Jane Frances de Chantal

married woman, religious founder (1572 – 1641)

(In Canada this optional memorial is kept on December 12.)

On the surface, the young Baroness de Chantal couldn't have been more of a contrast to the sick and homeless who, day after day, came to her door. She lived in a castle, dressed in rich clothes and enjoyed a loving family. But she felt a great connection with beggars. She knew that she too was a beggar who depended on God's continuing mercy and forgiveness. "What would I do," she asked God in prayer, "if you sent me away the second or third time?" So she was patient with those who repeatedly asked for her help.

Jane Frances was a beautiful young woman of the city of Dijon in France. At age 20 she married a gentle nobleman who loved her deeply. They had four children. Besides running a large household and raising her children, Jane found time to serve the needy. But all that changed one day when Jane's youngest child was two weeks old. Her husband, out hunting with a friend, was wounded accidentally. He died nine days later.

Jane was only 28. For months, she was overwhelmed with grief and depression. Realizing that her children needed her, she began to find ways to cope with her sadness. She spent time with them and redoubled her prayer and kindness to the poor. She prayed for a spiritual director to guide her next steps. At just this time Jane heard the lenten sermons of Francis de Sales (January 24). She convinced him to work with her, and they began a powerful, lifelong friendship.

Francis and Jane understood and complemented each other. He encouraged her to meet with the person who had caused her husband's accidental death. She did so, and later even acted as godmother to one of the man's children. When Jane's own children were grown, Francis convinced her to begin a new religious order. Both Jane and Francis taught that all people, not just a special few, are called to holiness.

19

Optional memorial of

St. John Eudes

presbyter, religious founder (1601 – 1680)

John Eudes was born in Normandy, a region of France. When he became a priest, France was caught in the bitter struggles of the Reformation. It was a time of misunderstanding and confusion.

Shortly after John was ordained, an epidemic of plague struck his diocese. He volunteered to nurse the victims, an act of great courage. So that he wouldn't transmit the disease to the other priests in his community, he lived in a large cask in the middle of a field until the epidemic had run its course.

John began traveling all over the country to preach parish missions, which were something like the parish renewal programs of today. He was such a dynamic preacher that his missions would sometimes last for months.

John's preaching was fiery. He stressed that Jesus loved everyone, regardless of their past failings. Wherever John went, he encouraged people to understand God's mercy through the image of the Sacred Heart of Jesus. When people came to John for the sacrament of reconciliation, he tried to model the healing love and forgiveness of Jesus.

John began a religious community to run places of refuge for reformed prostitutes. Today this community serves the needs of young women who have committed crimes.

Roman martyrology

St. Sarah

matriarch (c. nineteenth century BCE)

Originally Sarah's name was Sarai. She was the daughter of a sheik living in the city of Ur near the Tigris and Euphrates rivers. She married a prosperous herdsman named Abram.

Sarai was a person of faith. When God promised Abram that they would inherit the land of Canaan, Sarai willingly left familiar surroundings in Haran to make the long journey to Canaan.

The Lord gave Abram the name of Abraham, and to Sarai the Lord gave the name of Sarah, meaning "princess." Soon afterward, Abraham and Sarah were visited by three mysterious strangers. The visitors promised that Sarah would bear a child. She laughed when she heard this because she was now very old. But within a year, Sarah and Abraham had a son. His name was Isaac. This name means "laughter," and at his birth Sarah said, "God has brought laughter for me."

When Sarah died, Abraham and Isaac grieved for her. Abraham purchased a field in Canaan for her burial. The field was his first legal claim on the Promised Land. Centuries later, Canaan would come to be known by the name of Sarah and Abraham's grandson, Israel, who was also called Jacob (August 28). When Abraham died he was buried beside Sarah.

20

Memorial of

St. Bernard

abbot, doctor of the church (1090–1153)

Late one night at the abbey of Cîteaux there was a loud knock on the door. The abbot opened it to find over 30 people standing on the doorstep. One of the strangers spoke up. His name was Bernard and he seemed to be their leader. To the abbot's amazement, Bernard asked if they all could join the abbey.

It turned out that Bernard had been so enthusiastic about joining the abbey that four of his brothers, an uncle and a cousin felt drawn to join him. The rest of the group were friends. Bernard's family was French nobility. Most of them had been soldiers, so they knew what to expect from the stern way of life they were taking up. The abbot welcomed them all. Bernard's talent for leadership had found a home.

After a while even Bernard's father joined him. (His mother had died years earlier.) Soon so many new monks had joined the abbey that groups of 12 were sent out to found new houses. Bernard himself began a house called Clairvaux. The monks built it from scratch.

Bernard loved his quiet life at Clairvaux. He wrote hymns and meditations, and he helped the monks to live in harmony. But people from the outside world began coming to ask for his help. Even disputing princes sought out his peacemaking skills. St. Bernard is considered the greatest figure of the twelfth century. Many of his writings are beautiful, especially his reflections about the Blessed Virgin Mary. Like St. Ambrose, he is often pictured standing alongside a beehive, because his words were sweet.

Byzantine calendar

St. Samuel

prophet and judge (eleventh century BCE*)*

When Samuel was a child, his parents dedicated him to the Lord's service. He went to live with the priest Eli at Shiloh, where the ark of the covenant was kept. One night as he slept, Samuel heard a call. It was repeated three times so Eli told Samuel to respond to the voice by saying, "Speak, Lord, for your servant is listening." The voice was God's.

That was how Samuel became a prophet, a task he would carry out all through his life. When Eli died some time later, Samuel became the most important religious leader in the land.

When the great army of the Philistines threatened to overcome Israel, Samuel was convinced by the people to anoint a king. The person he chose was Saul, a skilled general who won lands for Israel.

But Saul was moody and unpredictable, and he often ignored the religious laws. Samuel warned Saul that God would take the kingship from him and give it to someone more obedient. Then he left King Saul, never to see him again.

After that Samuel secretly anointed a new king: an unknown shepherd boy, David (see December 29), who had never been a soldier. Samuel's choice turned out to be a wise one. When Saul was killed in battle some years later, David went on to build the 12 tribes of Israel into one powerful nation.

August

21

Memorial of

St. Pius X

pope (1835–1914)

Pope Pius X was baptized Giuseppe Sarto. He was one of ten children. His father was a postman. Giuseppe was ordained a priest and became known as a gentle pastor who loved to serve his people, especially the poor. He was also a talented leader. He was appointed bishop of the Italian city of Mantua and then archbishop of Venice. However, both of these positions were offered to him only after debate within the church. Some people thought such positions should be given only to priests from the upper classes.

Pius was elected pope, and he was the first peasant to hold that office since the Middle Ages. Pius was pope for 11 years, during which time he wished "to renew all things in Christ."

Pius thought that children should be allowed to receive communion as soon as they were old enough to understand its importance. He took steps to improve Christian education for children and adults. He improved church music and simplified the liturgical calendar. He encouraged people to read scripture every day.

A simple and unpretentious person all his days, Pius never got used to the formality of life in the Vatican. One day, when an old friend came to visit, he burst into tears, saying, "Look how they have me dressed up!"

Pius felt great compassion for people. On the eleventh anniversary of his election as pope, the First World War was declared. In Rome he said goodbye to a large group of students called back to their homes all over Europe because of the war. They were from England, France, Germany, Austria, Belgium and other countries. Soon they would be fighting each other. He asked them to be merciful, even as soldiers. He knew this huge war would bring great suffering The knowledge broke his heart. Three weeks later he died.

22

Memorial of

The Queenship of the Virgin Mary

In times past, most of the important church festivals were celebrated for eight days. This period of eight days is called an octave. Every week of the year is a kind of octave because Sundays always fall eight days apart.

In church tradition, an octave represents eternity. It may seem strange to us, but here's why: Seven days make a normal, run-of-the-mill week. But add an eighth day and you've got something special. You've got a week that ends and begins on the same day. In the early church, they thought that eight days was a symbol of perfection and of heaven.

Today is the eighth day after the solemnity of the Assumption. We honor Mary as the *regina caeli,* the queen of heaven. Psalm 45 was sung on Assumption Day and it is sung today as well. It speaks of a queen in a golden robe. Wherever she goes, she brings justice and splendor and great rejoicing. Jewish songs refer to the Sabbath that way. When it arrives, it is like a queen whose beauty chases away all sorrow.

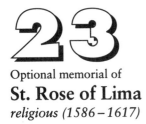

Optional memorial of

St. Rose of Lima
religious (1586–1617)

Rose was born in Lima, Peru. She was the youngest of a large family. She was never sent to school, so she spent her days gardening, and she learned to produce spectacular flowers. The birds and flowers of the garden reminded her of the love of God.

Marriage was the course young women were expected to take in those days, but Rose wanted to spend her life in prayer. To provide funds for her parents, she began selling her flowers and the beautiful embroidery and lace she made. She lived in a little hut in her beloved garden, and she spent many hours in prayer.

Rose became more and more aware of the poor of Lima. She opened a room of her parents' home to anyone who needed her care. She asked for no payment in return.

In those days people believed that to be holy they needed to punish their bodies by doing penances. Rose did such strict penances that she may have shortened her life by many years. She died at the age of 31, after a long illness.

During her quiet and short life, Rose had come to be thought of by the people of Lima as their treasure. Many of them believed that her prayers had saved the city from earthquakes that struck nearby. She was loved by both rich and poor. When she died, such great crowds gathered outside her home that her family was unable to bury her for several days. The city leaders took turns carrying her coffin to its resting place.

Rose of Lima was the first person to be named a saint of the church from the Western Hemisphere. She is a patron saint of South America, and she is widely honored throughout Central America, the Philippines and India as well. Each year the people of Lima hold a joyful procession in her honor. They carry a statue of her that is surrounded with the roses she loved so much.

Feast of

St. Bartholomew
apostle (first century)

St. Bartholomew is an apostle about whom not much is known. The gospels of Matthew, Mark and Luke mention him in their lists of the Twelve. The first chapter of the Acts of the Apostles mentions him waiting with the other disciples for the coming of the Holy Spirit.

The Gospel of John doesn't actually mention Bartholomew but includes the name Nathanael with the other apostles. If these two are the same person, we have a touching story of how he was called by Jesus to discipleship.

Chapter one of the Gospel of John describes the first meeting of Jesus and Philip (May 3). Afterward, Philip immediately went to tell his friend Nathanael the good news of this remarkable prophet. Nathanael joked that if Jesus was from Nazareth he couldn't be any good. (Nathanael was from Cana, and the two towns were neighbors and rivals.) When Nathanael came to see for himself, Jesus praised him as being "one in whom there is no deceit." Nathanael probably wondered how this teacher could possibly know such a thing. But as they talked Nathanael realized that Jesus must be from God.

Many countries claim to be the place where Bartholomew preached the good news after the descent of the Holy Spirit. The strongest traditions are found in India and Armenia.

Today is also called "Bartlemas Day." Because it comes at harvest time, in many places this is a favorite day for country fairs.

Optional memorial of
St. Louis
married man, king (1214–1270)

Louis of France was only 12 when he became king. He was 19 when he was married. Although the marriage had been arranged for political reasons, it was a happy one. Louis and his wife Marguerite had ten children.

Louis's reign was a peaceful time for the country. The Sorbonne, the first university to provide housing on campus, opened its doors. Grapevines that would produce the famous French wineries were being planted for the first time.

Though Louis was a very active king, he found time to spend several hours a day in prayer. He provided homes all over the country for orphans and widows. He fed the poor from his own table, sometimes waiting on them himself.

To ensure that he made fair judgments, he refused gifts from people who were bringing business before him. He sent counselors out into all parts of the kingdom. If local judges had been unjust in hearing cases, people could discuss the problem with one of these counselors, who reported back to the king. In fact, sometimes King Louis himself would sit under an oak tree and listen to the concerns of his subjects.

Optional memorial of
St. Joseph Calasanz
presbyter, religious founder (1556–1648)

Joseph was born to a rich family in Peralta in Spain. He became a priest and had a promising career ahead of him, perhaps as a bishop. However, he felt God calling him to a deeper kind of work than what he was doing. He moved to Rome and began to serve the poor. He noticed that in the slums, with no training or challenge, children's minds were wasted.

Joseph began spending his own wealth to set up free schools. He formed a religious order whose members would serve as teachers. He went out into the streets to beg for funds to support the schools, and he swept and scrubbed the schoolrooms himself.

His generosity met with resistance from rich people who knew that it was dangerous to educate the poor. If the poor were able to read and to speak for themselves, they might begin to struggle for their rights.

Joseph's last years were filled with troubles. When he was 86 years old, the work of the order was stopped by people who disagreed with him. His response to this was that he had done everything for God, so it didn't matter how other people judged him. He forgave his accusers and simply trusted that one day the good work would be allowed to continue.

Memorial of

St. Monica

married woman (332 – 387)

Monica was born in northern Africa, in what is now the country of Algeria. Her parents were Christian, and she took her faith seriously. But she had one grave problem growing up. In the world where Monica lived, pagans and Christians lived side by side. Her parents arranged for her to marry a pagan man named Patricius. He had a hot temper and his idea of marriage didn't include being faithful to his wife. After many years of patience and love on Monica's part, Patricius became a Christian shortly before he died.

Monica had much less success with her son, Augustine (August 28). Though brought up as a Christian, he stole, cut classes, lied, and engaged in casual sex. Monica tried to interest her son in a Christian way of life. But with her attempts to control him, she probably drove him even further from a peaceful and holy life. She asked a wise bishop to convince Augustine that his ways were wrong, but the bishop replied that only prayer could help. Monica prayed, and in time she was able to give Augustine's future completely over to God.

At the age of 28, Augustine was baptized. He would go on to become a great voice within the church. Mother and son began a joyful spiritual friendship. But only a few years later, Monica became ill unexpectedly and died far from home. Augustine, who was traveling with her at the time, was struck by the trust in God she had gained through her struggles. He later said that she had shown no fear of dying in a strange place. Monica was sure that God, who is always near, would know where to find her body on judgment day.

Memorial of

St. Augustine

bishop, doctor of the church (354 – 430)

Augustine was born in a town of northern Africa called Tagaste. His mother, Monica (August 27), was a Christian. She gave her son a basic Christian upbringing, but from childhood he seemed to take after his father, a selfish man who had nothing to do with the church. Augustine stole, lied and cheated.

But he was also brilliant, and in time he became a teacher. He had decided that Christianity was not for him. He believed in a pagan philosophy that allowed him to do whatever he wanted in his personal life without guilt. When his mother tried to convince him to return to Christianity, he only became more determined to avoid the religion of his childhood.

Things began to change for Augustine when he moved to a new teaching position in Milan in Italy. Ambrose, who was the bishop of the city, helped Augustine to think in new ways. After a long inner struggle, Augustine decided to be baptized. By this time he had a 15-year-old son, Adeodatus, who was baptized with him.

For the next several years Augustine lived with friends, doing works of charity and studying the scriptures. Then he was called to be the bishop of the town of Hippo not far from Tagaste.

As bishop, Augustine insisted that the priests of the diocese live simply. He himself lived in community and served the poor with kindness. He preached powerfully every day for 35 years. He found time to write many books. One famous book that is still read is his *Confessions,* which is the story of his life.

Augustine is honored as a doctor (a teacher) of the church. Here is a quote from one of his works: "What does love look like? Love has hands to help others. It has feet to hasten to the poor and needy. It has eyes to see misery and want. It has ears to hear the sighs and sorrows of others. That's what love looks like."

Roman martyrology
St. Jacob
patriarch (eighteenth century BCE)

Jacob's story begins in the 25th chapter of the Book of Genesis. The grandson of Abraham and Sarah, he was a bright young man. However, Esau, his older twin, was bigger and stronger and the favorite of their father Isaac. So Jacob tricked his brother Esau into giving up his inheritance. He also tricked his father Isaac into giving him the blessing intended for Esau. Then Jacob was forced to run from Canaan to escape Esau's anger.

Heading for refuge in a faraway land, Jacob lay down in the open fields one night to sleep. During the night he had a remarkable vision of a ladder that reached from earth to heaven, with angels ascending and descending on it. It seemed to signal God's coming to live with humankind. A voice promised to give Jacob land, many descendants, and a mission to be a blessing to everyone on earth.

Jacob found safety with his Uncle Laban, the brother of his mother Rebecca. Laban promised Jacob the hand of his lovely daughter Rachel in exchange for seven years' work. But when the time was up and the wedding was over, Jacob found that the woman under the bridal veil was Rachel's sister Leah. To marry Rachel, Jacob would have to spend seven more years working for Laban. But Jacob loved Rachel so much that he was willing to wait.

In time Jacob decided to return to Canaan with his two wives. He sent gifts ahead, in case his twin brother was still angry. On the way Jacob encountered a mysterious stranger who fought with Jacob and twisted his leg, leaving him with a limp. The stranger told Jacob that from now on his name would be Israel, which means "one who fought with God." Jacob realized then that the stranger was really God.

To Jacob's surprise, Esau welcomed him back. Jacob built an altar to God at the spot where he had seen the heavenly ladder. He committed his family to the worship of God alone.

God's promises to Jacob came true. Jacob's 12 sons became the founders of the 12 tribes of Israel. The land of his descendants was called by his new name, Israel.

29

Memorial of
The Martyrdom of St. John the Baptist

Herod Antipas was a weak and immoral king who had married Herodias, the wife of his own brother. John the Baptist was a prophet and a person of integrity, so he spoke out against this wrong. Herod was awed and puzzled by John, but Herodias was furious. John was a threat to her power. She had Herod throw him in prison.

At Herod's birthday celebration Herodias saw her chance to get John out of the way for good. Her young daughter Salome danced at the party, and Herod was so delighted that he foolishly promised her anything she wished as a reward, even half his kingdom. The daughter consulted her mother — and then she asked for the head of John the Baptist on a platter!

Herod had been outsmarted. He was afraid to kill John but saw no way out. So, for the sake of a dance at a birthday party, the great prophet John was murdered. (This story is told in the sixth chapter of the Gospel of Mark and the eleventh chapter of the Gospel of Matthew.) Some of John's disciples buried his body at Sebaste, a town some miles from Jerusalem.

Unlike the luxury-loving king who had him killed, John owned nothing. He ate only the simplest food and wore the skins of wild animals he caught in the desert. His one concern was to do the will of God. He devoted his time to prayer and the service of others. When people thought that he might be the Messiah, he quickly explained to them that one greater than he was coming. And when Jesus began his public ministry, John quietly stepped aside. "He must increase," John said of Jesus, "but I must decrease."

John's mission from the time he was born had been to prepare the way for the Lord. He had done so all his life, calling people to repent of their sins and to await the good news. Now he led the way in death as well — his martyrdom showed what lay ahead for Jesus. No wonder Jesus praised John as "a burning and shining lamp"!

We celebrate St. John the Baptist on June 24, the solemnity of his birth. Today we mourn for him. In the Eastern Church, today is a strict fast day, like Good Friday.

September

September is the ninth month, but the word September actually means "seventh month." Before the time of Julius Caesar the Roman year had ten months. The first month was March, which made September the seventh month. There was no January or February on the calendar. Calendars were used mainly by farmers, who weren't interested in keeping track of time during winter, when there was little to do. So during winter people lost track of days until their leaders announced the start of a new year each spring.

Julius Caesar reformed the calendar. Winter months were added. Now the year began on the first of January, not March. But the old names for the months continued to be used.

Many ancient calendars have the year beginning in spring. For instance, the Jewish people mark the first month of their religious year in early springtime, near the vernal equinox. (The Jewish New Year [Rosh Hashanah, page 195], however, begins on the first day of the seventh month.) In the Byzantine Christian calendar, September is the first month of the liturgical year.

The first Monday in September
Labor Day

Today marks the time when working people around the country come to the end of the summer vacation season and students return to school. We set aside this day to reflect on the work we do. Over the course of our lives, we spend more time working than we do at any other activity.

Until the last century or so, most people worked on farms. They worked long days, and the pace of life was slower. The Industrial Revolution changed that. New farm machines meant that fewer farming jobs were available. Farm workers moved to the cities, where they took low-paying jobs in factories. They worked as long as 16 hours a day. Their jobs were dangerous because the machinery had few safeguards against accidents. Even children as young as six or seven years old were forced to work because wages were so low and families needed many incomes to survive.

September

The labor union movement was born in response to these conditions. Unions gave workers a way to stand together and fight for safe machinery, better salaries and fair treatment. The first official Labor Day was celebrated in New York City in 1882. Peter J. McGuire, founder of the carpenters' union, suggested Labor Day at a union meeting. In its early years, it was a day when workers called attention to their grievances.

Eventually this day became a national holiday. Now Labor Day is celebrated in Canada on the same day as in the United States. Many other countries observe a day to honor workers on May 1.

Several popes of the last hundred years have written encyclicals, which are teaching letters, to speak for the dignity and rights of workers. The American bishops have also issued a letter about work. It's called *Economic Justice for All*.

1

Byzantine calendar
St. Joshua
(c. thirteenth century BCE)

The name Joshua means "the Lord is salvation." The life of Joshua proclaimed that message. He was a warrior in the service of God.

Joshua's story is told in the sixth book of the Hebrew scriptures, the Book of Joshua. He was the trusted lieutenant of Moses (September 4), who led the Israelites out of slavery in Egypt. When Moses died, Joshua took his place as leader.

Joshua led the Israelites toward the Jordan River. Past it was the first city in their path, Jericho. Suddenly the earth shook so that a bridge of dry land appeared over the river. The people walked across the river with dry shoes, just as

their parents had crossed the Sea of Reeds 40 years earlier when they escaped from slavery in Egypt.

As Joshua led his people, he had them form a procession. Priests walked in the front. They blew rams' horns to make an awesome noise. After them came more priests, carrying the sacred ark of the covenant. The ark held the stone tablets of the Ten Commandments. By carrying it before them, the Israelites placed their trust in God's power rather than in military might. The soldiers brought up the rear.

Each day for six days this odd procession circled the city. On the seventh day, the sound of the rams' horns was joined by the voices of all the Israelites, who shouted at the top of their lungs. At just that moment, the walls of the city fell to ruins, and the Israelites took the city.

Over time, the Israelites won enough land to divide among their tribes. They awarded Joshua a city in thanks for his bravery. Nearby, he built a permanent place of honor for the ark of the covenant. The place was called Shiloh. It was the first town built by the Israelites. From all over the land they came there as pilgrims. And there, two centuries later, the prophet Samuel (August 20) would be called by God.

Roman martyrology
St. Ruth
(eleventh century BCE)

"Do not press me to leave you or to turn back from following you. Where you go, I will go. Your people will be my people, and your God my God." With those words, the story of Ruth provides a model of faithful love.

The Book of Ruth, one of the shortest books in the Bible, is wonderful to read. The book is read in Jewish synagogues on the festival of Shavuot (page 199) in late springtime, when the barley harvest is ripe in Israel.

The story begins in a land called Moab. There a woman named Naomi settled with her husband after a famine struck their native land of Israel. Things went smoothly for a while. Their two sons married Moabite women who Naomi loved very much. One of them was Ruth. But then all three men of the family died, leaving the women to struggle on their own.

Naomi decided to return to Israel because she heard that the famine there had ended. Ruth knew that Naomi would need help and support. She refused to let Naomi return alone to her hometown of Bethlehem.

The two women came to Bethlehem in late spring, during the barley harvest. Ruth went to the field of a man named Boaz, a relative of Naomi's dead husband. Boaz, who was a kind and prosperous man, was touched by Ruth's care for Naomi. Ruth and Boaz married.

This story has a second happy ending. The great-grandson of Ruth and Boaz was King David, of whose line Jesus was born. The Gospel of Matthew mentions Ruth in tracing Jesus' family tree.

Memorial of
St. Gregory the Great
pope, doctor of the church (c. 540–604)

He described himself humbly as "the servant of the servants of God," but in the centuries since then he's come to be known another way — as "Gregory the Great." Pope Gregory earned that praise by a lifetime spent shepherding his flock.

Gregory was born into a family that had already produced two popes. He studied law, and by age

30 he became prefect (mayor) of Rome. But after only a year in his post, he divided his fortune in half. He gave one part of the money to the poor and used the rest to begin monasteries. He entered one of them himself, hoping to live the simple life of a Benedictine monk.

However, Gregory's hope didn't last long. Soon he was named one of the seven deacons of Rome and was sent to represent the pope in the court of the emperor in Constantinople. After seven years there, he moved back to Rome to become the pope's secretary. When the pope died, Gregory was elected to take his place.

Gregory served the people in many ways in his 14 years as pope. He worked to improve the church's worship. Gregorian chant is named in his honor. Gregory taught a great deal through his writings and preaching. He tended lovingly to the poor and had ruined churches rebuilt.

One of Gregory's last acts was to send a warm winter cloak to a bishop who needed one. He called the care of others "the art of arts."

Byzantine calendar
St. Moses
lawgiver, prophet (c. thirteenth century BCE)

Throughout the scriptures one event emerges as most important in the memory of the Jews: their journey from slavery in Egypt to freedom in the Promised Land. In this great undertaking, God was assisted by the great prophet Moses. No wonder the Book of Deuteronomy describes him as "unequaled."

The story of Moses is told in the Book of Exodus and the books that follow. When he was born, the Jews were slaves in Egypt. The Pharaoh was

September

so afraid of their numbers that he ordered all male babies of the Jews slaughtered at birth.

Moses's mother concealed him in a waterproof basket and hid him in the shallows of the river. Pharaoh's daughter discovered the tiny ark and fell in love with the baby inside. Moses's sister, who had been watching nearby, offered to find a nanny for the baby. In this way Moses's mother became his nursemaid. Over time she told her son about his real family and their sufferings.

Moses grew up as a prince, but he felt sympathy for his people. Once, seeing a Jewish slave mistreated, Moses killed the slave owner. Then he ran from Egypt to save his life. Years later, while tending flocks in the desert, Moses happened upon a bush that burned but was not consumed. God spoke from the bush and commanded Moses to return to Egypt and to lead his people to freedom. Though Moses had no idea how that could be accomplished, he obeyed. He followed the Lord's instructions day by day.

Pharaoh stubbornly refused to let the Israelite slaves go. One night, the angel of God passed through Egypt, slaying the firstborn son of every Egyptian family and even the firstborn of all their cattle. The Israelites had marked their doors with the blood of a lamb so the angel would see the blood and pass over them. They ate the first Passover meal in haste that night before fleeing Egypt. That meal is remembered every year during the festival of Pesach (see page 199).

On their journey, Moses led the people safely through many trials. First their lives were spared when the marshy waters behind them closed in on the pursuing Egyptian army. Then, when the people were hungry and ready to give up, food and water were miraculously provided for them. They fought and won their first battle by looking up at Moses's outstretched arms for encouragement. Most important of all, on Mount Sinai God gave Moses the Law for the Israelites.

Moses did not live to enter the Promised Land with them. But before he died God took him up to a mountaintop where, to his great joy, he saw all the beauty and richness of this land spread out before him.

Anniversary of the death of
Albert Schweitzer
(1875–1965)

Dr. Schweitzer was born in Alsace, on the border between France and Germany. As a child he loved to wander the beautiful countryside. He was bright and had great musical talent. His father was a minister, and by the time Albert was 16 he was playing the church organ at services. He stood out in other ways. Even at a young age he refused to take part in games that injured animals or made fun of people.

Albert studied religion and music, and in time he became well-known in both fields. He became a preacher and lecturer in Strasbourg. He wrote a book about the life of Christ, and he also wrote the life story of his favorite composer, Johann Sebastian Bach. He played Bach's music all over Europe. By the time Albert was 30, his books were a success and he had many famous friends.

Albert wanted to share in the life of Christ by easing some of the suffering of the world. He decided to study medicine and to use his skills in Africa, where they seemed to be needed most. Many who knew him were baffled by his decision to leave the beautiful life he had made for himself.

After earning his degree he headed for the village of Lambarene in French Equatorial Africa (now the republic of Gabon). The morning after he landed patients were already standing in line to see him. His first hospital building was an abandoned chicken coop.

There was no electricity, and the heat and humidity in the low-lying, deeply forested country were oppressive. Every day he treated diseases he had never seen in medical school, such as malaria, dysentery and leprosy.

During the First World War, Dr. Schweitzer was forced to leave Africa. When the war was over he returned. He would spend the rest of his life working at the hospital and raising money for its upkeep. In 1953 he was awarded the Nobel Peace Prize, a high honor. He used the opportunity of his prestige to speak out against white oppression of black peoples. He also said that reverence for life must lead to every nation on earth eliminating nuclear weapons.

Dr. Schweitzer loved all living creatures. He often used his medical skills to treat injured or sick animals. He lived to be 90. On his last walk through the compound he said goodbye to the trees he had planted. He was buried with a bag of rice, which he always carried to feed chickens. His battered sun hat was also tucked into his coffin.

Feast of
The Birth of the Virgin Mary

No word of Mary's birth is recorded in scripture, so there's no way to know where or when it took place. But it is fitting that we honor her birth in the harvest season, because Mary is the model for all who wish to bring forth Christ in their lives.

In some parts of Europe, the summer harvest and the seed for the winter crops are blessed today. For centuries, Catholic wine growers have used this day to bring the grape harvest to church to be blessed. Alpine farmers drive their cattle and sheep down from summer pastures today.

Mary's birth was first kept by Byzantine Christians. By the seventh century the Roman church began celebrating this feast, too. Like other feasts of Mary, it was a day for processions.

We don't know who Mary's parents were. Tradition has named them Ann and Joachim (July 26). During the fifth century, a famous church named for St. Ann was dedicated in Jerusalem on September 8. The church was said to be built on the site of the house where Mary was born.

The Immaculate Conception of Mary is celebrated on December 8, which is nine months before this day.

In the U. S. A., memorial of
St. Peter Claver
presbyter, religious, missionary (c. 1581 – 1654)

Peter Claver was born in Spain, where his parents were farmers. He became a Jesuit novice. He sailed for the Americas as a missionary at age 29, never to see his homeland again. When he took his final vows he committed his life to serving slaves.

At that time large numbers of people were being kidnapped in Africa and then herded onto ships. They were chained below deck in cramped spaces. They were fed only corn and water once a day, and they suffered from all kinds of diseases. Many of them had serious wounds. There was no medical treatment, and a third to a half of the people died during the two-month voyage to the Americas. Once on land, the survivors were carried off to pens where they were held like cattle.

For 38 years Peter Claver would meet the slave ships at Cartagena in what is now Colombia. He went down into the holds where the slaves were trapped. He brought gifts of medicine, bandages and fresh fruit. He washed the slaves, dressed their wounds and made beds for them to lie on. He assisted imprisoned slaves by convincing lawyers to plead their cases. If a slave was condemned to death, Peter Claver would stay by his or her side until the end. He tried to protect young African women from the slaveowners. He fought to uphold the laws that allowed slaves to marry.

In the seasons when the weather was too dangerous for slave ships to sail, Peter went inland to the coffee and cotton plantations and to the mines. There, where the slaves toiled, he would witness marriages, baptize babies and hear confessions. He also held preaching missions for the plantation owners and the sailors. Peter was known as a very simple, quiet person. That may explain why he never spoke out against slavery itself. He called himself the "slave of the slaves."

At age 70 Peter caught the plague. After that his arms and legs trembled and he was unable to take care of himself. His brother Jesuits were so busy nursing other plague victims that sometimes there was no one to tend Peter. But when word got out that he was dying, people of all races broke through the gates of the Jesuit college for a last glimpse of the person they considered a saint.

13

Memorial of
St. John Chrysostom
bishop, doctor of the church (c. 347 – 407)

Have you ever heard a two-hour-long sermon? People used to come in droves to hear John Chrysostom explain the scriptures for hours on end. His homilies meant so much to people that Christians of later centuries gave him the name "golden mouth," which is what "chrysostom" means in the Greek language.

John was born in the city of Antioch, in what is now the country of Turkey. He was raised by his mother, a widow. As a young man he went out into the wilderness to live in prayer, as many other people of his time were doing. But after six years his health was damaged by this difficult way of life. He moved back to live in the city.

Antioch was a large and busy city where the emperor lived part of the time. As a young priest there, John quickly gained fame for his preaching. After 12 years he was named bishop of Constantinople, the capital of the eastern half of the empire. As bishop, John insisted that the priests of his diocese live simple and moral lives. He fought for the poor and for those treated unjustly, and he built hospitals with his own money.

John died at the age of 52. His last words were, "Glory be to God for all things."

14

Feast of
The Holy Cross

The most common symbol of the Christian religion is what used to be a device for murdering criminals. The Romans set up crosses outside the city walls. Criminals were nailed or tied to them and left there to suffocate slowly. After they were dead, their naked bodies were left hanging as a warning to anyone who passed by.

Since then, many writers of the church have reflected on the meaning of the cross on which Jesus died. A sign of shame has become a sign of honor. In dying on the cross, Jesus became one with the poorest, the outcast, the least among us.

A beautiful legend is told about the cross: When God sent Adam and Eve out of paradise, they carried with them a seed from the tree of life. After they died, their children buried them with the seed. From their bodies grew a new tree, which in time was cut down to make the wood of Jesus' cross, a new tree of life. The cross spread its four beams to wrap around creation, to join earth and heaven.

We Christians make the sign of the cross when we enter or leave a church, when we eat our meals, when we go to sleep at night and when we awake in the morning. The cross is our protection in danger and a constant reminder of God's love. Before we were baptized, we were marked with the sign of the cross. That stamped each of us as a Christian.

The feast of the Holy Cross began in the year 335, when churches in Jerusalem, built on the sites of the crucifixion and resurrection of Christ, were dedicated. It became a major feast, and any Christian who could make the pilgrimage to Jerusalem would try to be there for the celebration. The whole 40-day period between Transfiguration Day (August 6) and Holy Cross Day became a time of pilgrimage to welcome the autumn season.

Christians in Ethiopia have a special love for this day. Crosses are put on poles and decorated with wild flowers. Every household sets one up outdoors. People sing and dance around the holy cross. But they do not feast. Today is a strict fast day, like Good Friday, on the Eastern Christian calendar. In the presence of the tree of Paradise, no one eats. Adam and Eve's sin of eating the fruit of the tree will not be repeated this day.

15

Memorial of
Our Lady of Sorrows

Yesterday we honored the cross of Christ. Today we continue the feast of the cross in company with Mary, the sorrowful mother.

Mary lived in a country oppressed by the Romans. She knew how it felt to be an unwed mother, a refugee, the mother of a political prisoner and criminal. She experienced poverty and she was a widow. Her sufferings have been shared by many people of our times, especially in places around the world that endure political oppression and war.

In Italy in the thirteenth century, Jacopone da Todi wrote a "sequence" song in honor of this day. This song is often sung when people pray the stations of the cross. Here are a few verses:

> At the cross her station keeping,
> stood the mournful mother, weeping,
>   close to Jesus to the last.
>
> Through her heart, his sorrow sharing,
> all his bitter anguish bearing,
>   now at length the sword has passed.
>
> Christ, when you shall call me hence,
> be your mother my defense,
>   be your cross my victory.

September

16

Memorial of

Ss. Cornelius and Cyprian

Cornelius, pope, martyr (died 253), and Cyprian, bishop, martyr (c. 200–258)

Cornelius and Cyprian, fellow bishops, lived in difficult times. Though separated by distance, they dealt with the same issues and they encouraged each other. Their feast days have been celebrated together since the fourth century.

Cornelius was a Roman who was elected pope after Pope Fabian (January 20) was martyred. The election was delayed 14 months because Emperor Decius was continuing to persecute Christians.

An important issue during Cornelius's time in office was how to treat large numbers of Christians who had abandoned their faith during the persecution. Some bishops took them back as if nothing had happened, while others wouldn't allow any of them to return to the church. Cornelius said that people who gave up their faith should be welcomed back, but only after doing penance. This was a wise middle course between the two extremes. Cornelius was supported in this by his friend Cyprian.

When the persecution began again, the emperor sent Cornelius away from Rome. When Cyprian heard about this he wrote Cornelius a beautiful letter of support. He said, "If one of us dies before the other, may our friendship continue in the Lord's presence." Cornelius did die shortly afterward, from the hardships caused by his exile. He had been pope for only two years.

Cyprian was a rich pagan teacher and lawyer in the town of Carthage in northern Africa. When he became a Christian in the year 246, many people were amazed because he had been famous for his worldly lifestyle. He studied the Bible and

many religious writers to learn about his new faith, and he was named bishop soon afterward. When Emperor Decius began the persecution, Cyprian went into hiding, but he sent letters to his flock back in Carthage.

Later, after Cyprian returned to Carthage, an epidemic struck the city. Cyprian organized the people of his diocese to nurse the sick. They helped all the sick, even those who had persecuted Christians. Cyprian's teachings were important to the churches of Africa. After he refused to sacrifice to the pagan gods, Cyprian was beheaded during the persecution of Emperor Valerian.

17

Optional memorial of

St. Robert Bellarmine

bishop, doctor of the church (1542–1621)

Robert Bellarmine grew up in a little town in the region of Tuscany in Italy, where his father was the chief judge. Robert decided to become a Jesuit priest. After he was ordained, he was sent to teach Greek in a boys' school. Since Robert himself had never studied this difficult subject, he learned it little by little, one lesson ahead of his students. Later he wrote a book to help university students learn Hebrew. His students loved him because he was funny, inspiring and gentle.

Robert lived during the bitter and confusing time of the Protestant Reformation. Even as a young man he was known for his fine homilies that explained the Catholic point of view. He was able to deal with complicated subjects in a way that ordinary people could understand. Because of his skill, people came from as far away as England to hear him preach. When people heard what he had to say, they knew that he had a great spirit and a generous heart.

One of the happiest times in his life was the four years he spent as archbishop of Capua. In his scholarly way he studied the lives of the great bishops for ideas about how to serve the people. During the week he traveled to outlying villages to teach the faith, but he was always back in Capua by Sunday to preach. He gave generously to the needy and made himself available to anyone who wanted to talk with him. He lived simply, eating the diet of the poor — plain bread and garlic.

Roman martyrology
St. Hildegard of Bingen
abbess (1098 – 1179)

Hildegard of Bingen served as the conscience of the church in the twelfth century. Not only that — she was also a physician, writer, poet, preacher, musician and playwright.

Hildegard was born to noble parents in a village near Bingen in the Rhine River valley in Germany. The tenth child in her family, she seemed odd to her parents because at the age of five she began to have religious visions. They sent her to live with a spiritual director named Jutta.

Over time, other young women came to join them and an abbey was built for them. They adapted the Rule of St. Benedict. When Jutta died, Hildegard was elected abbess. She was about 38 years old, and she would serve in that role for the rest of her life.

Hildegard was blessed with a deep understanding of God and creation. In spite of Hildegard's humility, her wisdom and goodness were becoming known. Many gifted young women came to join the abbey, which provided a haven for people in many ways. Most came to work and pray. Other people also came for medical care. Poor elderly women who had nowhere else to go were welcomed in as permanent guests.

People poor and rich, anonymous and famous, came for guidance from Hildegard. When larger quarters were needed, she decided to build a new abbey at Bingen. In time another new abbey would be built nearby. It is still in existence and is now called the Convent of St. Hildegard.

When the abbeys seemed well-organized, Hildegard began the first of four preaching journeys she would take during her life. These duties took her to many towns in Germany and into France as well. She was into her 70s by the time the last of these journeys took place.

In many ways Hildegard seems to be a saint for our time. She spoke of her concern for the environment, saying, "All nature is at the disposal of humankind, but we are to work with it because without it we cannot survive."

18

Anniversary of the death of
Dag Hjalmar Hammarskjöld
(1905 – 1961)

Dag Hammarskjöld's family had been Lutheran ministers, scholars, soldiers and public servants. His father was prime minister of Sweden. Dag decided as a student that service to humanity would be a rewarding life. He had a deep sense that all people were equal in the sight of God, and he had a special commitment to peace.

In 1953, after a career of high posts in the Swedish government, Dag Hammarskjöld was elected the second Secretary General of the United Nations. He treated his staff kindly and took on the hardest tasks himself. He was unanimously elected to a second five-year term.

September

Dag Hammarskjöld was not afraid to speak out when he saw nations misusing their power. He traveled constantly, especially to spots where misunderstandings led to "brush fire" war that could flame up into world conflict. He was very gifted at providing fair solutions to crises.

He was flying to a trouble spot in central Africa when his plane crashed and he was killed. His unexpected death was a crisis in itself. He was sincerely mourned by all at the United Nations, even those from countries he had opposed. His loss was felt especially by people from small, powerless nations who felt that he had understood their needs.

Two years after his death, his personal journal, *Markings*, was published. Only then did the world learn that Dag Hammarskjöld's commitment to peace was the result of his deep Christian faith.

19

Optional memorial of
St. Januarius
bishop, martyr (died c. 305)

Not much is known about Januarius. By the time he died he had become the bishop of the city of Benevento in Italy, and he was martyred in the persecution of the Roman emperor Diocletian.

St. Januarius is patron saint of the city of Naples, where he is called San Gennaro. When the Roman persecutions ended, Januarius's relics were enshrined in Naples. The people of Naples ask for San Gennaro's intercession when Mount Vesuvius threatens to erupt and when epidemics break out.

In New York City's Little Italy, the memorial of San Gennaro has become "the festival of all festivals." There are processions and dancing in the streets under lighted arches.

Memorial of
Ss. Andrew Kim Taegon, Paul Chong Hasang, and companions
Andrew Kim Taegon, presbyter, martyr (1821–1846), Paul Chong Hasang, catechist, martyr (1794–1839), and their companions, martyrs (died 1839 to 1867)

In the eighteenth and nineteenth centuries, Korea was a country closed to outside influences. The government did not welcome European ideas. But Christian missionaries managed to enter the country, and many Koreans were baptized. At times the government persecuted the Christians and many were martyred.

The parents of Andrew Kim Taegon were converts to Christianity. Andrew left Korea to enter a seminary in Macao in southern China. While still a seminarian, Andrew ventured back into his homeland, disguised as a beggar, to prepare the way for other missionaries. He learned that his father had been martyred and his mother was homeless.

Many times Andrew almost was arrested, once escaping from pursuers over an ice-covered river. After crossing the border into Manchuria, he was ordained a priest. He set sail to return to Korea. Less than a year later, he was arrested and martyred.

Paul Chong Hasang was 45 years old when he was killed in 1839. Both men were part of a large number of people who died for the faith in Korea. One hundred and three of these martyrs were canonized by Pope John Paul II when he visited Korea in 1988. Most of them were married women and men. Today Korea has many Christian people.

Feast of
St. Matthew
apostle, evangelist (first century)

Tax collectors have never been popular people, but in our day at least they are considered respectable. In the time of Jesus, tax collectors were social outcasts. They worked for the Romans, who had conquered and oppressed the Jewish people. Worse, many tax collectors were dishonest, forcing people to pay more than they really owed.

We do not know what kind of tax collector Matthew was. Jesus chose to call him to be one of the Twelve, in spite of what people would think. Jesus attended a party at the home of his new disciple. (The story is told in the ninth chapter of the Gospel of Matthew.) Matthew invited all his friends, the other outcasts of society — tax collectors and public sinners. The religious leaders were horrified that a teacher like Jesus would keep such company. When Jesus was questioned about it, he said, "I did not come to call the virtuous, but sinners."

After the death and resurrection of Jesus, when the Holy Spirit brought gifts of courage and wisdom to the apostles, Matthew preached the gospel. Some traditions say that he worked in Judea, the southern part of the Holy Land, for many years. But others say he traveled as far as Germany, Greece, Syria, Persia or Ethiopia. Tradition says that he was martyred, but where or when that happened is no longer known.

The gospel that bears Matthew's name was written in Greek, perhaps around the year 80. Matthew's gospel was written for a community of Jewish and Greek Christians. Many of the stories in this gospel remind us that all people are welcome to follow Christ. An example is the story of the Magi who were led by a star to visit the infant Jesus. The Magi were not Jews, and yet they came to honor this Jewish child, Jesus. The story of the Magi is found only in the Gospel of Matthew.

Byzantine calendar
St. Jonah
prophet (eighth century BCE)

The story told in the Book of Jonah starts with God calling Jonah to travel to Nineveh, a wicked and powerful city in the pagan land of Assyria (in what is now the nation of Iraq). Jonah's task was to warn the people there to repent of their sins. But he didn't want to do this because he knew that God would be merciful to them once they did repent, and Jonah thought these people didn't deserve such good treatment.

Instead of traveling east to Assyria, Jonah boarded a boat heading in the opposite direction. A terrifying storm came up, and Jonah realized that it was his disobedience to God that had brought it on. He told the sailors to throw him overboard, which they did. At once the sea grew calm.

Jonah was saved from drowning by a giant fish that swallowed him whole. After three days and three nights, the fish spit him out onto dry land. Jonah headed straight for Nineveh. As he had suspected, his preaching was effective. Everyone showed God sorrow for their sins, and God pardoned them all.

The Book of Jonah was probably written at a time when people in Israel had suffered a great deal because of their contacts with outsiders. The Book of Jonah showed that God's mercy is great enough for all the peoples of the earth.

September

The Conception of St. John the Baptist
herald of the Lord

The Eastern church celebrates a most joyful event today: the conception of John the Baptist. He was a prophet and a martyr, and he prepared the way for the Lord Jesus.

The wonderful story of the conception of John is told in the first chapter of the Gospel of Luke. Zechariah and Elizabeth, an elderly couple, had yearned for a child for many years. The angel Gabriel, who "stands in the presence of God," came to bring amazing news: Zechariah and Elizabeth were going to have a son. His name was to be John. He would be great in the eyes of God. It would be his solemn task to prepare the people for the Lord.

Elizabeth did conceive a child. She was filled with wonder and joy that such a blessing could come her way. When John was born, Zechariah sang praises to God. The people of the country-side all around were amazed. They wondered, "What then will this child become?" It was clear that God's power had been at work.

Every morning of the year the church sings Zechariah's song once again. It is called the *Benedictus*, which means "blessed" in Latin. The first words are "Blessed be the God of Israel."

In the calendar of the church year, the autumn equinox is linked to the conception of John the Baptist. His birth will be celebrated nine months from now (June 24), near another change of seasons, the summer solstice (June 21).

Autumnal equinox

This celestial event marks the official change of seasons. After today, nights will be longer than days in the Northern Hemisphere. Autumn is beginning. (Of course, in the Southern Hemisphere the opposite is true and the season of spring begins.)

The full moon closest to the autumnal equinox is known as "harvest moon." In the old days, the light of the full moon helped farmers harvest crops during the night. The next full moon, about a month later, is called "hunters' moon." It is a second harvest moon.

St. Cleopas and companion
disciples of the Lord (first century)

Three days after the death of their beloved teacher, Cleopas and a companion not named in scripture walked from Jerusalem toward Emmaus, about seven miles away. The 24th chapter of the Gospel of Luke tells their story, which began on the road as they talked about all the sad and puzzling events of the past few days.

A stranger joined them. They were amazed that this person hadn't heard about Jesus' death, since everyone in Jerusalem was talking about it. They told him what a great prophet Jesus had been, and how their hopes had been crushed when he died. Then they described the rumors that Jesus' body had disappeared from his tomb because he was alive.

The stranger responded by explaining the scriptures, from the time of Moses forward, and how the Messiah had to suffer and die.

At sunset, the two begged this wise stranger to have supper with them. When he broke the bread, they suddenly recognized that he was Jesus, risen from the dead. He vanished from their sight, and they knew that the story they had heard earlier that day was true. Cleopas and his companion were filled with joy that they had been chosen to be witnesses of the resurrection.

Though it was difficult to travel at night in those days, they hurried the seven miles back to Jerusalem. There they poured out their wonderful news to the other disciples.

Not much else is known about Cleopas and his companion. Some people think that the two were husband and wife.

Byzantine calendar

St. Sergius of Radonezh
abbot (c. 1315 – 1392)

When he was young, the noble-born parents of Sergius of Radonezh were driven from their home in the city of Rostov because of political unrest. They settled in Radonezh, not far from Moscow, where they became farmers.

By the time Sergius was 20, both his parents had died, so he followed his dream of becoming a hermit. Invasions by a tribe called the Tartars had ruined many of the monasteries, so people like Sergius who wanted a life of prayer were retreating into the northern forests of Russia.

Word got around about Sergius's wisdom, holiness, and kindness to the poor. Monks joined him and built little huts and a chapel. The place was called Holy Trinity, and Sergius was its abbot. People came from far and wide for his advice, his peacemaking skills, or just to experience his warm and gentle spirit. Sometimes Sergius had to travel long distances. He always chose to go on foot.

Several times he was offered the chance to be a bishop, but he preferred life at the monastery. There he taught the peasants new and better ways to farm their land.

Over time his monastery became the center of a great spiritual renewal that affected all of Russia. As many as 75 new monasteries were born from the parent monastery Sergius had founded.

Sergius is considered one of the greatest Russian saints. His feast is an important day for the church in Russia.

Optional memorial of

Ss. Cosmas and Damian
martyrs (died c. 303)

Beautiful legends have grown up around these two saints. It's been said that they were brothers, maybe even twins, who were trained physicians. In Christian charity, they would take no money for their services. They refused to sacrifice to idols, and so they were tortured by government police and then thrown into the sea.

Cosmas and Damian are patron saints of doctors, surgeons and druggists. People pray to them in times of epidemic diseases.

Because the legends describe them as twin brothers, they are also the patron saints of twins. In Africa the legend of Cosmas and Damian got mixed up with other legends about twins. In the past, some people thought that being a twin was a curse. But African Christians pointed to the stories of Cosmas and Damian to say that being a twin is a blessing and a joy. Nowadays among Christians in Africa, twins are considered a special sign of God's grace.

September

27

Memorial of

St. Vincent de Paul
presbyter, religious founder (c. 1580–1660)

The parents of Vincent de Paul were peasant farmers in the village of Pouy, in France. They worked very hard to keep their six children fed. Because they knew Vincent was bright, they made sacrifices so that he could be educated.

Vincent was determined to use his intelligence and charm to earn a good living for himself. He became court chaplain to Queen Margaret of Valois and used his connections to make other important friends. But then Vincent found a fine spiritual director who opened his heart to a concern for others. He began to develop a spirit of compassion. At that time, ordinary people lived in misery, disease and violence. Rich people were completely unaware of the suffering that surrounded them.

Vincent began to work in a small country church where he organized members of the parish to provide food and clothing for the poor. It was the first of many such organizations, which today are called St. Vincent de Paul societies.

Vincent came to realize that country people also needed spiritual care. He organized an order of priests that would be trained to go out to the villages and work with the peasants. The order came to be called the Vincentians, and it was soon at work all over France. Many of the priests who volunteered gave up promising careers for this humble work.

Vincent established homes for orphans, for reformed prostitutes, for physically handicapped persons, and for the elderly. He believed that the rich and noble had a need to share their wealth and to give service, and he boldly reminded them to do so.

At that time women religious were cloistered. They spent their lives in their convents. Vincent became a great friend of Jane Frances de Chantal (August 18) and Francis de Sales (January 24). From them he got the idea for a new kind of religious order "whose convent is the sick room, whose chapel is the parish church, whose cloister is the city streets."

Vincent assisted Louise de Marillac (1591–1660) in founding the order. It was called the Sisters of Charity. Among its members were women from the richest families in France, now devoted to serving the poor wherever there was a need.

Vincent worked on all these projects until he was 80 years old. On his deathbed he said, "I believe, I trust, I am ready."

28

Optional memorial of

St. Wenceslaus
king, martyr (c. 907–929)

Good King Wenceslaus looked out
on the feast of Stephen,
When the snow lay round about,
deep and crisp and even.

Wenceslaus was born shortly after the great saints Cyril and Methodius (February 14) brought the gospel to Bohemia. The country was part pagan and part Christian. Wenceslaus's grandmother, Ludmilla, brought up her oldest grandson as a Christian. She knew he would rule the country some day.

Wenceslaus became king at age 18 and took steps to make Christianity stronger. With his own hands he used wheat from his fields and grapes from his vines to make bread and wine for the liturgy. He brought back priests who had been exiled from the country, and he invited missionaries from other countries to come and help in Bohemia. He built new churches and he passed new laws that protected the poor and outlawed violence.

Some of the pagan nobles of the country hated him. His own brother Boleslaus sided with them. As the king was on his way to Mass one day, Boleslaus and some of the other nobles struck him down with swords. Wenceslaus said, "Brother, may God forgive you," and he died at the door of the church. He was only 22 years old.

Immediately the people acclaimed him as a martyr, and the country rapidly became Christian. Boleslaus repented of what he had done. He built a shrine for Wenceslaus's body in Prague at the Church of St. Vitus.

Memorial of

St. Lawrence Ruiz and companions

Lawrence Ruiz, married man, martyr
(c. 1600–1637), and his companions, martyrs

Lawrence Ruiz lived at a time when Europeans were turning Asian cities into colonies. A European warship would land, the captain would claim the place for his country, the local leaders would be captured and a new government set up. Often whole regions and whole nations were being conquered by European countries with powerful navies, such as England, Spain and Holland.

The Japanese were afraid that this might happen to them. Japanese leaders tried to shut out influence from other countries. They also shut out European religions. Christians were murdered or forced to leave Japan.

Lawrence was born in Manila in the Philippines. His parents were Christians. He married and had three children. Then he joined a secret missionary team of Dominicans sailing for Japan.

A storm blew the ship aground on the small island of Okinawa, which is off the coast of Japan. Lawrence and his shipmates were taken to the Japanese city of Nagasaki, where they were tortured and killed. Nagasaki had once been the site of a large but secret Christian community. (See St. Paul Miki and companions, February 6.) Over 50,000 Catholics there had been killed or driven from their homes.

Lawrence Ruiz is the first Filipino martyr to be canonized. He and his companions are patron saints of Japan, the Philippines and Taiwan.

Feast of

Ss. Michael, Gabriel and Raphael

archangels

This great day is a triple celebration of the glory of God. The feast days of Michael, Gabriel and Raphael, who used to be remembered separately, have been combined into one joyful feast. It is called Michaelmas in some places.

Although angels are mentioned in the Bible many times, only these three are specifically named. They are messengers of God, which is the meaning of the word "angel." St. Michael's role was to defend Christians from the powers of evil. This day, which comes as the nights grow longer and longer, is the church's fearless welcome to the dark and cold.

Michael's name means, "Who is like God?" The 12th chapter of the Book of Revelation tells of Michael casting out of heaven those angels who

September

presumed that they were like God. Michael is considered the special protector of Israel and also the protector of the church. The Book of Daniel tells us that Michael will lead the dead to God on the day of resurrection.

Gabriel was the archangel who brought the news that John the Baptist would be born to Zechariah and Elizabeth. It was Gabriel who appeared to Mary to ask her to become the mother of God. His name means "hero of God." The Book of Daniel says that Gabriel announced the end of the Jews' exile in Babylon. According to tradition, Gabriel will sound the trumpet to awaken the dead on the day of judgment.

Raphael's name means "God has healed." Raphael plays an important part in the Book of Tobit, where he guards a young man on a journey and restores sight to the man's elderly father. He describes himself as one of the seven angels who stand in the presence of God. In the Gospel of John, the healing pool where Jesus cured a paralyzed man was said to be a place where Raphael stirred the waters.

For centuries, this day has been an occasion for a holiday feast. Perhaps the cooler weather stirs the appetite. In many countries, goose is the traditional dish to serve, because geese are migrating at this time. In Poland, it is served with sour cream and apples, in England with onions and sage. However, in Germany roast pig is served. The Scots keep the feast of the angels with oatmeal cakes.

Memorial of
St. Jerome
hermit, presbyter, doctor of the church
(c. 341 – 420)

Jerome was born in Dalmatia, along the coast of the Adriatic Sea. His parents were Christians, and they sent him to Rome for a good education. Jerome developed a passion for collecting books (which were very rare and expensive objects in those days).

After his schooling Jerome lived as a hermit in the Syrian desert for five years. Later he was invited to Rome to become the secretary of Pope Damasus (December 11). But only three years later, Damasus died. Jerome's feisty personality had made him many enemies in Rome by then, so he traveled to the Holy Land. He settled in the city of Bethlehem, where he would remain for the rest of his life.

In Rome, he had preached some very outspoken homilies criticizing the wealthy. He had also begun a scripture study group for women of the upper classes. It was the first group of its kind that we know of. He knew that contact with scripture would transform people's lives.

One woman of the group, Paula, became a brilliant scholar in her own right. Like Jerome, she studied Greek and Hebrew so that she could better understand the Bible.

Paula and many other followers of Jerome went with him when he settled in Bethlehem. Paula and Jerome founded two monasteries, one for men and one for women, and a church to be used by both houses.

In Bethlehem Jerome devoted his life to study and meditation. Assisted by Paula and others, he completed the enormous task of translating the Bible from Hebrew and Greek into Latin. Latin was spoken by most people at that time. Jerome's translation was called the Vulgate, from the Latin word for "the common people." There had been no careful Latin translation available before. Jerome's was used for many centuries.

Despite his hot temper, Jerome was always kind to needy persons. When Rome was attacked in the year 410, many refugees came East to the monasteries. Jerome laid aside his studies to serve them, saying, "Today we must translate the words of scripture into deeds, and instead of speaking saintly words we must act them."

When he died, Jerome was buried under the Church of the Nativity in Bethlehem.

October

October means "eighth month" in Latin. Why is that? In the old Roman calendar, the year began in spring, not in winter.

September was rich with feast days. November also will have several important days. But October was cut from rather plain cloth. There are valleys between mountains and ordinary days between extraordinary ones.

The second Monday in October
Columbus Day (U. S. A.)

October 12 marks the day in 1492 when three wooden ships landed at the tiny island of what is now San Salvador in the Bahamas. The ships had been provided by the king and queen of Spain. Their Italian captain, Christopher Columbus, was sure he had just reached "the Indies" (Japan and China) as he'd set out to do. His bold plan was to reach the Far East by sailing west.

The "new world" Columbus found was filled with cultures older than those he had left behind in Europe. Many of these cultures were destroyed by diseases spread by the Europeans. Many more Native Americans died because of the cruelty of Columbus's sailors. When the Europeans realized they would not find gold mines, they turned to capturing and selling slaves as a source of income.

The course of history would be changed by the blending of the "old" and "new" worlds. The native people of the Americas, their gifts and their cultures, have proven to be the new world's greatest treasure. In many Latin American countries October 12 is called "the Day of the Race." This refers to the new race of human beings formed by the marriages of Native American people and European people as a result of Columbus's voyages.

In large cities of the United States, Columbus Day is a time for Italian Americans to celebrate their famous countryman with parades and church services. Parades are held in Chicago and New York City. San Francisco holds its "Festa Italiana" over the weekend before this day. Activities include a street fair, a waterfront cavalcade based on the life of Columbus, and ceremonies at Telegraph Hill, where a statue honors the explorer.

The second Monday in October
Thanksgiving Day (Canada)

Few people know that the first formal Thanksgiving service in North America was celebrated in Newfoundland. It was held in 1578 by Sir John Frobisher and the European settlers after their safe landing. However, Thanksgiving Day didn't become an annual event in Canada until much later.

October

The tradition returned to the province of Nova Scotia with travelers who had celebrated Thanksgiving Day in New England. The tradition spread to the rest of the country, and in 1879 a day of thanksgiving for a good harvest and other blessings became an official holiday in Canada.

Traditional Thanksgiving feasts include dinners of venison, waterfowl and other wild game, as well as other North American foods, such as wild rice, corn, cranberries and potatoes.

1

Memorial of
St. Thérèse of the Child Jesus
religious, doctor of the church (1873 – 1897)

Marie Françoise Martin grew up in Lisieux in France. Her parents were wealthy and religious. Marie was their youngest daughter, so she received a lot of attention from her parents, sisters and the family servants.

Marie was raised by her sister Pauline after their mother died. When Marie was nine Pauline entered the Carmelite convent nearby. Marie began to long for the life of poverty and prayer at Pauline's convent. She obtained permission to join at the unusually early age of 15.

Marie was given the name Thérèse. (Many English speaking people use the form Theresa.) Those in charge of the young nuns were especially strict with her. They wanted to make sure she didn't receive special treatment. In addition to her housekeeping tasks, she cared for the convent chapel and later took on much of the work of guiding the young nuns who had come into the convent after her.

Thérèse's life centered around the gospels. She believed that any life could be a holy one. "To pick up a pin for love can convert a soul," she said. So she did her drab everyday chores with joy and love.

Thérèse's patience was put to its greatest test when she developed tuberculosis, a deadly and painful lung disease. Just before she died, at the age of 24, she made a startling statement: "I promise to spend my heaven doing good on earth."

Thérèse wrote down her story because the leader of the convent had instructed her to do so. It wasn't intended for outside publication, only for the enjoyment of the sisters at other Carmelite convents. But they found it so helpful that they passed it on to their friends, and soon it was being read in many countries of the world. Thérèse's story gave its readers hope that they, too, could become saints, even if their lives were not spectacular in any way.

2

Memorial of
The Guardian Angels

In the 18th chapter of the Gospel of Matthew, Jesus advises his followers to become like little children. "Take care that you do not despise one of these little ones," he says, "for, I tell you, in heaven their angels continually see the face of my Father in heaven." His words are one source for the belief, held since the days of the earliest Christians, that every human has a guardian or protecting angel.

"Angel" means messenger in Greek. Angels are mentioned often in scripture, where they are not only messengers but defenders, companions, guides and guardians. The Letter to the Hebrews describes them as spirits whose work is service. Guardian angels have a special task — to assist human beings in their journey toward God.

All the angels used to be remembered on the feast of Michaelmas (September 29). But people wanted a day to honor their own special protectors. And so today we continue the feast of the angels. The joy of this day is based on our sure knowledge of all the ways that God lovingly cares for us.

Memorial of
St. Francis of Assisi
deacon, religious founder (c. 1181 – 1226)

Francis of Assisi was the son of a wealthy cloth merchant in Italy. As a teenager, Francis sold cloth in his father's shop. He was very good at charming the customers. At night he went to parties with the young nobles of the town. He loved fine clothes and everything else that went with being rich. He wasn't much of a student, but he loved the tales of King Arthur and his knights in armor.

Francis wanted to be a knight himself. When the town of Assisi went to war with Perugia (a neighboring town), Francis joined the campaign. A year as a prisoner of war changed his outlook. When he came home he was ill for months. He was confused because everything that had given him joy now seemed empty. Francis spent hours praying for guidance in San Damiano, an old, rundown chapel on the outskirts of town. One day guidance was provided. "Repair my house," said the voice of Christ, "which, as you see, is falling into ruin."

He carried bricks on his back to the chapel and began to repair its stonework. Only much later did Francis realize that the house that God was talking about was not the small chapel but the entire church.

The church of Francis's day was wealthy and powerful, and most people did not have the courage to take the words of the gospels literally. But Francis followed Christ's example. He became the "Poverello" — the "little poor one." He owned only one tunic, a plain brown robe with a rope for a belt, which was the garment worn by peasants when they labored in the fields. He worked with lepers, the most despised people of society. He acted as a peacemaker between warring towns.

Soon others began to join Francis, earning their bread by working in the fields or by doing odd jobs. They preached not just to the rich but to the poor as well. Francis helped his friend Clare (August 11) begin an order of religious women. And Francis invented something called the Third Order, a way for people to live the religious life while continuing their ordinary work.

Francis had an understanding of the unity of all creation that was way ahead of its time. He addressed every created thing as Brother or Sister and treated everything with reverence. He allowed the beauty of creation to fill him with joy.

Francis became ill and died when he was only about 45 years old. On his deathbed he composed the Canticle of the Sun, a hymn of praise still sung to this day. Then he asked to be laid on Brother Earth naked so that he could welcome Sister Death as simply as possible. The pope who canonized him two years later described him as "the most perfect image of Christ." His body rests in the basilica that was built at Assisi after his death.

Francis of Assisi is a patron saint of Italy. In 1979 he was also named patron saint of ecologists and all people who work to protect the environment.

October

6

Optional memorial of
St. Bruno
presbyter, religious founder (c. 1030 – 1101)

Bruno was born in the city of Cologne. He became a well-known theology teacher in the cathedral school of Rheims. This school was a forerunner of the modern university. Many fine young students came to Rheims just to study with Bruno, who had become the head of the school by the time he was 30.

Later Bruno felt called to live a life of quietness and prayer. With the help of a former student who was now the bishop of Grenoble in France, he found the valley now called the Chartreuse. Bruno and six friends built a chapel with seven small wooden dwellings clustered around it. They copied books by hand, grew their own food, and spent many hours a day in silent prayer.

Bruno loved this place, but he enjoyed it for only six years before being called away. A new pope, Urban II, another of Bruno's former students, was working to reform the church, and he needed the wisdom and guidance of his old teacher. Urban persuaded Bruno to come live in Rome. However, after the profound silence of the mountains, Bruno found the city much too noisy for prayer. The pope allowed him to build another monastery in a quiet spot in the southern tip of Italy. There Bruno would be close to Rome if his advice was needed, and there he spent the last 10 years of his life.

The motherhouse of the Carthusian Order, the order of monks founded by Bruno, still stands in the Chartreuse. Now it is a great monastery. Once a week its monks take a long walk together in the wild countryside just as Bruno enjoyed doing many centuries ago.

In the U. S. A. and Canada, optional memorial of
Bl. Marie-Rose Durocher
religious founder (1811 – 1849)

When Eulalie Durocher was growing up in a little town outside Montreal, she wanted only a quiet and simple life for herself. She enjoyed riding her horse Caesar.

Marie-Rose (the name she took when she became a religious) was the tenth of 11 children. Even as a teenager, she was so competent that when her mother died she was able to take over the household. Then her brother, a priest in the town of Beloeil (near Montreal), asked her to become the housekeeper and host at the rectory where he lived. Although she was never very healthy, she had a great deal of energy and she worked hard at serving others.

In those times most Canadians lived in rural areas. The huge country had about half a million Catholics, most of whom had received no religious education. There was a severe shortage of clergy to serve the needs of this large, spread-out population.

Marie-Rose had the advantage of a few years of formal education as well as the religious education she had been given by her mother. Realizing that the children of the parish needed catechesis, she began to teach them. After encouragement from her spiritual director and the bishop of Montreal, she founded a religious congregation to do this work. She was then 32 years old.

Marie-Rose lived only six years longer. She would have been surprised to learn that some day her actions would touch not only her homeland of Canada but also the United States, South America, Africa and Japan. Those are the places that have been served by the Sisters of the Holy Names of Jesus and Mary, the religious congregation she founded.

7

Memorial of
Our Lady of the Rosary

"His mother treasured all these things in her heart." This is how the Gospel of Luke describes Mary's reflection on the mystery of Jesus. The rosary is a tool that helps Christians to reflect on the life, death and resurrection of Christ. People have prayed the rosary in its present form for more than 500 years.

The most important and most beautiful prayers for Christians are the psalms. Some people try to pray all 150 psalms each week. Many people learn a few psalms by heart and pray one psalm before going to bed at night. Some people even sing them in the shower.

A long time ago, when many people couldn't read, they would pray the "Hail Mary" instead of singing psalms. That is why the full form of the rosary has 15 groups of ten beads, which totals 150, one for each psalm in the Bible. This is often shortened to five groups of ten beads.

8

Roman martyrology
St. Mechthild of Magdeburg
religious (1207–1282)

Mechthild was a wise woman. Her joyful book, *The Overflowing Light of God,* is a collection of poetry, stories, visions, reflections and dialogues. Throughout, she reaffirms her confidence in God's constant loving presence. She thought that this sure knowledge of God's presence was something all believers were meant to have.

Being able to know God's love, Mechthild said, had nothing to do with how educated we are. In fact, God wants most to bless the humblest and simplest. This understanding of God's kindness consoled many people of her time.

Of Mechthild's early life we know only that she was born to a noble family somewhere near Magdeburg in Germany, and she was well educated. When she was about 12 years old, she experienced the Holy Spirit in a way that had a strong effect on her. She had mystical experiences all her life, which were the source for her writings.

At about age 20 Mechthild became a "beguine." Beguines were women who lived in community and spent their time in prayer and works of service to the needy. But, unlike nuns, they did not make vows to remain in this life.

At about age 60 she joined a Cistercian convent at Helfta in Germany. Her style of spirituality and prayer influenced other women who lived at the convent. Her writings were translated into Latin and read by other great writers of her day.

9

Optional memorial of
St. Denis and companions
Denis, bishop, martyr, and his companions, martyrs (died c. 258)

Twentieth-century tourists in Paris like to climb the hill of Montmartre for a great view of the city. But in the earliest centuries of Christianity, Montmartre was a place of execution. The word Montmartre means "Hill of Martyrs" in French. According to legend, St. Denis was martyred there.

Denis probably was Italian. He was sent from Rome after many Christians had been martyred in Gaul (an old name for France). His task was to

October

encourage the Christians who had survived the persecution and to spread the gospel. Denis was chosen because of the goodness of his life and because he understood the faith so well. He may have been the first bishop of Paris.

It was said that Denis lived on an island in the Seine river, in the center of the city, with a priest and a deacon. They assisted him with his preaching and other Christian service.

Denis was beheaded during the persecution by the Roman emperor Valerian. Denis's assistants were martyred with him. A few centuries later, when Christianity became the religion of the Roman Empire, a great abbey church named after Denis was built over his tomb. It became the burial place of the kings of France, who wanted to be close to their country's patron and hero.

Optional memorial of
St. John Leonardi
presbyter, religious founder (c. 1541 – 1609)

As early as the thirteenth century, groups of lay people began transforming their world by praying together and serving those around them who were in need. To begin with, these groups of people usually had a social connection with each other. They might be relatives, neighbors or members of the same profession. Their groups were called confraternities, a term that comes from the Latin word for "brother."

Some confraternities took on the work of feeding the poor or staffing a hospital. Others provided burials for the dead. This was an especially important service in times of plague when great numbers of people died at the same time.

John Leonardi was a pharmacist's helper in Lucca in Italy, where he was born. His work led him to begin caring for people in hospitals and prisons. At the age of 25 he began training to be a priest. He was ordained when he was 40. Then he began to teach young people, while he continued to assist those in hospitals and prisons.

John began the Confraternity of Christian Doctrine at Lucca. He trained people in the rewarding and important service of teaching about the Christian faith. He also wrote a collection of Christian beliefs that would be used by catechists for 300 years. John died in Rome from the plague, which he caught while caring for other victims during an epidemic.

14

Optional memorial of
St. Callistus I
pope, martyr (died c. 222)

Callistus was a young slave whose master, a high official of the emperor, saw that he had talent. The master put him in charge of a large amount of money. Somehow the money was lost or stolen. Frightened, Callistus ran away but was caught and thrown into a dungeon. Eventually he was sent to do hard labor in the mines of Sardinia.

In time he was freed. When he returned to Rome, Pope Victor saw that he was a good person who had been unjustly treated. Victor's successor, Pope Zephyrinus, also respected Callistus. He appointed the ex-slave to be the deacon in charge of the Christian cemetery on the Appian Way. (To this day the cemetery is called the catacomb of Callistus.) Later Callistus became the pope's secretary. In the year 217, he was elected pope himself. He served in that position for only five years before being killed in a riot.

But during that short time he proved his skill and compassion as a leader. Some historians think Callistus was among the greatest of all popes.

Callistus was criticized for being too forgiving. Probably because of the sufferings he had been through, Callistus wisely felt that people who denied their faith under persecution should be allowed to return to the church if they repented. He believed that the church had been given the power to forgive every kind of sin. Many Christians disagreed. They thought that forgiveness made the church weak.

Callistus died a martyr as did some of those Christians who had opposed him.

Memorial of
St. Teresa of Jesus
doctor of the church (1515 – 1582)

Teresa was a constant amazement to the other people in her convent in the city of Avila in Spain. She was a mystic, a person with a gift for deep prayer. According to stories told about her, sometimes she would sink into union with God so intense that she actually rose off the floor and floated in the air. This would happen unexpectedly, for instance, when she was helping with the dishes. But she was also romantic and enthusiastic. She would grab a set of castanets and dance around the room when things seemed dull during recreation time.

Teresa of Avila was born in Spain during the years when Martin Luther was beginning the Reformation in Germany (February 18). The young Teresa wasn't that interested in religion. She preferred romance novels and beautiful clothes. At the age of 21 she decided to enter the Carmelite Convent of the Incarnation, which was like a club for young women. The richest nuns received special treatment, and the place was filled with visitors, gossip, games and good food. Teresa enjoyed

the distractions. But after 20 years, she realized how much she longed for a place where the real Carmelite life would be lived — a place of prayer, silence and fasting. Boldly she asked for and received permission to begin such a community.

This reformed Carmelite convent was called "discalced." That means shoeless. The women who lived there wore simple rope sandals. Everyone shared in the chores equally, including Teresa.

When the Carmelite Father General came to visit Teresa's convent, he was so impressed that he asked her to begin discalced houses for Carmelite men. Through the work of reform Teresa met her friend John of the Cross (December 14), who shared her passion for prayer and simplicity.

In the midst of all this activity, Teresa also did a lot of writing. Her books about the spiritual life are considered classics. She wrote seven major works and several smaller ones. For that scholarship she is called a doctor — a wise teacher — of the church. She is the first woman to be given this title. She is also one of the most beloved saints of Spain and Latin America.

Optional memorial of
St. Hedwig
married woman, religious (c. 1174 – 1243)

Hedwig was born in Bavaria. Her large family were nobles; two of her sisters married kings. She received an education that prepared her to be a noble's wife. Her parents arranged for her to marry Henry I, the duke of Silesia in central Europe. The young couple developed a strong marriage and had seven children.

Henry was a wise ruler. He came to rely on the good judgment of his wife, who was a gifted peacemaker.

October

When Hedwig went out to work with poor people, she would give her slippers away if she saw a woman walking barefoot. (Sometimes this meant that Hedwig herself walked barefoot for the rest of the day.) She encouraged her husband to care for the poor. One way he provided funds was to sell all the gold and silver in the house.

Hedwig and Henry provided hospitals, monasteries and the first convent and school for young women in their region. Prisoners built the convent, and in exchange for their work they were given their freedom.

After Henry died, Hedwig spent the remaining years of her life at the convent. She prayed with the sisters, dressed simply and lived their life of poverty in every way that she could. She kept her money in order to make sure that it was spent on the poor, and she often left the convent to serve the sick and needy as she had always done.

Optional memorial of
St. Margaret Mary Alacoque
religious (1647 – 1690)

In the seventeenth century, many Christians in France were being taught that perhaps only a few people could ever reach heaven. This false idea was called Jansenism. At just the time when this idea was doing its greatest damage, Margaret Mary and other people came to a special understanding of God's mercy.

Margaret Mary Alacoque was born in a small town in Burgundy in France. She had many difficulties in childhood, including the death of her father, a serious illness, and trouble with relatives of the family.

When Margaret Mary was 20, she joined a convent of the Visitation sisters. During prayer she saw the image of the Sacred Heart of Jesus filled with mercy for every human soul. This was a

much different understanding of Christ than the one taught by the Jansenists. Margaret Mary felt called to let people know about this love. She suggested ways that people could show devotion to the loving heart of Jesus, and she suggested that a feast day in honor of the Sacred Heart be started.

After some initial doubts about whether or not Margaret was imagining things, the convent began to observe a feast of the Sacred Heart of Jesus. Later a chapel was built there to honor Christ under that title. Other Visitation convents began to keep the feast, and before long the dioceses of France did so as well. Another person who helped to spread this devotion was John Eudes (August 19). After Margaret's death, the observance became a feast of the whole church.

17

Memorial of
St. Ignatius of Antioch
bishop, martyr (died c. 107)

Not much is known about the early life of Ignatius of Antioch. He is believed to have been a disciple of John the Apostle (December 27). For perhaps as long as 40 years Ignatius was bishop of Antioch in the ancient kingdom of Syria, in what is now Turkey. Antioch, a major city, was the place where the word "Christian" was first used.

During the reign of the Roman emperor Trajan, Ignatius publicly refused to worship pagan gods. Although he was by then an old man, he was a powerful witness to the Christian faith. The Romans wanted to eliminate his influence. They sentenced him to be fed to wild beasts in the Colosseum at Rome.

Ignatius was put in chains as though he were a dangerous criminal. Ten soldiers were assigned to guard him during the long ocean voyage from Antioch to Rome. At every port where the ship stopped along the way, the Christians of the city came out in great numbers to meet him. Everyone received the blessing of the beloved bishop and extended their prayers to him.

During this journey, Ignatius was allowed to write seven letters. They still exist and are considered some of the greatest treasures of Christianity. The letters were addressed to some of the churches he visited, to the church of Rome, and to Polycarp (February 23), the bishop of Smyrna and a dear friend.

The letters show Ignatius's concern for others, even while he was in the midst of great suffering himself. "My love for you overflows all bounds," he wrote to the Philadelphians. The letters call for harmony among Christians and encourage loving service to all the needy.

Ignatius's letters also show the thoughts that went through his mind as he prepared for death. "I am the wheat of the Lord," he said. "May I be ground by the teeth of the beasts to become the pure bread of Christ." He described himself as "a setting sun on its way to God."

Byzantine calendar
St. Hosea
prophet (eighth century BCE)

Hosea's image for God came from the pain of his own life. His wife had left him and their three children, yet he never stopped loving her. From his anger and pain Hosea came to a new understanding of God's faithfulness and love.

As people were changing their way of life from herding to farming, many of them fell into worshiping the pagan god Baal, as their neighbors the Canaanites did. The farmers thought that Baal could bring them a better harvest.

The nation used military force unjustly, made alliances with pagans, and mistreated the poor of their own land. In all this, Hosea realized, they were forgetting the law of Moses. He called them to rely on nothing and no one except God. He promised that God would redeem them from waywardness, asking only for repentance in return.

Feast of
St. Luke
evangelist (first century)

Tradition gives each of the four gospels a name: Matthew, Mark, Luke and John. But this was a century or two after the gospels were written.

The gospel that bears Luke's name was written sometime after the year 80. In the beginning of the gospel, the author says that he had spoken with eyewitnesses to the events. He also had Mark's gospel, written earlier, as one of his sources. The author's other work, the Acts of the Apostles, continues the events told in the gospel. It records the story of the church as it unfolded after the descent of the Holy Spirit.

The Gospel of Luke displays Jesus' sensitivity to the concerns of women and all others who are oppressed in society. The importance of prayer is stressed: Jesus spends time in prayer before making any important decision. The gospel notes many examples of the times Jesus healed the sick in mind and body. And both the gospel and the Acts of the Apostles make it clear that Jesus came to save everyone — Samaritans, lepers, tax collectors, Roman soldiers, public sinners, even shepherds.

The Gospel of Luke is symbolized by an ox, like the oxen that were sacrificed at the Temple. The gospel begins with the story of John the Baptist's father offering sacrifice in the Temple.

But just who was St. Luke? We know about him from Paul and other early Christian writers. Luke never knew Jesus personally. He was a well-educated Greek. He may have been a doctor. Paul was his catechist, and in return he became Paul's loyal friend and assistant. He joined Paul at Troas during his second missionary journey and stayed with him through his travels, except during the times when Luke was assigned to stay with a community. When Paul was imprisoned, Luke stayed close by to assist him and watch over his health. Paul described him as "the beloved physician."

Some people say that Luke was an artist as well as a physician. Perhaps this tradition began because the Gospel of Luke and the Acts of the Apostles are so descriptive. They are filled with colorful details. An excellent exercise is to read these two books through as a continuing story.

19

Memorial of
Ss. Isaac Jogues, John de Brébeuf and companions

Isaac Jogues (1607–1646) and John de Brébeuf (1596–1649), presbyters, religious, missionaries, martyrs, and their companions, martyrs (died 1642–1649)

(In Canada this memorial is observed on September 2.)
When Europeans explored and conquered the Americas, the French settled in the regions north of the St. Lawrence River and around the Great Lakes. They called this area New France. The French were more interested in trading than in mining or farming. So they were somewhat less envious of the Native American lands than were the Spanish or English settlers. Still, like other European settlers, they took the best hunting grounds. The Native Americans learned to distrust them.

Into this difficult situation Jesuit missionaries came from France to preach the gospel to the Native American peoples of the area. The missionaries started with the Hurons, whose way of life was more settled than the other tribes. A mission base was built at a place called Sainte-Marie some distance from the Indian villages. A small hospital, a fort and a cemetery were built there, and sometimes the Jesuits visited other tribes from this headquarters.

After more than 20 years of work with the Hurons, the Jesuits found increasing acceptance of the Christian message. The missionaries looked for ways to be of service to the people, especially in times of illness. However, because of their friendship with the Hurons, the Jesuits earned the hatred of the Iroquois, the enemies of the Hurons.

Over an eight-year period, seven lay missionaries and priests were murdered. Most of them were tortured before they died. René Goupil was the first to be killed. Isaac Jogues was held captive over a year before he was ransomed by Dutch Protestants. Later he returned, hoping to help work out a peace treaty between the Hurons and the Iroquois. When it was completed, he was captured by a war party and killed, along with lay missioner John Lalande.

Gabriel Lalement and John de Brébeuf were killed only four or five weeks after Lalement's arrival at the Huron missions. De Brébeuf, the leader of the team, had worked there for 24 years. He had composed catechisms and a dictionary in the Huron language.

Anthony Daniel, the parish priest at the settlement of St. Joseph, went out alone to meet the Iroquois when they attacked. He hoped that the Hurons would be spared because of his death.

Charles Garnier was shot down when the settlement of St. Ignace was raided. Noël Chabanel was killed by a Huron Christian angry about the changes brought by the Europeans.

These men were the first Christian martyrs of the North American continent. Every year many pilgrims visit their shrines at Auriesville, New York, and at Midland, Ontario.

Byzantine calendar

St. Joel
prophet (c. 400 BCE)

Not much is known about Joel, who probably lived after the return of the Jews from exile in Babylon. The Book of Joel seems to build on the work of some of the other prophets, so this prophet may have been one of the last to write.

The Book of Joel is unusual. It is like a reconciliation service. Joel calls the people—even the oldest and the youngest, even brides and grooms—to fast and assemble in prayer. The fast may have been called in connection with the Jewish New Year and Day of Atonement (page 195), a traditional time of fasting in sorrow for sin.

Joel wrote that repentance must be from the heart, not just for show. He encouraged people not to tear their clothing, which was a customary way to show sorrow, but to open their hearts to change and to trust that God will honor their sincere sorrow for sin. Then Joel records an extraordinary promise. "I will pour out my spirit on all flesh; your sons and your daughters shall prophesy, your old shall dream dreams, and your young shall see visions."

20

In the U. S. A., optional memorial of

St. Paul of the Cross
presbyter, religious founder (1694–1775)

(This memorial falls on October 19 in the universal Roman calendar and is transferred to this date in the U. S. A. because of the obligatory memorial of Ss. Isaac Jogues, John de Brébeuf and their companions.)
Paul Francis Danei, called Paul of the Cross, reflected all his life on the passion of Jesus.

When he was 26 Paul founded a religious order called the Barefoot Clerks of the Cross and Passion—the Passionists for short. They would live the strict life of monks but would also preach parish missions. Missions were something like the parish renewal programs of our time. During a mission, people of the parish would participate in processions, and they would listen to long sermons that might help them better their lives.

In time the new order became well-known among the people of Italy for fine preaching. Paul himself traveled over a large area, always speaking of the passion of the Lord. Huge crowds of people came to hear him. He was said to touch the hearts even of hardened sinners and criminals. After his preaching, he would minister to people through the sacrament of reconciliation, always stressing the mercy and love of God.

October

21

St. Ursula and companions
martyrs (third century)

How does a legend grow? The legend of St. Ursula and her companions took shape over time. There were several versions of this legend. Most of them say that a young British princess named Ursula, along with 11,000 companions, sailed up the Rhine River. They left their ships near the city of Cologne to make a pilgrimage to Rome. But when they returned to Cologne they were martyred by the Huns, a fierce tribe that had captured the city.

Some brave women really were martyred in Cologne, probably at the end of the third century or a little later. We know this because the other Christians of the town built a church over the tomb of the martyrs.

An early version of the story said that eleven women died. But in the ninth century, someone mistakenly translated that number as 11,000. The name Ursula was found on the tombstone of an eight-year-old girl, and people began to think that Ursula must have been the name of the leader of the women. After another century, an old cemetery surrounding the church was found. People thought the bones buried there must be the relics of the 11,000 martyrs.

This story was popular during the Middle Ages. The legendary St. Ursula came to be thought of as a leader of all women and a rousing teacher.

When Angela Merici (January 27) founded the first order of religious women dedicated to teaching children, she named the new community after St. Ursula; they are called Ursulines.

23

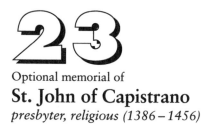

Optional memorial of

St. John of Capistrano
presbyter, religious (1386 – 1456)

The life of John Capistrano can be summed up in one word: conversion. He was a lawyer and became mayor of Perugia in Italy at the age of 26. But all that meant nothing when he was taken as a prisoner of war a few years later. In the loneliness of his cell he resolved to change his life.

Once freed, John became a Franciscan novice. His teacher was Bernardine of Siena (May 20). Over time John became Bernardine's assistant in preaching throughout Europe. John also helped in Bernardine's task of reforming the Franciscan order, which had moved away from Francis's ideals. After Bernardine died, John wrote his life story and continued preaching, addressing thousands of hearers each day.

John served as a diplomat and adviser to popes. He worked for harmony between the Eastern and Western churches.

St. John of Capistrano's Day is known in California as the day the swallows begin to fly south from the Franciscan missions. The birds are bid farewell today, but they'll be welcomed back next spring on St. Joseph's Day, March 19.

Episcopalian and Lutheran calendars

St. James of Jerusalem
brother of the Lord (first century)

Did Jesus have brothers? Over time many people have wondered that, because scripture mentions James and several other "brothers of the Lord." However, Aramaic, the language spoken by Jesus and his first disciples, uses the same word for brother and for cousins. (There is no word for cousin in Aramaic.)

The James we remember today has been confused with James the son of Alphaeus (May 3), who was one of the Twelve. However, James the brother of the Lord was not one of the Twelve.

James became the first leader of the Christians of Jerusalem after the risen Christ appeared to him. In that important role he is mentioned several times in the Acts of the Apostles and in the letters of Paul. James played a part in the Council of Jerusalem, where Paul and Barnabas were told to preach the gospel to Gentiles — people who were not Jews.

Around the year 62, James of Jerusalem was martyred. The Letter of James may have been written by him or by the person who replaced him as leader of the church in Jerusalem.

Optional memorial of

St. Anthony Mary Claret

bishop, religious founder (1807–1870)

Anthony Mary Claret had been a weaver in Barcelona in Spain. He traveled all over the country for ten years preaching parish missions. The missions went so well that he gathered five young men to do this work with him. They were called the Missionary Sons of the Immaculate Heart of Mary (now called the Claretians).

During this time Anthony's fame spread. Against his will he was called away from his work for a tough assignment as bishop of Santiago in Cuba. The diocese covered half the island. In the eight years he spent there, he began new parishes, started religious education and worked to reform the priests of the diocese. He also began credit unions

to loan money to the poor. He had such an effect on Santiago that to this day he is called the spiritual father of Cuba.

Many of the problems in Cuba were caused by racism and slavery. The church there did not treat black people as human beings. Anthony insisted that interracial marriages were valid marriages.

In those days a few wealthy farmers forced the people to grow only one crop — sugar cane. That way the people had to buy all their food and supplies from the rich. People became trapped in poverty. Anthony believed that the country should be made up of small family farms so that people could produce their own food. His efforts to help the poor made him so unpopular that 15 attempts were made on his life.

Moves and upheaval continued through Anthony's life, yet he found time to write over 200 books and pamphlets. He began a publishing house in Spain. He died in exile in France at the age of 63.

Feast of

Ss. Simon and Jude

apostles (first century)

The scriptures say very little about either Simon or Jude, the two apostles whose feasts are celebrated today.

In the Gospel of Luke, Simon is called a zealot. A zealot is a person of strong beliefs and actions. In those days there was a radical group among the Jews called the Zealots. These radicals hated the Romans for taking control of Israel. They wanted to remove the invaders by force. However, in Simon's case the word zealot may have meant that he took the Jewish law very seriously. According to legends, Simon the Zealot spread the gospel in Egypt.

In the gospels of Matthew and Mark, Jude is called Thaddeus. We call him Jude to distinguish him from Judas Iscariot, who betrayed Jesus. He is called the patron saint of hopeless cases.

It is believed that Jude and Simon each traveled to Persia, where they were martyred. Their bodies were carried to Rome for burial in St. Peter's.

Today's feast comes just before All Saints' Day. There are old customs for today that are about getting ready for "Hallowtide." It was once a custom today to go from door to door begging for the ingredients of "soul cakes," which were eaten in early November as a way to share a meal with the dead. People would sing, "For the love of Simon and Jude, give us fixings for our food!"

31
Reformation Day

On this day in the year 1517, Martin Luther (February 18) posted some of his ideas on the door of the castle church of All Saints in Wittenburg, Germany. Luther taught theology at the university there. The teachers often invited discussion of their theories by posting them publicly. On October 31 pilgrims arrived in town for the celebration of All Saints' Day. Luther thought they would help get a lively debate going.

Over the next few years the debate turned into a division within the church. This chaotic time became known as the Protestant Reformation. For hundreds of years a gulf remained in place between Catholic and Protestant believers. Reformation Sunday (the Sunday before October 31) is held in Protestant churches, especially Lutheran churches, to remember what the reformers had done. Usually the service includes the singing of Luther's great hymn, "A mighty fortress is our God."

During the Second Vatican Council, held in the 1960s, the Roman Catholic church dealt with many of the issues raised during the Reformation. Since then, Catholic and Protestant churches have been talking with one another in an official and ongoing way. Because of this dialogue, Reformation Day has taken on new meaning. It's now a time when many churches meet to celebrate the beliefs they share and to pray for understanding and unity.

On the Eve of All Saints' Day, the churches are reminded of the constant need for reform, for debate, for dialogue, for building up the communion of saints.

Halloween

By the end of October, in most of North America and Europe, days have become short and cold. The church keeps a great festival at this dark time of year — All Saints and All Souls, the first and second days of November. And, like every other Christian festival, the holiday begins at sunset on the day before.

An old name for All Saints' Day was All Hallowmas. ("Hallow" is another word for saint.) The eve of All Saints was called All Hallows' Eve, which got shortened to Halloween (from Hallowe'en, i.e., Hallows' evening).

This festival has an interesting history. Many of the peoples of northern Europe divided the year into four seasons based on the length of days, but these were a bit different from the seasons as we know them. "Winter" was the period of the shortest days. It began on November 1 and ended on February 1.

Tonight, huge bonfires were lighted on hilltops to welcome the dead who would return home for a bit of comfort by the warm hearthside. Food was set out. Any stranger was welcomed into the home. Who knew? Maybe the stranger was really a dead relative.

But the annual return of the dead brought trouble, too. Not all of them were friendly. So everyone stayed together all night for protection, and they told stories of the dead and of narrow escapes from cranky ghosts. People dressed up like the dead to make any ghostly visitors feel more welcome and also to confuse the angry ones.

In the earliest days of Christianity, the remembrance of the dead and the celebration of the saints was kept at Eastertime. We Christians look forward to the day of resurrection of all who have died. But in the tenth century in western Europe, the church began to keep the remembrance of the dead in November, in autumn, when it seems as if the earth itself is dying.

In most of Europe, Halloween is strictly a religious event. Sometimes in North America the church's traditions are lost or confused. Still, All Hallows has been kept by the church for over 1000 years.

Halloween night still can be a Christian celebration, kept as the holy eve of All Saints' Day. Halloween customs reflect the gospel. Trick-or-treat is just good, old-fashioned hospitality. In the name of Christ, we welcome all who knock on our doors. Walking in the streets in masks and costumes reminds us of our journey to heaven. Once our journey is done, we will take our masks off and see ourselves as we truly are — the beloved children of God, the saints in glory.

November

The name for the eleventh month really means "the ninth month." In the ancient Roman calendar November was the ninth month because the year began in March.

In church tradition, November is a month to remember the dead and to pray for them. The month begins with All Saints' Day and All Souls' Day. Either in the last days of November or the first days of December, the season of Advent begins.

In folklore, November had a strange name. It was called "Gossamer," which means "goose summer." That meant something like Indian Summer, which is a time of warm weather after the first frost.

St. Martin's Day, the 11th day of the 11th month, was a time to feast on roast goose. Perhaps that's where "goose summer" comes from.

The first Tuesday after the first Monday in November
Election Day (U. S. A.)

Every fourth year on this day in the United States, people choose their next president. Every second year, some United States senators and members of the House of Representatives are chosen. Many local elections are held today, too.

In colonial times, only about 15 percent of the American people had the right to cast a ballot. At first, suffrage (the right to vote) was limited to free males age 21 and over who owned land. In some colonies, Catholics and Jews were not allowed to vote. Many years passed before women and African Americans were granted suffrage. In some states it was 1948 before Native Americans were given the right to vote, and in 1970 suffrage was granted to those between the ages of 18 and 21.

November

The fourth Thursday in November
Thanksgiving (U. S. A.)

Thanksgiving Day in the United States comes at the end of November, a bit late in the year for a typical harvest festival. The growing season is over. In some parts of the country snow has already fallen.

The Pilgrims, the Calvinist settlers in New England, held the first Thanksgiving Day celebration in 1621. Many of the English settlers did not celebrate Easter or Christmas. They had abandoned Catholic feast days and seasons, but they were devoted to the Bible. They based their laws and customs on it.

After landing in Massachusetts the Pilgrims had a tragic winter. They found the New England winters far colder than in England, and half the settlers died. In the spring, help came from a Pawtuxet Indian named Squanto, who showed them how to plant corn and other native crops. Because of this, they had a bountiful harvest.

Inviting their Native American saviors to join them, they prepared turkeys and other wild game, seafood, corn, dried berries and vegetables. Their harvest festival lasted three days.

Thanksgiving Day didn't become an annual event until much later. In 1789, President George Washington proclaimed a day of thanksgiving for the new country. For many years after that, some states celebrated on one day, some on another. In 1863, in the midst of the Civil War, Abraham Lincoln proclaimed the fourth Thursday of November as the official Thanksgiving Day of the nation.

The Law of Moses calls the people to share their bounty with family, servants, strangers, widows and orphans. Today in America many people have no way to share in Thanksgiving Day because they are hungry, homeless or isolated from family and friends. On Thanksgiving Day we remember them and welcome them with our prayer and our service.

1

Solemnity of
All Saints: Hallowmas

"There was a great multitude that no one could count, from every nation, from all tribes and peoples and languages, standing before the throne and before the Lamb, robed in white, with palm branches in their hands." Today's first reading at Mass, from the seventh chapter of the Book of Revelation, describes the reason for our glorious rejoicing today.

Agnes and Maria Goretti were only 12 when they were martyred; Anthony of the Desert died at 105. God's saints come in every size, shape, color and age. Some saints are remembered by name, but most are unknown to us. Known or unknown, honored or forgotten, they have one great thing in common: During their lives, all helped to announce the dominion of God. St. Bernard of Clairvaux said, "Calling to mind the saints arouses in us above all else a longing to enjoy their company."

The idea of holding one feast to celebrate all holy women and men seems to have been born in the early centuries of Christianity. In the Byzantine rite, All Saints' Day is celebrated in spring. It is held on the first Sunday after Pentecost, as if to say that holiness is a gift of the Holy Spirit.

In the Latin rite, in 844 Pope Gregory IV set November 1 as the date for a festival in honor of all the saints. Why this date was chosen is something of a mystery. Historians tell us that there were pre-Christian feasts on this day: a pagan Roman festival for the fruit harvest, and the Celtic New Year — a celebration of the harvest and of the dead.

Whatever the reason, All Saints' Day is a celebration perfectly suited to autumn. As we draw toward the end of the agricultural year, we celebrate God's great harvest of all people throughout history who have shown love, joy and service to others. That's why All Saints and its holy eve, Halloween, are made bright with autumn fruits, vegetables and flowers. That's why it's customary to celebrate with apple-bobbing and pumpkin carving and other harvest games. And that's why All Saints' Day is begun with a night of trick-or-treating. People give and receive hospitality, the hallmark virtue of the saints.

In the early years of the church, saints were proclaimed by the members of their villages and towns. In about the tenth century the first canonizations took place. These were official statements by the pope that someone was clearly a saint. For the past several centuries the process of canonization has been a very thorough procedure involving years of investigation and reflection.

The number of canonized saints is relatively small. And yet the martyrology, the list of the saints, includes over 10,000 names! But today is something far more than a remembrance of the good people who lived on earth. Today we rejoice in the communion of saints. We're part of this communion. All creation is united in the Spirit. We link arms with all the people of every time and place. We look forward to the day of resurrection, the final day, when creation will be transformed. Perhaps our celebration actually hastens that great day.

2

The Commemoration of
All the Faithful Departed: All Souls

This is the day we set aside to pray for all the dead who have gone before us. Christians dead and living are all one body. Our love and work on earth can be a blessing to those who have died, just as their love is a blessing for the living.

To prepare for All Souls' Day, graves are weeded and planted with flowers or decorated with gravel. In some places today, cemeteries are filled with burning candles. Many families remember the dead each year by giving alms to the poor or by planting a tree or by donating to a hospital. In some places families have a picnic in the graveyard. Extra portions of food are set aside for the dead to share.

In Latin America, the Day of the Dead is not gloomy or sad. It is filled with life. Vendors sell candies in the shapes of skulls, skeletons and coffins. Newspapers have fake death notices for politicians and movie stars as a way to poke fun at people in power. People make little figures of skeletons going about day-to-day activities. People bring candles and foods to cemeteries and spend much time there.

A long time ago in England, people went from door to door on this day and begged for "soul cakes." The people sang a carol, "Soul, soul, soul cake! Please, good people, a soul cake! One for Peter, two for Paul, three for God who made us all." This is how the custom of trick-or-treat probably started. All Souls' Day can be spent telling the stories of the dead. Photo albums, scrapbooks and anything that helps spark memories are all part of the celebration.

For many Christians in Mediterranean lands, on All Souls the dead arrive with gifts. Children

November

especially receive treats so that they're happy to be visited by the dead. Many Christians set up shrines for the dead. Everything that reminds people of the departed can be collected in a shrine. Chrysanthemums and marigolds and fragrant herbs have a place, too. Their aromas are said to assist the memory.

All Souls reminds us that it's good to speak about the dead, and to remember and to pray. The church continues the remembrance throughout this month of November and into Advent. Days are short and growing shorter. The growing darkness can remind us of the end of days, when time will be no more. At this season we ask God to speed up the coming of the kingdom, where justice will flower, where life will be lived in all its fullness, where death itself will die.

3

Optional memorial of
St. Martin de Porres
religious (1579 – 1639)

The birth certificate of Martin de Porres said "father unknown." In fact, Martin's father was a wealthy Spanish noble. But Lima, Peru, where Martin was born, was a segregated city. The Spanish had enslaved native Indians and kidnapped blacks from Africa to work in the mines and plantations. The city of Lima was composed of the homes of rich *conquistadores* (conquerors), surrounded by slums crowded with poor people, including blacks and native Indians. Martin's mother was black. Martin's father, a wealthy Spanish noble, abandoned his wife and children. So Martin and his sister, Juana, lived in poverty for the early years of their lives.

By the time Martin was 12, he had become the apprentice of a local barber. In those days, barbers did not only cut hair. They also set broken bones, dressed wounds, prescribed healing herbs for the sick, and listened to people's troubles. Martin soon earned the trust of his patients.

At 15 he volunteered to be a *donado* or lay helper at a Dominican monastery in Lima. He was given responsibility for jobs no one else wanted. Some of the priests thought that, because Martin was black, he shouldn't be there at all. Others, noticing his talent and goodness, tried to talk him into advancing to the priesthood. At age 24 Martin became a brother. But he continued to do the simplest tasks. He knew that this work gave him the flexibility to do great good. He cared for sick members of the monastery, scrubbed floors, fed the horses and donkeys, tended the gardens and cleaned the toilets. He also gave guidance, often showing a puzzling knowledge of people's secret concerns, and made peace between people in conflict.

Brother Martin fed many needy people each day with the monastery's leftovers. He began to lodge the sick and the homeless there, too, until every vacant room and even the halls were filled. When his fellow Dominicans complained, he found other places for people.

Martin began a home for abandoned street children. The home was the first place of its kind in the Americas. It was open to all, regardless of race. It had a paid staff of chaplain, doctor, nurse and counselors.

Martin planted orchards for the poor on unused land. This made figs, olives and oranges available to people who couldn't afford them otherwise. Then he showed poor people how to care for the trees. Martin's closeness to God gave him a reverence for all creation. He treated all creatures — from mice in the monastery to a raging bull that charged at him one day — as brothers and sisters.

Martin died of a fever at age 60. People of every race turned out together to mourn him. The poor considered him their hero. He is the patron of interracial justice.

Roman martyrology
St. Malachy O'More
abbot, bishop (1094–1148)

Ireland had been cut off from the churches of Europe by a series of invasions. Many people became confused in their practice of Christianity. They needed guidance and renewal. Malachy was ordained a priest at age 25 and had the task of bringing the word of God back into people's lives.

When Celsus, the bishop of Armagh, knew he was dying, he asked Malachy to replace him and reform his diocese. But Celsus's cousin wanted the title of bishop because it had been in the family for generations. Supporters of the old bishop's heirs were armed and willing to fight. Showing remarkable patience, Malachy refused to set foot inside the diocese for three years. During that time he did everything he could to restore Christian life to its people from the outside, but he wasn't willing to cause bloodshed. Finally he was allowed to take his rightful place as bishop.

Later in his life Malachy traveled to Rome to ask for the pope's blessing on the work he had done in Ireland. Along the way he stopped at Clairvaux, where Bernard (August 20) had established a monastery. The two became friends.

A few years later, on a second trip to Rome, Malachy again stopped at Clairvaux. While he was there he became ill and died. Bernard presided at his funeral liturgy. Later Bernard recorded Malachy's life story.

Like Martin (November 11), Clement (November 23) and Nicholas (December 6), St. Malachy is sometimes pictured as old man winter who descends to earth to bring the frost.

4

Memorial of
St. Charles Borromeo
bishop (1538–1584)

Charles Borromeo was born into a life of wealth and high status. When he was only 12 years old, his uncle, who would later become Pope Pius IV, gave him title to valuable church properties. At the age of 22 Charles was named a cardinal! He wore fine clothes and, for relaxation, he hunted with his friends. In a way, Charles's early life was an example of the abuses of power in the church. These abuses were what caused Martin Luther and other reformers so much concern.

However, Charles was also a hard-working student who already had earned his doctorate by the time he became cardinal. He lived in Rome, where Pope Pius gave him many responsibilities. One of Charles's greatest accomplishments was the work he did for the Council of Trent, an attempt by Catholic leaders to correct the wrongs named by the Protestants.

The Council had been suspended, but upon Charles's insistence was reopened. Many important reforms resulted.

When Charles was 25, he made a retreat based on the *Spiritual Exercises* of St. Ignatius (July 31). He experienced a deep change in his spirit and began to live a life of strict poverty. Soon he became the bishop of Milan. Living by the guidelines the Council had created, Charles became a kind and wise bishop.

Almost no religious education existed then, but Charles wanted everyone, especially children, to understand their faith. He began the Confraternity of Christian Doctrine and soon had trained enough catechists to teach 40,000 students.

November

He also made himself available to the poor and needy. After a famine in Milan, from his own money he kept thousands of people fed for three months. And when the city was hit by an outbreak of plague, Charles nursed many victims, giving to them what remained of his possessions.

Charles Borromeo died at the age of 46. He is a patron saint of catechists and catechumens.

Roman martyrology

Ss. Elizabeth and Zechariah

parents of St. John the Baptist (first century)

We know Elizabeth and Zechariah from the first chapter of the Gospel of Luke. They are described as "righteous" people who "lived blamelessly before God." This is very high praise.

On June 24, the church celebrates John the Baptist's birth. On September 23 (nine months before June 24), Eastern Christians remember John's conception. Turn to those dates in this book for the stories of John's conception and birth. Or, better, read all about it in the Gospel of Luke.

Nearly every time Elizabeth and Zechariah speak, they are praising God. Zechariah's song of praise, the *Benedictus,* "Blessed is the Lord God of Israel," is sung by the church every morning.

People don't begin a whole new way of behaving as they get older. They react from the habit of thousands of small actions over the years, from the way they have lived their lives. Elizabeth and Zechariah provide for us a holy example of growing old gracefully.

9

Feast of

The Dedication of the Lateran Basilica in Rome

Today we honor a church that counts the world within its parish boundaries. The basilica of St. John Lateran is the cathedral of Rome. That means it is the church of the Rome bishop, who is the pope. And so St. John Lateran is a spiritual home of Catholics everywhere.

The earliest Christians met in homes. When that became too dangerous in Rome because of persecutions, they met secretly in underground burial places called catacombs. That situation didn't change until the fourth century, when the emperor Constantine made Christianity the official religion of the Roman Empire.

Constantine made generous gifts of property to the church of Rome. Among them was a palace with grounds that had once belonged to the Laterani family. In 324 he added to the site a large rectangular building that could be used for public gatherings. It was called a basilica, which means, literally, a building fit for a king. It was to be a Christian church and was called the Basilica of the Savior.

Legend says that the basilica was dedicated on November 9 that year. The baptistry was dedicated to St. John the Baptist, and generations later the whole building was dedicated to John, so it became known as St. John of the Lateran.

The Lateran basilica reminds us of our history as a people. It is filled with treasured Christian relics. Its high altar is built over a wooden table on which Peter himself is said to have celebrated the Lord's Supper with the Christian community of Rome.

However, on this November feast day we celebrate not a building but a loving God who provides a home for us on earth and in heaven. According to St. Paul, we are God's building. We are living stones that are built up into God's house.

10

Memorial of

St. Leo the Great

pope, doctor of the church (died 461)

One of the most powerful scenes in history would have to be the gentle, scholarly Pope Leo the Great going forth unarmed and alone to meet Attila the Hun and his huge army. The invaders had come through northern Italy, leaving destruction in their wake. They were heading straight for Rome. The emperor and his generals were as terrified as the rest of the citizens. But Leo trusted in God's providence. His courage and faith somehow convinced the warlord to turn his troops away from Rome.

Leo was pope for 20 years. In those days that was an unusually long time to remain in office. He knew that in this role he held a great deal of power to serve the people of God.

Only two years after he had convinced Attila's armies to turn back toward the Danube river, another tribe called the Vandals threatened Rome. Again Leo pleaded for mercy. He was unable to prevent these new invaders from taking the city, but they did agree not to loot it, burn its buildings or murder its people.

Leo was a gifted pastor. In between invasions, he helped the church understand why it celebrates feasts and holy seasons. Many of his homilies spoke boldly against false teaching and encouraged people to provide for the poor. Leo wrote, "If God is love, as St. John tells us, then charity should have no limits, because God cannot be contained."

11

Memorial of

St. Martin of Tours

bishop (c. 316–397)

"I am a soldier of Christ. It is not lawful for me to fight." With these words Martin of Tours identified himself forever as a saint of peace. How fitting that his feast day has become a celebration of peace and a day of thanksgiving for its blessings!

Martin's parents were pagans. They lived in Pannonia, in what centuries later would become the nation of Hungary. After he became a catechumen at the age of ten, Martin's parents would not allow him to be baptized. His father was a soldier. At that time Roman law required that sons follow their fathers' line of work. So Martin had to join the army. He served in Gaul for three years.

According to a legend, as a young officer he met a shivering beggar on a cold, snowy evening. On a kind impulse he cut his military cloak in two and gave the beggar half. Afterward he had a vision of Christ wrapped in the cloak. Then Martin decided to be baptized.

Later, when a barbarian invasion threatened, Martin made his famous statement of peace. He was speaking to the emperor at the time. Today we would call him a conscientious objector. Centuries later, in the 1980s, the Catholic bishops of the United States wrote a teaching letter on peace. They mentioned Martin as an example of someone with the courage to refuse to do violence.

Martin laid down his weapons and spent the rest of his life as a soldier for Christ. Because of his generous life and the miracles of compassion that he worked, people all over Gaul became Christian.

Martin was made bishop of the city of Tours. He visited every parish in the large diocese every year. When he was dying, the people begged him

November

not to leave them. Ever the soldier, Martin prayed, "Lord, if your people still need me, let me stay with them. But surely I have already fought long enough." Then he died peacefully.

Until that time only martyrs had been celebrated as saints. Martin was so loved that he became the first person who was not a martyr to be honored as a saint. His day is known as Martinmas. It became a great harvest festival. Because Tours was located on a trade route, the fame of St. Martin was carried all over Europe. Pilgrims came in great numbers to visit his grave.

Veterans' Day (U. S. A.)
Remembrance Day (Canada)

In the early years of the twentieth century, a war called the Great War involved most of the countries of the earth. Millions died as a result of new and terrible weapons. Everyone hoped that it was the "war to end all wars." A very special time was chosen as the hour when the guns would be stilled and peace declared: the eleventh hour of the eleventh day of the eleventh month. By this choice, the signers of the peace treaty suggested that humankind had waited until it was nearly too late. The war would come to be known as the First World War.

The day chosen for the beginning of peace was special for another reason. It was the memorial of St. Martin of Tours. Martin had been a soldier in the army until he laid down his weapons. His feast day, Martinmas, was a celebration of peace. That day had also been a thanksgiving festival in Europe since the Middle Ages. Now there was even more reason to be thankful.

In Canada, Armistice Day became known as Remembrace Day after the Second World War. It became a time to honor those who died in both conflicts. In the United States, this day is now called Veterans' Day. All Americans who have fought in wars during this century — those who survived as well as those who died — are honored.

Memorial of
St. Josaphat
bishop, martyr (c. 1580 – 1623)

Josaphat was born in Poland. When he was in his teens, a council of bishops representing millions of Byelorussians and Ukrainians decided to seek reunion with the church of Rome. They had been part of the Orthodox church, which for several centuries had been separated from the Roman church. Today these people are called Byzantine Rite Catholics. They have the same rituals as the Orthodox but they are in union with the pope. People were bitterly divided about this reunion with Rome.

Josaphat became archbishop of Polotsk. The diocese had been neglected for years. Some of its priests had grown careless in their commitment to the people, and the churches were falling into ruin. Josaphat worked hard to correct these wrongs. He set up meetings for all the priests, prepared a catechism, and became an example to all. He traveled to the most out-of-the-way villages to preach and teach, and he visited prisoners and the sick.

A group who didn't approve of what Josaphat was doing set up an Orthodox bishop side by side with him. For the next three years the group spread false rumors about Josaphat's motives. Even some of the Roman Catholics were angry at Josaphat because he insisted on fair treatment for the Byzantine Catholics.

In 1623 Josaphat decided to go to the city of Vitebsk, where his opposition was strongest. He refused to take a military escort, although he knew he was walking into a dangerous situation. For two weeks he preached in churches and homes. After several attempts had been made on his life, he said to the people, "I am here among you as your shepherd, and you ought to know that I shall be happy to give my life for you."

Finally a large crowd of people gathered at the house where he was staying. When they started beating his servants, Josaphat offered himself in place of them. The crowd hit him with an ax, shot him and dumped him in the Dvina river. He is the first Byzantine-rite saint to be formally canonized.

13

In the U. S. A., memorial of

St. Frances Xavier Cabrini
religious (1850–1917)

"The whole world is not wide enough for me," remarked the small woman. The travels of Frances Xavier Cabrini covered the United States from New Jersey to Seattle, from Chicago to New Orleans.

Frances was the youngest child in a large family in Italy. Her dream from early childhood was to spread the faith in China, as her patron saint Francis Xavier had done (December 3). After training to be a schoolteacher, she applied to join a religious order but was refused. After working with orphans for a few years, Frances decided to start the first order of missionary sisters. Soon an abandoned friary became the new home of the Missionary Sisters of the Sacred Heart.

Seven women who had joined Frances in service at the orphanage became the first members of the order. Their special work was teaching young girls anywhere education was needed. In a few years so many women had come to join the order that the friary became severely overcrowded. Like Frances, many of these women had been refused by other religious communities. New convents were begun in Milan and Rome.

To her surprise, Frances began to receive encouragement to look west instead of east for her missionary work. Of the 50,000 Italians newly arrived in New York, many had never had any religious education and most didn't go to Mass. Their lives were spent in crowded tenement neighborhoods. Archbishop Corrigan of New York City sent Frances a formal invitation to begin her missionary work there.

When Frances and her sisters got to New York, the archbishop's plans for them had fallen through. He wanted them to return on the next boat, but Frances was determined to stay. Soon she had earned a reputation as a shrewd bargainer in her handling of money. Always she trusted that God would provide, and she was right.

By the time Frances died, she had begun 67 badly needed schools, orphanages and hospitals. These were located in the United States, Central and South America, Italy, France and England. In all, Frances crossed the ocean 30 times. After she died, her sisters fulfilled her dream and did missionary work in China.

Mother Cabrini, as Frances came to be called, became the first American citizen to be canonized. She is a patron saint of immigrants.

November

15

Optional memorial of
St. Albert the Great
bishop, religious, doctor of the church
(1206 – 1280)

Women and men training to be scientists have their own patron. His name is Albert the Great. He lived at the time when the first universities came into being. He studied every field of knowledge that was taught in those schools.

Albert was born in his family's castle on the Danube river in Germany. After studying at a university, he decided to join the Dominican Order.

Albert soon had a reputation as a great teacher at the University of Paris and at other schools. One of his students was a young Dominican named Thomas Aquinas (January 28), who was brilliant but also very shy. Albert saw his greatness and encouraged him.

Besides teaching, Albert wrote 38 large volumes (not counting his Bible studies and sermons). He studied logic, mathematics, ethics and astronomy. He did studies of plants and animals. In the field of geography, he was the first to study the mountain ranges of Europe. Many people of his time feared that study would destroy Christianity. Albert had no such fear. His faith and hard work paved the way for a new age of scientific exploration.

Albert believed that we must try to understand God so that we can grow in love for God. His work became the foundation of important writings by his pupil Thomas. But Albert also served the people of God in other ways. He became a bishop, and he worked for reconciliation between the Greek and Roman churches.

Albert the Great is sometimes called by the Latin translation of his name, Albertus Magnus.

16

Optional memorial of
St. Margaret of Scotland
married woman, queen (c. 1046 – 1093)

Margaret of Scotland was a member of the English royal family, who came to Scotland when England was conquered by the Norman French. Her family lived in exile for most of Margaret's early life. Uncertainty about her future and even her safety had taught her a humility that was unusual in royalty. She placed her trust in God and treated everyone with great courtesy.

Malcolm, the king of Scotland, fell in love with Margaret, and she agreed to marry him. The new queen encouraged her husband to rebuild ruined churches and monasteries and provide new ones. She imported builders and stone masons to bring beauty to a country where worship spaces had always been bare and cold. The royal couple prayed together, and during Advent and Lent they filled their dining hall with 300 poor people each evening. Malcolm would serve those on one side, Margaret those on the other.

Margaret and Malcolm had eight children. Among them were three future kings of Scotland and a future queen of England. Margaret saw to their religious education herself and encouraged them to love and care for the poor.

Margaret made charity fashionable. When out riding, she would give away her shoes and cloaks to the poor. Then the knights accompanying her would compete among themselves to be first to give away their cloaks.

The poor of the nation loved Margaret and clustered around her whenever she appeared. Near the town of Dundermline still sits a rock called St. Margaret's Stone. It was said that she sat there while hearing the cases of poor people treated unjustly by the courts.

Because of the affection that Margaret had for her family and the entire kingdom, she is one of the patron saints of Scotland.

Optional memorial of
St. Gertrude the Great
religious (c. 1256 – 1302)

We know nothing of Gertrude's parents. However, they must have realized what a gifted child she was because when she was only five years old they brought her to the Benedictine convent at Helfta to have her educated. She proved to be an excellent student. She became a member of the Benedictine order and probably never left the convent for the rest of her life.

A woman named Mechthild took Gertrude under her wing. In time, the two women worked together as writers. By the age of 26 Gertrude was taken seriously as a scholar. She thought this would be her life's work until one day in prayer she experienced the presence of Christ as she never had before. For the first time Jesus became real to her as a person and a friend. She later said it was as though Jesus picked her up and lifted her over a wide hedge of thorns, placing her close by his side.

From then on Gertrude allowed the Lord Jesus to make his home in her. She abandoned all her earlier studies to focus on scripture and theology.

Gertrude lived only to the age of 45. In the later years of her life she was ill, but she continued to be blessed with deep experiences of Jesus' love. Her most famous work is called *The Herald of God's Loving-Kindness*. Her visions gave spiritual directors new images that helped them to explain the Trinity and the love of God.

17

Memorial of
St. Elizabeth of Hungary
married woman, religious (1207 – 1231)

For political reasons, the marriage of Elizabeth of Hungary was arranged shortly after she was born. The future husband chosen for her was Louis, a German prince. When she was four years old she was taken to live in Wartburg Castle to be raised by Louis's family. Some of them didn't care for her because she was so concerned about others and so pious. They tried to talk Louis into sending her back to Hungary, but he refused.

By the time they were married, Louis had become the ruler of three German provinces. He was proud of Elizabeth's kindness to the poor and sick, and he understood when she gave away all her rich clothing and jewels. Once there was a terrible famine while Louis was away. When he returned, members of the court complained that Elizabeth had given away the family's store of corn to feed 900 people a day. Louis made it clear that he thought she had done the right thing.

Elizabeth treated poor people with respect. If they were capable of working she found ways for them to earn their bread. She was godmother to many children of people she had helped. She encouraged them to keep a Christian home.

Louis died in an epidemic. Elizabeth, who had just given birth to their fourth child, was overcome with grief. Those who opposed her took this opportunity to seize control and have her driven out of the castle. For awhile, she and her children were very poor.

Later, after providing for her children's future, she built a little hospice. There, in the spirit of St. Francis (October 4), she cared for the sick, the poor and the elderly. In her spare time she fished to earn money for them. She died before reaching the age of 24. She was buried in the Church of St. Elizabeth, built in Marburg to honor her memory.

Optional memorial of

The Dedication of the Basilicas of the Apostles Peter and Paul in Rome

Christians rejoice on the "birthdays" of their parish church and the cathedral of their diocese. The birthday celebration of a church is held every year on the date when its dedication was held.

The basilica of St. Peter and that of St. Paul were built over the spots where these great saints were martyred by the Roman emperor Nero. The emperor Constantine, shortly after his conversion to Christianity, is said to have dug the first 12 baskets of earth for the foundation of the earliest church of St. Peter. Since then both churches have been rebuilt. St. Peter's was first dedicated in the year 324, and St. Paul's in 390.

St. Peter's has always been considered a destination for pilgrims who travel to Rome from all over the world. It is visited especially on the great feasts when the church celebrates its mission to the world, such as Epiphany and Pentecost.

Optional memorial of

St. Rose Philippine Duchesne
religious, missionary (1769–1852)

Native Americans who knew Rose Philippine Duchesne called her "the woman who prays always." In prayer as in everything else, she was a person of great determination.

Rose was born in Grenoble in France where her parents were prosperous merchants. As a young woman, she joined an order of sisters. Shortly afterward, the French Revolution began, and all convents and monasteries were closed. Rose went home to her parents, where she spent her time teaching neglected children and caring for the sick and the dying. She treated them all as if they were Christ.

When the war was over, Rose and a small group of nuns from her old convent joined a new religious order, the Society of the Sacred Heart. This brought her a spiritual director and lifelong friend, Mother Madeleine Sophie Barat, who herself was canonized after her death.

At the age of 49 Rose was sent to the United States with five other sisters. They had been invited to assist the archbishop of St. Louis with religious instruction in that huge diocese.

In the village of St. Charles, Missouri, Rose founded a convent in a small log cabin and began a free school for girls. During the next few years, as she founded schools in Mississippi and Louisiana, she and her sisters suffered all kinds of hardships, from forest fires and epidemics to hunger and a lack of fuel. In Rose's work with settlers, she fought prejudice against African Americans.

When she was 71 years old, Rose went with those who opened a mission for Potawatomi Indians at Sugar Creek, Kansas. She prayed while the other sisters taught. It was said that children tiptoed into church and sprinkled little slips of paper on the back of her habit as a prank. Hours later the paper was undisturbed because she hadn't moved from the spot. After only a year at the mission, she became ill. She died at St. Charles at the age of 83.

Rose Philippine Duchesne is one of the newest saints on the calendar. She was canonized — named as a saint by the church — in 1988.

Byzantine calendar
St. Obadiah
prophet (c. fifth century BCE)

Sometime after the Jews returned to Jerusalem after their exile in Babylon, the prophet Obadiah spoke. We know nothing about Obadiah's life. The book that bears this prophet's name is the shortest book in the Hebrew scriptures; it is only 21 verses long. In it the prophet describes the day of the Lord, when God's judgment will fall on all pagan nations.

We remember Obadiah at a time of year when the church looks forward to the day of judgment. The prophet tells us, "As you have done, it shall be done to you. Your deeds shall return on your own head." Obadiah's desire for revenge may seem mean-spirited, but it comes from a deep concern for the people of Israel and a sense of confidence in God's justice.

Memorial of
The Presentation
of the Virgin Mary

Many celebrations honoring Mary began in the Eastern church in the early centuries of Christianity. A church in Jerusalem was dedicated to Mary on this day in the year 543. In the fifteenth century the feast of the Presentation of the Virgin Mary was brought to the West.

That title came from an ancient legend that Mary's parents, Ann and Joachim (July 26), had offered her to God when she was three years old. They brought her to the Temple to consecrate her to God's service.

For Christians in the East, this day is an important holiday, and it is called the "Entrance of the Mother of God into the Temple." Mary herself is called God's temple, the place where God came to live. The feast turns our thoughts to Advent. When Christ comes in glory, all of us will be God's temple.

Memorial of
St. Cecilia
martyr (second or third century)

Cecilia probably was martyred sometime during the third century. The earliest information about her, a writing from the late fourth century, refers to a church that was named after her. The church had been Cecilia's home, so she probably was a person of wealth.

Later legends portray Cecilia as a young woman of a noble Christian family in Rome. Against her wishes she was given in marriage to a young pagan named Valerius, who later became a Christian. Valerius and his brother were arrested while burying martyrs, and then they, too, were martyred. Cecilia buried them but was caught. Because she was a noble, the authorities put her under house arrest instead of throwing her into prison. An executioner came to her home and struck her with a sword.

It was said that on her wedding day, while the musicians played, she "sang in her heart to Christ" in prayer. Perhaps this is why for centuries she has been considered the patron saint of musicians. When the Academy of Music was founded in Rome in the sixteenth century, it was named for her. To this day, many choirs and music societies bear St. Cecilia's name. Her remembrance day has become a celebration of music and song.

Optional memorial of
St. Clement I
pope, martyr (died c. 101)

Clement served the people of God as pope during the last decade of the first century. He probably died around the year 101, but the details of his life are no longer clear. A letter Clement wrote that has been preserved shows him as the shepherd of the church. It was addressed to the Christian community at Corinth in Greece.

At the time the Corinthian community was divided. Clement urged everyone involved to practice kindness and peace. He told them, "Without charity nothing is pleasing to God."

In the ninth century, Clement's body was brought to Rome by the missionary saints Cyril and Methodius (February 14). There it was laid to rest in a church that had already been known for hundreds of years as San Clemente (St. Clement).

St. Clement's Day, like All Saints and Martinmas and several other feast days at this time of year, was a time to welcome the winter. Someone would dress up in a long beard and get dubbed "Old Clem." Then he or she would go with others from house to house tapping on doors and windows. This was called "clemencing." They begged as they sang, "Clemany, Clemany, Clemany mine! A good red apple and a pint of wine! Some of your mutton and some of your veal, and if it is good, pray give us a deal!"

Optional memorial of
St. Columban
abbot, missionary (c. 540 – 615)

Pagan tribes had destroyed the Roman Empire. In the process they had also set Christianity in Europe on its ear. After the invasions, with social structures a mess, people had to make due on their own. Roads were in ruin. There were no markets, no health care, no churches, no police. People lived in fear of bandits and burglars. Surprisingly, help would come from distant outposts of the former empire, from places such as Ireland.

Columban (sometimes called Columbanus) was the most famous of a group of Irish missionary monks who helped to renew the Christian faith in Europe. Columban was born in West Leinster in Ireland. He became a monk at Bangor (on the east coast of Ireland, near Belfast). Bangor was the most famous school in Ireland. He stayed in that safe, quiet place for 20 years or more.

At about age 45 Columban was sent with a group of 12 monks to renew the Christian faith in Gaul (now France). They began at a ruined Roman fort called Annegray. Nobles and peasants alike flocked to join them, and within a very short time Columban had founded two more monasteries nearby.

Columban, strict and not always tactful, spoke out against the immoral life of Theodoric, king of Burgundy. For his boldness he earned the hatred of Theodoric and of the local bishops who had never spoken up against the wrongs. Soon Columban and the other Irish monks in the area were deported — they were ordered to go back where they came from.

Columban escaped across the Alps to northern Italy with his only possession, a copy of the gospels in a leather case that hung from his shoulders. A few year later, he died at Bobbio in Italy, where he was helping people build a church.

The monasteries founded by Columban and his companions led to the founding of other monasteries all over Europe. These places became havens of learning and prayer. The monastery at Bobbio developed one of the finest libraries of the Middle Ages.

Optional memorial of

Bl. Miguel Agustín Pro
presbyter, religious, martyr (1891 – 1927)

The father of Miguel Pro was a mining engineer in the poor mining town of Concepción del Oro in Mexico. The miners worked hard in dangerous conditions. Most of the other workers in Mexico were also oppressed. Widespread anger led to revolution, which broke out when Miguel was entering the seminary.

The revolutionaries directed much of their anger at the church in Mexico, because it had sided with the rich. Miguel's seminary was closed for safety's sake. Its students left in disguise. Miguel, who loved disguises, was dressed as a peasant and pretended to be the servant of some of his classmates. He continued his studies in Spain. Later he taught at a boys' boarding school in Nicaragua, where the students enjoyed his sense of humor, his love of sports and his kindness to their parents.

Meanwhile, things continued to grow worse in Mexico, where all religion had been outlawed. Miguel was sent to Belgium, where he studied ways to bring the gospel to working people and the poor. He was ordained a priest but soon became very ill, so his superiors sent him home to Mexico.

Soon after he arrived there, the government ordered that all priests be arrested and tried. But he was unknown as a priest, so for the next year he worked hard to serve people. Riding everywhere on his bike, he baptized, witnessed marriages, and prayed with the dying. He also distributed food to the poor, arranged places for homeless people to live, and cared for abandoned children. Totally committed to working people, he ministered to truck drivers, plumbers and office workers. During this time his life was in constant danger.

When a bomb was thrown at the car of a government official, Miguel and his two brothers were arrested and shot, even though it was clear to the authorities that they had not committed the crime.

Miguel Agustín Pro has been given the title "Blessed." This means he is close to being declared a saint.

Memorial of

St. Andrew Dung-Lac and companions
Andrew Dung-Lac, presbyter, martyr (1785 – 1839), and his companions, martyrs (died 1820)

Christianity was first brought to Vietnam over 350 years ago by a French Jesuit priest. Since that time, a great number of Christians have died for the sake of the faith in that country. The martyrs we honor today are a representative group of more than 100 in number. They include French, Spanish and Vietnamese Catholics.

Andrew Dung-Lac was Vietnamese. His parents were Buddhist, but they allowed him to be brought up in the Catholic faith. Later he became a catechist. Then, when he was nearly 40 years old, he was ordained a priest.

Andrew worked in several parishes. One day he was arrested. Members of his parish collected funds to ransom him from jail. After that he changed his name from Dung to Lac for safety's sake, and he moved to a new area to work. In 1839 an edict was issued that was designed to root out all Christians. The law demanded that all citizens take part in ancestor worship and the building of temples.

Soon after that Andrew was captured with another Vietnamese priest, Peter Thi. They were beheaded in Hanoi. They were canonized, with the other martyrs remembered today, in 1988.

29

Anniversary of the death of
Dorothy Day
(1897–1980)

As a child, Dorothy Day didn't have the advantage of a religious education. Her parents weren't churchgoers. Her father was a newspaper writer who changed jobs frequently, so the family moved often. By the time she was 16 Dorothy had decided that there was no God. Still, she wanted to use her writing talent to work for justice and somehow to improve the world. So after two years of college she moved to Greenwich Village in New York City, where many other young artists and writers had gathered.

Dorothy's new friends fought for women's rights and protested the draft. Some of them were communists. They believed in working for change, and they scorned religion. Like many of her friends, Dorothy had love affairs. She met a man with whom she wanted to spend the rest of her life, and she became pregnant.

The experience of carrying a new life within her called forth in Dorothy a deep new faith in a loving God. When she decided to become a Catholic and to raise her child as one, the father of her child broke off the relationship. This was

very painful for her, but she was consoled by prayer and by the birth of Tamar, her daughter.

These were the years of the Great Depression, a time of hardship for many people. Dorothy had become a noted writer and began to report on the sufferings of the poor for Catholic magazines such as *Commonweal.* In 1932, covering a hunger march in Washington, she prayed in tears that she might find some way "to change conditions, not just report them."

When she got back home to New York, it seemed that her prayer had been answered in an unusual way. A stranger named Peter Maurin was waiting to see her. He suggested that she start a newspaper that combined her old ideals of a just society with her Catholic faith. Thus was born *The Catholic Worker.* It sold on the streets of New York for one cent so that everyone could afford it.

People who felt inspired by the paper began stopping by to volunteer their help. Hungry people would join the staff for soup and bread or a cup of coffee. With the only money she had, Dorothy rented an apartment to house homeless people. It became the first of many Catholic Worker Houses of Hospitality. In time, Catholic Worker Houses would also be set up in Boston, Detroit, Chicago, St. Louis, Los Angeles and other cities.

Dorothy and the other staff members lived in voluntary poverty. They depended on God to meet their financial needs. Dorothy herself dressed in the used clothing that people donated to the house.

Dorothy was a pacifist—she believed that war was not compatible with the message of Jesus. She based this belief on her lifelong study of the gospels, the lives of the saints and the great teachers of the church.

In the 1950s and 1960s she was repeatedly arrested for refusing to go into a shelter during New York City's annual air raid drill. These drills were supposed to show people how to protect themselves in the event of nuclear attack, but Dorothy believed their real purpose was to give the American people a false sense of safety. Each year, more and more people realized that shelters could not protect them from nuclear warfare. Eventually New York City canceled the drills.

Because of her remarkable spirit, Dorothy Day has come to be thought of by many as a twentieth-century prophet.

Feast of
St. Andrew
apostle (first century)

Andrew lived a quiet and simple life as a fisherman. He worked with his brother Simon in the town of Bethsaida in Galilee. One day Jesus walked by as they cast their nets and invited them to become fishers of people. Soon afterward Jesus worked a miracle in Andrew and Simon's house, healing Simon's mother-in-law of a fever. (All this is told in the first chapter of the Gospel of Mark.)

In the gospels, Andrew is often shown bringing others to Jesus. It was Andrew who brought forward the boy with the five loaves and two fishes when food was needed for the crowd. In the Gospel of John, Andrew tells his brother Simon, "We have found the Messiah." After Jesus marched triumphantly into Jerusalem, Andrew helped some Greek men who wanted to speak with Jesus.

After the descent of the Holy Spirit, Andrew brought others to Christ in a new way. He became a missionary. To this day, several countries in far-flung parts of the world claim to have been visited by Andrew. However, it isn't known for sure where he preached or where he died.

Tradition says that Andrew was crucified on an X-shaped cross, called a "saltire cross." Because of legends that he preached in Scotland, that country put his cross on its flag. Thistle flowers are worn by the Scots today, the way shamrocks are worn by the Irish on St. Patrick's Day (March 17) and leeks are worn by the Welsh on St. David's Day (March 1). Andrew is a patron saint not only of Scotland but of Greece and Russia as well.

December

The word for the last month of the year means, in Latin, "tenth month." The ancient calendar of the Romans began in March, which made December the tenth month.

In ancient times, people of northern Europe stopped counting the days during winter. There wasn't any farm work to do, so there wasn't any reason to keep track of time. They called this free time "Yule." This word comes from the same root word as the word "wheel." The days of Yule connected the old year to the new.

1

Byzantine calendar
St. Nahum
prophet (seventh century BCE)

Assyria was a rich and proud nation that had oppressed the Jews and other peoples with great cruelty. But then the tables were turned. Nineveh, Assyria's capital city, was about to be overrun by the armies of the Medes and the Babylonians.

At just this time the prophet Nahum wrote a poem reflecting on God's justice and the fall of the

December

Assyrian Empire. The poem contains everything we know about this prophet. Nahum expressed feelings of triumph that the hated enemy would be destroyed. This attitude was probably common at that moment among all of Assyria's enemies.

Nahum's prophecy shows both anger and faith. The long period of oppression had been a great trial to the faith of the Jews. The prophet believed that the fall of Nineveh would prove that God governs history and punishes unjust acts.

Anniversary of the day
Rosa Parks kept her bus seat
(1955)

Montgomery, Alabama, was called "the cradle of the Confederacy." On its courthouse steps in 1861 Jefferson Davis was sworn in as president of the southern states. These states refused to give up slavery. The Civil War was fought to bring them back into the United States.

Montgomery was the site of another historic refusal. In 1955 Rosa Parks refused to give up her seat to a white man on a segregated bus. Segregation was a system of unjust laws and practices. For example, black citizens were forced to use only the rear seats of a bus. Rosa's courage marked a turning point in the struggle for equal rights for all Americans.

Rosa came to Montgomery as a little girl in the early 1900s. She had some fearful moments in her early life. Groups of white men called the Ku Klux Klan tormented black families. Dressed in white sheets to hide their faces, the Klansmen set fire to houses and barns. Sometimes they even dragged people from their homes and killed them. The white men did this to terrify the black people: When people are afraid, they are less likely to ask for justice and fair treatment.

When Rosa grew up, she did volunteer work for a group that defended the rights of black people. On the day she refused to give up her bus seat, she was arrested and fined. The black citizens of Montgomery were outraged. They decided not to use the buses again until black and white riders were treated as equals. They were led by a young minister, Martin Luther King, Jr. (page 26). After a year of protests, the unjust rules of the bus system were changed.

This victory helped to build the civil rights movement all over the United States. But Rosa Parks and her husband Raymond both lost their jobs because of her stand. They moved to Detroit, Michigan. There she continued to work for civil rights, for the rights of women and for the poor of the city.

Rosa Parks's favorite activity has been speaking with schoolchildren about freedom and civil rights. In 1987 she won a $10,000 award for her work. She used the money to begin the Rosa and Raymond Parks Institute for Self-Development. The Institute encourages young people to use their talents to work for change.

2

Byzantine calendar
St. Habakkuk
prophet (late sixth century BCE)

Why does God allow evil people to prosper? This question has been asked for centuries by those suffering unjust treatment. One person asked this question in a way that was especially stirring: the Jewish prophet Habakkuk.

Habakkuk wrote at a time when the Jews were being oppressed by the Babylonians. Nothing is known about Habakkuk except what can be guessed from the writing itself. Although the Book of Habakkuk is only 56 verses long, we can tell that this prophet was deeply concerned about the sufferings of others.

Habakkuk begins the prophecy by asking God why injustice exists. God answers that faith provides enough security for a person of virtue. God also reminds Habakkuk that justice will triumph in the end. During the course of this conversation Habakkuk seems to journey from doubt to faith. The book closes with the prophet's song of victory and praise.

Anniversary of the deaths of
Maura Clarke, Ita Ford, Dorothy Kazel and Jean Donovan
(died 1980)

El Salvador is a tiny country in Central America. For many years the poor of that country have been greatly oppressed. Many who tried to oppose the rich and the government have been killed.

In late 1980, the residents of the seacoast town of La Libertad all knew the white Toyota van driven around the countryside by Ursuline Sister Dorothy Kazel and Maryknoll lay volunteer Jean Donovan. Dorothy and Jean were known as the "Rescue Squad" because they often helped Salvadoran refugees move to places of safety.

On December 2, Jean and Dorothy drove to the airport to pick up Maryknoll Sisters Maura Clarke and Ita Ford, who were returning from a meeting in Nicaragua. Maura and Ita were also religious sisters on a mission to El Salvador from their homes in the United States.

After they left the airport, none of the four were seen alive again. The white van was found the next morning, a stripped and burned-out shell. Later the bodies of the women were found. They had been shot to death.

Until a few months before they died, the four women felt safe because they were citizens of the United States. More recently they realized that their lives were now in danger. Their dear friend Archbishop Oscar Romero (March 24) had been shot while celebrating the eucharist. Other friends had also been killed or threatened.

However, the four women also knew that poor people depended on them. So they delivered food, they led Bible study and health classes, and they assisted those searching for loved ones who had been arrested by the police. Knowing how much they were needed, the four chose to stay and work, whatever the cost. All were known for their joyful spirit in the grim situation.

Memorial of
St. Francis Xavier
presbyter, religious, missionary (1506–1552)

Francis Xavier was born in a castle in Spain. He experienced a radical change in life which came about when he was a student at the University of Paris. It was there that he met another student named Ignatius of Loyola (July 31).

At first, Francis thought that Ignatius was a strange person. Ignatius was an ex-soldier. He challenged those around him to take Christianity more seriously than they ever had before. In time he invited Francis and five other young men to form a new religious order, the Society of Jesus (also called the Jesuits).

Shortly after Francis was ordained a priest, he began his life's work of bringing the gospel to the Far East. Even though he often got seasick and had trouble learning foreign languages, he eventually taught and baptized people in India, Ceylon, the Philippines and Japan.

December

Francis refused any comforts that weren't available to the people he served. Often he slept on the ground and lived on rice and water. Despite his noble birth, he never allowed himself to be waited on by servants. Wherever he went, he sang to the children and cared for the sick. He spread the gospel by dealing with people in a gentle and courteous way.

For years Francis dreamed of working in China. At age 46 he finally boarded a ship sailing to the city of Canton. But he caught a fever, and the frightened sailors left him on an island near the mainland. There he died.

St. Zephaniah
prophet (seventh century BCE)

The prophet Zephaniah lived at a time when many people had become casual about the way they worshiped God. They thought that it wouldn't matter if they loosened up on their Jewish way of life. And so they ignored many of God's laws and began to live no differently than the pagans.

Zephaniah called the people of Judah to obedience and humility. King Josiah responded to Zephaniah by beginning religious reforms. The altars to the sun and moon were taken down. The people returned to the worship of God alone.

The book that bears Zephaniah's name is short. Throughout, the prophet speaks of "the day of the Lord," when all nations will be judged. On this day of doom, God will punish those who oppress others. But God will gather the faithful and there will be a great homecoming. The guests of honor will be the misfits and outcasts, the handicapped and the suffering.

During Advent we also wait for the day of the Lord. We live our lives out of tune with the rest of the world. And we prepare for a homecoming, when all God's people will live fairly and in peace.

4

Optional memorial of
St. John Damascene
presbyter, doctor of the church (c. 676 – c. 749)

An icon is a painted or mosaic picture on a flat surface. Magnificent icons of Jesus, the saints and scenes from the Bible have existed since the early days of Christianity. These images fill Eastern Christian churches and homes to this day. But in the time of John Damascene, some people believed that venerating icons was the same as worshiping idols. The clear thinking and teaching of John Damascene helped to lay their mistaken ideas to rest.

John is called "Damascene" because he was born in Damascus. The city was ruled by Muslims. The powerful post of treasurer to the caliph was held by John's father, a Christian. He spoke at the caliph's court for the other Christians of the city. John inherited this position. Like his father, he was respected by everyone because he was humble and kind. He was a monk at the monastery of St. Sabas, near Jerusalem. He lived quietly, writing hymns and reflections. When the emperor issued an order that all sacred images be destroyed, John wrote brilliant essays explaining that sacred images were not the same as idols. Christians don't *worship* icons. Instead, he explained, looking at an icon helps them to enter into the mystery it shows.

John wrote beautiful poetry and songs. We still sing the English versions of some of John's songs. He wrote the beautiful hymn "Let all mortal flesh keep silence" and the Easter carol "Come, you faithful, raise the strain."

Roman martyrology

St. Barbara

martyr (date unknown)

Legends about Barbara say that she was a beautiful and bright young pagan woman who lived in the time of the Roman emperor Maximilian. Her father, who did not want her to marry, shut her up in a tower. She used her time of imprisonment to read works of philosophy, and she eventually decided there must be only one true God.

In time Barbara was baptized by a Christian who disguised himself as her doctor to gain entrance to the tower. Her father, when he found out about this, was furious and had her killed.

These stories about Barbara became popular centuries later when the fatal disease called the black death was an epidemic, killing more than a quarter of the people of Europe. Those who survived were afraid and depressed. They thought that perhaps the end of the world had come. They turned to prayer and devotions.

Barbara is one of a group of favored saints called the Fourteen Holy Helpers. So are St. Blase (February 3) and St. George (April 23). These saints were invoked in times of illness and other troubles. Barbara was considered the patron of a happy death.

Optional memorial of

St. Nicholas

bishop (died c. 350)

Nicholas may be the most popular saint of all time. Thousands of churches are named after him. He seems to be portrayed by artists more than any other saint, with the exception of Mary. There are hundreds of delightful legends about him. However, historians know almost nothing for sure about his life.

Nicholas was the bishop of the city of Myra in Asia Minor, in what is now the nation of Turkey. Centuries after he died, his bones were brought to the city of Bari in Italy. People came to his tomb to pray, and many were healed of their illnesses.

According to a legend, when Nicholas was a baby and his parents brought him to church to be baptized, he jumped eagerly into the water. When he grew up and was named bishop, he became known as the "wonderworker." He could heal the sick and calm storms.

A story is told about a man who was so poor that he could no longer buy food for his family. He was going to sell his daughters into slavery so they wouldn't starve. Bishop Nicholas found out about this. So at night he tossed three bags of gold into their house through a window.

In many places, families are visited today by someone dressed up like St. Nicholas. His visit is usually scary. He is accompanied by a devil, who snorts and groans and who rattles chains. Bishop Nicholas tells each person in the family about the things they do wrong, and he encourages them to do better in the coming year. When he leaves, there is a feast. Tangerines are eaten as reminders of the gold he gave to help the poor women. Candy canes are reminders of his crosier, the shepherd's staff that bishops carry.

The name Santa Claus means St. Nicholas. In the 1800s, New York department stores began to hire men to dress up as St. Nicholas so that more shoppers would come in to buy Christmas presents. The writer Thomas Nast drew pictures of St. Nicholas, but he mixed up legends about the saint with myths about the Norse god Thor. That's why Santa Claus is shown traveling by reindeer and living with elves at the North Pole.

December

7

Memorial of
St. Ambrose
bishop, doctor of the church (c. 339–397)

Feisty little Ambrose, the bishop of Milan in Italy, confronted emperors of Rome on a regular basis. His early years prepared him for this task because his father was the governor of Britain, Spain and Gaul. Ambrose studied in Rome, then joined the emperor's service. Soon Ambrose himself was appointed governor of northern Italy, and he moved to Milan.

When people gathered there to select a new bishop, an argument broke out. Ambrose, who was never shy, stepped in to calm the dispute. To his shock, he was promptly chosen bishop himself. In those days, many people were not baptized until they were settled in life. So although Ambrose had received Christian training, he had never been baptized. Then, within a week, he was baptized, ordained, and made bishop! He immediately found the finest teacher available and made an intense study of scripture and theology in the midst of his busy life.

Ambrose held a position of influence as bishop of Milan. He used his power to speak boldly for justice. He convinced the warrior Maximus not to invade Italy. He forced Emperor Theodosius to do public penance for allowing soldiers to kill a number of innocent citizens. But the most important people in Ambrose's life were the people of his diocese. They admired and trusted him.

When he was pressed by the mother of Emperor Valentinian to abandon two churches, Ambrose led a protest. His people supported his bold stand and for an entire week they refused to leave the cathedral. To keep them occupied, Ambrose taught them new hymns he had written.

8

Solemnity of
The Immaculate Conception of the Virgin Mary

Christians remember the conception of Christ on the solemnity of the Annunciation of the Lord (March 25). Because John the Baptist prepared the way for Christ, Eastern Christians celebrate his conception on September 23. Today's solemnity of the conception of Mary falls nine months before the celebration of her birth, on September 8.

Mary's conception day became a feast in the seventh century. The church teaches that Mary was free from sin from the moment she was conceived. This special grace prepared her to be the mother of God. Mary did not earn this freedom in any way. It was simply a gift bestowed by God. The medieval scholar Duns Scotus explained that "no one owes more to Christ than Mary the immaculate one."

9

In the U. S. A., optional memorial of
Bl. Juan Diego
hermit (1474–1548)

Juan Diego was an Aztec Indian who lived in Mexico when the country was conquered by the Spanish. With his wife and uncle, he had been among the first Aztecs baptized by the missionaries. His Aztec name was Cuatitlatoatzin (kwah-TEE-tlah-toe-ah-tzeen) which means Singing Eagle.

He lived in a village near what is now Mexico City. His one-room hut had a dirt floor and a roof woven of cornstalks. He was among the poorest people in his village. He lived on the corn and beans he grew himself, and he made his own sandals from deerskin.

One day in December, 1531, Juan Diego encountered a magnificent young woman, dressed as an Aztec princess. She asked him to give a message to the bishop. She wanted a church built where she stood. She wanted to be a source of consolation for the people.

In Mexico City where the bishop lived, the bishop's servants taunted Juan, and the bishop put him off. Juan returned to the spot where he had first seen the lady. He was convinced that he had failed her. Tenderly she assured him that he was the best person for this task. The next day, Juan returned to the bishop's house. This time the bishop asked Juan to obtain some kind of sign from the woman.

In the morning, the woman guided Juan to a patch of brilliant roses growing in the winter cold on the bleak hill where they spoke. He gathered them into his cloak and took them to show the bishop. When Juan unfurled his cloak in the bishop's presence, they saw that it had been imprinted with the woman's image.

A chapel was built for the image and people streamed to see it. It is called the image of Our Lady of Guadalupe, whose feast is December 12 Juan became the caretaker of the chapel. He spent his time in meditation and prayer. He died at the age of 74 and was buried in the chapel, along with his beloved wife and uncle. His life had been a sign of good news: God calls the poor to preach the gospel to others.

10

International Human Rights Day

In 1945, when the Second World War ended, world leaders realized that new and better ways of solving disputes among nations must be found. They created the United Nations to provide a forum where countries can debate peacefully, rather than taking up arms to settle grievances. The United Nations works for peace. It works against hunger, disease and poverty.

In 1948, after much hard work, the United Nations produced a document called the Universal Declaration of Human Rights. Delegates from member nations all over the world hammered out their definition of 30 rights that all human beings need to live a decent life.

The Declaration says that everyone on the planet, regardless of race, sex, language or religion, has a right to certain basic freedoms. Among these freedoms are the right to life, health care, education and privacy. People also are entitled to freedom from imprisonment without trial. They have a right to leave and reenter their country. They have a right to seek protection in another country if they are persecuted in their own.

Each of those freedoms is being denied to some of the world's citizens even as we celebrate the Declaration today. The United Nations will continue working for these basic human rights. They will also work to get the Declaration into the hands of people everywhere. People need to know that they deserve these rights and that the United Nations has pledged to uphold them.

December

Anniversary of the death of

Thomas Merton
monk (1915–1968)

In the United States the 1960s were troubled times. Christians felt confused about how to behave and what to believe in a world of racism, riots, assassinations, and the bloodshed of the Vietnam War. But many found guidance flowing from an unlikely place: a monastery in Gethsemani, Kentucky, where Father Louis, better known as Thomas Merton, had been praying and writing for the previous 20 years. From this remote spot he challenged American Catholics to live as active, committed and prayerful Christians in a time of confusion.

Thomas Merton was born in France. Both his parents died by the time he was a teenager. Then he lived with various relatives or attended boarding schools.

Young Thomas was a bright student and he won entrance into Cambridge University in England. After one year he came to New York City, where he enrolled at Columbia University. Majoring in journalism, he met all sorts of people and heard their ideas. For a month or two he even joined the Communist Party, since it seemed to stand for values he believed in. But soon he found an idea that seemed even more radical to some of his friends: prayer.

Thomas had very little religious upbringing. Now he decided to become a Catholic. He taught college for a couple of years, worked with the poor in New York, and then entered the Trappist monastery at Gethsemani (near Louisville) in Kentucky.

Life at Gethsemani consisted of hard work, prayer several times a day, and study. Thomas was also encouraged to use his writing gifts. In 1948 a book of his was published. It was about his life and his search for God. *The Seven Storey Mountain* was a best seller. Many people began to find wisdom in his life story and in his later books on spirituality, liturgy and prayer.

Thomas said that a true Catholic is someone who listens to all points of view with reverence. He believed that Christians of different denominations need to converse with each other and that Christians need to talk with people of all religions. He spoke out against the dangers that would make global understanding less possible: the arms race, poverty, unjust governments.

At the age of 53 Thomas Merton went to Southeast Asia to learn and to teach about prayer with leaders of oriental religions. In Bangkok, Thailand, he was found electrocuted in his room. When his body was brought home to Gethsemani, the usual rules of the monastery were lifted so that his friends from many faiths and backgrounds could enter to witness his burial. His books continue to teach and to challenge readers everywhere.

11

Optional memorial of

St. Damasus I
pope (c. 305–384)

Pope Damasus was a talented man. He appeared at just the place and time where his gifts were most needed. He was born in Rome and remained its most devoted citizen all his life.

At the time of his birth, Christians were still being persecuted by the emperor Diocletian. As a child Damasus loved to hear stories about the courage of the martyrs. Soon the new emperor, Constantine, granted religious freedom to Christians. When Damasus became pope, he helped Christians adapt to this new, more peaceful age. He built several of Rome's most famous churches.

At his request Emperor Gratian removed the pagan altar from the Roman senate.

Damasus spoke strongly against false teachings that were confusing believers. But when those who had been misled by these teachings came back to the church, Damasus welcomed them.

Damasus decided that Latin would be the official language of the Western church. He ordered his secretary, Jerome (September 30), to provide a clear, new Latin translation of the Bible. This famous translation was called the Vulgate. It replaced many less accurate versions.

Damasus was pope for 24 years. During that time he helped to shape Rome and Christianity.

In the U. S. A., feast of
Nuestra Señora de Guadalupe
(Our Lady of Guadalupe)

Every year pilgrims stream to a great church near Mexico City. There, over the altar, is a simple tilma (a cloak) made from two pieces of cactus cloth. Though that kind of cloth seldom lasts 20 years, this tilma has survived intact for centuries.

In 1531, the tilma belonged to Juan Diego (December 9), an Aztec Indian. Juan had been baptized a Christian after the Spanish invaded Mexico. One December morning he was walking past an old shrine of the Aztec goddess of the corn harvest. The Spanish had smashed the shrine and renamed the place Guadalupe. There Juan saw a vision of Mary, the mother of God. She was dressed as an Aztec princess. She had olive skin and black hair like an Aztec. She was clothed in magnificent colors. Around her waist was a sash, which women wore when they were pregnant.

Mary spoke to Juan with affection. She gave him a message for the local bishop. Mary wanted the bishop to build a church where she stood. She promised to grant help to all who would call on her there.

When Juan Diego delivered the message, the bishop didn't believe him. Mary provided Juan with a sign to take to the bishop. She guided Juan to a spot where wild roses were blooming. He was amazed to see roses in winter.

Juan Diego gathered an armful of the flowers into his cloak and hurried off to show them to the bishop. But when he opened his tilma in the bishop's house, an even more amazing sign had been provided. Somehow the image of Mary, just as she looked when she appeared to Juan, filled the tilma.

Only 12 years before, the Spanish explorer Hernán Cortés had first made contact with the Aztecs. He and his soldiers were Christian, but the Aztecs didn't want to be like them. The Christians were brutal and greedy. They had brought great suffering to the native people and had shown particular cruelty to Aztec women.

The Mother of God brought a much brighter message, one of hope and compassion. Her appearance was a rebuke to the Spanish and a consolation to the poor. She brought new dignity to the Aztec people, especially to the women. In the seven years following her appearances, eight million Aztecs were baptized.

Since then many miracles have been credited to her. Peace treaties have been signed in the church built in her honor. She is the patron of Mexico. She is honored throughout the Americas and all over the world.

December

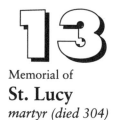

Memorial of
St. Lucy
martyr (died 304)

Lucy's name means light. Coming midway through Advent, her feast day guides our hope toward the coming of Christ our Light.

Lucy was a young woman of Syracuse in Sicily (an island off the southern coast of Italy). We know that she died a martyr during the persecutions by the Roman emperor Diocletian.

Legends that sprang up long after she died centered around ways she stood up to the violence in her world. One legend said that she was engaged to marry a young pagan. However, when she told him that she wanted to devote her life to the poor, he reported her to the government police. They arrested her and then tortured and killed her.

To this day Lucy is still considered the patron saint of Sicily, and especially the city of Syracuse. In another Italian city, Venice, the gondoliers consider her their patron. They sing a famous song in her honor, *Santa Lucia,* as they guide their boats through the city's canals.

Lucy is honored in northern countries, where at this time of year the nights are long and cold. Lucy the light-bearer is remembered there with "Lucy candles" and "Lucy fires."

In Sweden, on the morning of St. Lucy's Day, the eldest daughter in many families rises before dawn. Dressed in a white gown with a red sash and a crown of lighted candles, she leads the other children of the family. Younger girls carry candles and boys wear pointed caps studded with stars. They carry freshly-brewed coffee and sweet saffron breads baked in swirls, called "Lucy cats." As they serve breakfast in bed to their parents, the story of Lucy is retold. A beautiful Swedish carol is sung in the chilly, pale light of St. Lucy's morning: "Soon shall another morning dawn, an everlasting day, when Christ the Lord in glory comes, to chase the night away."

In Hungary children plant wheat seeds in small pots on this day. By Christmas the wheat has sprouted, and they can carry its green shoots to church to the manger of the Christ child. The wheat is a powerful sign of the promise of spring. It is "living straw."

Geminid meteor shower

During the long nights around the remembrance of St. Lucy, the sky is graced with a meteor shower. It is called the "Geminid" shower because the meteors seem to radiate from the constellation of Gemini, the Twins.

The best times to look for meteors are after sunset and before dawn. Early in the morning this month, the constellation of Gemini is in the northwest sky. If the sky is moonless and clear, it's possible to see 50 meteors an hour.

As the earth's orbit crosses the orbit of a comet, specks of dust left over from the comet hit the earth's atmosphere, where they quickly burn up. From earth this looks like shooting stars. The Geminid meteor shower is sometimes called St. Lucy's Lights.

14

Memorial of
St. John of the Cross
presbyter, doctor of the church (1542 – 1591)

John was born in the village of Fontiveros in Castile, Spain. His father died when he was young. His mother was poor. At about the age of 20 John became a Carmelite friar.

Most Carmelites of his time lived by a relaxed version of the original rule of their order. John wanted to live by the original rule, which was strict. He hoped that would draw him closer to God.

Teresa of Avila (October 15), who was also a Carmelite, had received permission to begin convents with a simple lifestyle like the one John had chosen for himself. Teresa asked John to become the spiritual director of the nuns at Avila, where she lived.

Despite John's gentle nature, he had made powerful enemies within the Carmelite Order. These friars thought he was rebellious. To teach him a lesson, they had him imprisoned in Toledo. His cell was tiny, hot and filthy. Light came in through one small slit high on the wall, so John had to stand on a stool in order to read his prayer book. During the nine months that he was held in prison, he wrote some of his greatest spiritual poetry.

"Where there is no love," he said, "it is for you to bring love." He thought of prayer as a tool to help us become more loving toward others. His books about prayer and spiritual direction are used by people all over the world. John also is considered to be one of the greatest poets of the Spanish language.

16

Las Posadas ("lodgings") begin

During these last and most intense days of Advent, many Mexican families observe the custom of *Las Posadas,* "lodgings." For the next nine days groups of neighbors and friends will gather each evening to remember Mary and Joseph's journey to Bethlehem.

Many other nationalities also observe the last nine days of Advent. These days, called in Latin a *novena,* remind us of the nine days when the disciples waited for the coming of the Holy Spirit on Pentecost. They also remind us of the nine months of pregnancy, when parents await the birth of a child.

During *Las Posadas,* groups of people wander through the neighborhood singing. They may be accompanied by a guitar, maracas, a harp or shepherd's pipes. Sometimes they carry small figures of Mary and Joseph, or perhaps a boy and girl are dressed as the pilgrim couple. Candles light the way. The procession stops at each home to ask for shelter. From within, a rude voice tells them to go away. They respond kindly that Mary is about to give birth to the king of heaven. Finally a door is flung open and everyone is welcomed in.

The nativity figures are placed on a small altar set up for the occasion. Traditional songs are sung and prayers said. *Las Posadas* helps everyone remember that Jesus came as a poor and humble child. Unless there is hospitality to all strangers, unless we open our doors to Christ, Christmas cannot come.

On Christmas Eve, the last night of *Las Posadas,* everyone will go together to Midnight Mass. Then the Christmas celebration begins. There will be parties and singing every day from Christmas until Epiphany.

December

Byzantine calendar

St. Haggai
prophet (sixth century BCE)

When the holy city of Jerusalem was destroyed, the Jewish people were taken from their homeland and brought to Babylon. All during this exile, the Jews yearned for their home. They remembered everything they loved about Israel, and they told its stories again and again.

Even after they were allowed to return, however, they felt sad and discouraged. The great Temple of Solomon lay in ruins, and harvests were poor. They did not prosper as they had hoped to.

Haggai was the first prophet to speak after their return. He understood how disheartened people felt. With another prophet, Zechariah (February 8), he rallied them. Haggai challenged the Jews to begin work on a new temple. He reminded them that their greatest need was to worship together. He hinted at a new kingdom to come. In the work of rebuilding the Temple, he seemed to say, they themselves would be rebuilt as a people.

17

Byzantine calendar

St. Daniel and the Three Youths, Ss. Hananiah, Mishael and Azariah
(date unknown)

You might say that the Book of Daniel was written in code. When it appeared almost 2200 years ago, the Jews needed something to rely on. Their nation and their faith seemed to be falling down around them. They weren't even allowed to gather for worship. How could they keep trusting God in times like these?

The king of Syria, Antiochus IV, had taken over the land. He was trying to force the Jews to abandon God. He killed many people, punished the high priests and misused the holy Temple.

To the police and spies of Antiochus, the Book of Daniel probably seemed to be only some strange stories from the Jews' past. But the people knew that the stories were a reminder of God's constant care for them, even in the worst of times. Just as God had helped their ancestors, so would God help them.

The stories in the Book of Daniel are set in the kingdom of Babylon during the time of the Jewish exile there hundreds of years earlier. They tell of the prophet Daniel and his three young friends, who were selected from among the Jewish exiles to serve in the court of the Babylonian kings. The three youths are known by their Babylonian names — Shadrach (Hananiah), Mesach (Mishael) and Abednego (Azariah) — but Daniel is known to us by his Hebrew name.

At court, Daniel and the three youths were ordered to eat food forbidden to Jews. (Antiochus had forced the high priests to do the same thing.) But Daniel and his friends resisted the rich food of the court; instead they thrived on vegetables and water.

Later, the three young men faced a more difficult test. After refusing to worship an idol of their king, they were thrown into a fiery furnace. But the three young men did not die. The flames burned only the ropes that tied their hands. They began to sing a song of praise to God, and suddenly an angel appeared in the middle of the fire. The angel made the flames as cool as dew.

The events retold in the Book of Daniel assured the Jews that Antiochus would not succeed in destroying them. And, in fact, he did not. The Jews regained their independence soon after the Book of Daniel appeared. This new freedom is celebrated by the Jews each year during the feast of Hanukkah (see page 197), which comes at this time of year.

The O Antiphons begin

See pages 4–6.

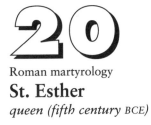

Roman martyrology

St. Esther

queen (fifth century BCE)

The Bible is not a book but a whole library — a collection of every kind of literature. The Book of Esther can be compared to a novel or short story.

Esther was the heroine's Persian name. Her Hebrew name was Hadassah, which means myrtle, a fragrant flower. In the story, God placed her in a position to save her people from destruction. She did her best, in spite of her fears. The Jewish festival of Purim (see page 198), celebrated in late winter, recalls the story of her courage.

Optional memorial of

St. Peter Canisius

presbyter, religious, doctor of the church
(1521–1597)

The town where Peter Canisius was born, Nijmegen, was then a German town. Peter's father was a town leader who thought his son should be a lawyer. Instead, Peter chose to become a priest of the Jesuit Order, newly founded at that time. He committed himself to a life of prayer, study, reflection and writing. However, he also spent a lot of time visiting the sick and people in prison.

People came in large numbers to hear Peter preach. He also founded colleges and seminaries.

He became known as the second apostle of Germany. (The first was Boniface, June 5.)

Peter's letters fill 8000 pages. He had many friends and wrote to people of every walk of life. Some of his letters were criticisms addressed to church leaders, but even here Peter was tactful.

One of Peter's greatest concerns was instructing people in their faith. During the course of his life he wrote three books called catechisms to fill this need. Even in the last years of his life, when he had been paralyzed by a stroke, he worked on a very simple catechism for children. Throughout his life he wrote many other works, and he encouraged others to write as well. For that reason he is considered one of the founders of the Catholic press.

Winter solstice

Today marks a turning point in the year. For people of the Northern Hemisphere, the winter solstice is the shortest day and longest night. From now on days will lengthen. For the ancient peoples of Europe, the winter solstice was one of the greatest feasts of the year.

Once the harvest was in, there was little farm work to do, and so there was plenty of time to relax and celebrate. Sometimes the festivities lasted for two months! Many northern Europeans called these days "Yule," from the word "wheel." They thought that the year was like a wheel. When the days started to get longer, it was as if someone had given the year a fresh turn.

At Yuletide there were special songs and dances, and hospitality. Circle dances called carols helped to celebrate the renewal of the circle of the year.

December

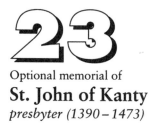

Optional memorial of
St. John of Kanty
presbyter (1390 – 1473)

John of Kanty dedicated his life to teaching. A professor for many years at the University of Kraków in Poland, he advised his students to "Fight false opinions, but let your weapons be patience, sweetness and love. Roughness is bad for your own soul and spoils the best cause."

John was a country boy born in the small town of Kanty in Poland. His parents sent him to study in Kraków, where he received his degree when he was only 19. He was ordained a priest and became a lecturer at the university.

John spent most of his life there teaching about the scriptures. But even as a distinguished professor, John was a friend of the poor and was known to them because he shared everything he had.

He lived very simply. In fact, on one occasion when he went to dine with rich people, the servants turned him away because his cassock was old and patched. He made four journeys to Rome, alone, on foot, carrying his luggage on his back.

One Christmas Eve the whole town of Kraków went into mourning when news got around that John was dying. He comforted those around him when he saw them grieving. He was 83 years old. He is a patron saint of Poland and Lithuania.

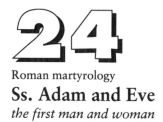

Roman martyrology
Ss. Adam and Eve
the first man and woman

The story of Adam and Eve, which begins in the second chapter of the Book of Genesis, is the first Bible story most of us learn about. To us it may seem familiar and comfortable. But when it was first written down, it must have sounded strange.

The story is about a couple who were equals and who remained faithful to each other all their lives. Just as important was the suggestion that all humans came from one mother and father. That meant that people from every tribe and nation were brothers and sisters. We are all children of Eve and Adam.

On December 24 we remember the sadness of Adam and Eve as they left paradise. It was once a custom on this day to toll church bells, as at a funeral. But at midnight the tolling stopped and the bells began to peal the good news: Christ is born!

Christmas Vigil
See page 6.

Solemnity of
The Birth of the Lord
(Christmas Day)
See page 7.

26

Feast of

St. Stephen

first martyr (died c. 34)

Stephen was so sure of Jesus that he staked his life on him. Stephen's powerful story is told in the sixth and seventh chapters of the Acts of the Apostles.

Stephen was a Greek-speaking Jew. When the apostles needed seven people to help them, he was the first person they chose. This was a sign that Stephen was trusted by everyone. We call him a "deacon," a word that means servant and helper. He had to be a person of integrity, because his job was to distribute funds to needy members of the community.

In honor of Stephen's faithful service to poor people, today has become the customary day in Christmastime to give gifts to people in need. Many people save money each day of Advent and then give this money to charity today.

Stephen was the first martyr. The word "martyr" means "witness." The martyrs' lives and deaths give witness to their faith. Stephen's name is the Greek word for "wreath." Famous athletes and military heroes and anyone who won a great victory were given leafy wreaths to wear like crowns on their heads. The martyrs often are shown wearing leafy crowns.

When we hang a Christmas wreath on our front door, we announce the victory of Jesus. We welcome the victory of peace, of love, of justice. And we remember deacon Stephen, the first witness to lay down his life for Christ.

The Twelve Days of Christmas

See page 8.

27

Feast of

St. John

apostle, evangelist (first century)

There are several people called John in the Christian scriptures. There is John the Baptist. There is the man named John who wrote the Book of Revelation. And there is John the apostle, the son of Zebedee.

To make matters a bit more confusing, there is the "beloved disciple" we read about in the Gospel according to John. The gospel doesn't tell us the disciple's name, but later generations of Christians began to call him John because they thought the beloved disciple mentioned in the Gospel of John was the same person as the apostle John mentioned in the other three gospels.

In many ways this Gospel of John is very different from the other three. Most of the stories in John's gospel are not found in the other gospels. Also, the stories are more poetic, which sometimes makes them harder to understand. Each story seems to have many different meanings. The church reads John's gospel especially during Lent and Eastertime, when we put extra effort into understanding the stories. The symbol of John's gospel is the eagle who flies to the heights.

Who was John the apostle? He was a fisherman. His father was Zebedee and his older brother was James (July 25). Jesus called both brothers to follow him. Immediately they left their nets and became Jesus' disciples. (See Matthew 4:21.)

John and his brother sometimes misunderstood their role. Jesus gently teased the two with the nickname "Sons of Thunder" because they once wanted to call down God's wrath on some people who mocked them. At another time they hoped to get the seats of honor next to Jesus when he came into his kingdom. Jesus explained to them that the way to the kingdom was through suffering.

Along with James and Peter, John was present when Jesus was transfigured in glory on Mount Tabor. These three disciples were also with Jesus during the agony in the garden of Gethsemane.

It's clear from the Acts of the Apostles that John played an important role in the early church. He was with Peter when the first miracle was done in Jesus' name. Traditions say that John later became the bishop of Ephesus (in what is now Turkey). There he lived to be a very old man, calling the Christians in his care to love one another.

Feast of
The Holy Innocents
martyrs (first century)

The story of the Innocents is told in the second chapter of the Gospel of Matthew. Herod, the king of Judea, held the throne only because the Romans kept him there. Herod was bloodthirsty and had even murdered several members of his own family, including three of his sons. He would have no scruples about taking the lives of other people's children if he thought his throne was in danger.

When the Magi told him about a newborn king, Herod ordered the death of all male babies in Bethlehem. In the meantime, Joseph, having been warned of the danger in a dream, fled with Mary and Jesus to Egypt.

Matthew quotes the prophet Jeremiah (May 1) to describe the sorrow of the mothers of Bethlehem: "A voice was heard in Ramah, wailing and loud lamentation. It is Rachel weeping for her children, and she will not be consoled, because they are no more."

Only a few days after one of the gladdest days on the Christian calendar, we remember one of the most tragic events told in the Bible. In every generation there will be innocent victims and their weeping mothers.

Optional memorial of
St. Thomas Becket
bishop, martyr (1118–1170)

Young Thomas Becket was a sportsman. He loved hunting, training hawks and taking risks. But Thomas had a serious side, too. He studied law in London and then he became the assistant of the Archbishop of Canterbury. The bishop trusted Thomas's good judgment.

When young Henry II became king, he named his fellow adventurer Thomas as chancellor. This meant that Thomas was the second most powerful person in England. He was only 36 years old. Thomas enjoyed the luxury of his post. He took many friends along on his trips to other countries. But he also made frequent retreats into prayer, and he convinced Henry to make the legal system more just.

King Henry wanted Thomas to accept the title of Archbishop of Canterbury. Thomas reluctantly agreed to take the title. He changed his fine clothes for a simple black cassock. He began to get up early every day to read scripture and to visit the sick. He gave large sums of money to the poor.

The king began making unjust demands, and Thomas and Henry began to clash. Henry called Thomas a traitor, and Thomas was forced to escape from England. He stayed in hiding for six years. When he returned, four of King Henry's knights paid him an unexpected visit. With their swords they struck him down in his cathedral.

Roman martyrology
St. David
king, prophet (died c. 970 BCE)

Today the city of Jerusalem is the spiritual home to Jews, Christians and Muslims. This city was established for Israel by David. Although he was a savage military leader, he also was a capable ruler, a man of prayer, and a repentant sinner. His story spans the First and Second Books of Samuel and the First Book of Kings.

A young shepherd boy might seem like an unlikely candidate for ruler. David was a herder still in his teens when the prophet Samuel (August 20) secretly anointed him king.

David became a public figure when he fought Goliath, a giant from the Philistine tribe. Though David was much smaller than Goliath and armed only with a slingshot, he felled the giant with one smooth stone.

Later, King David drove the Philistines out of the land of Canaan. He brought the 12 tribes into one nation for the first time. Wisely he chose Jerusalem as its capital. Situated midway between north and south, the city was a place where all the tribes felt equally represented.

David gave stability and honor to Jerusalem by bringing the ark of the covenant there. The ark had been the sacred shrine of the Jews from the time of Moses, centuries before. Mighty King David was not afraid to dance in delight and praise when it was carried to the city.

When David died, all Israel mourned. David's son Solomon succeeded him, but throughout the centuries no king would be as loved as David.

Anniversary of
The Massacre of Native Americans at Wounded Knee, South Dakota
(1890)

Native Americans have lived throughout North America for more than 20,000 years. Starting in the sixteenth century, Europeans began to move farther and farther west across the continent. As they went, they destroyed the Indian way of life.

The Native American tribe called the Lakota (Teton Sioux) were hunters. For centuries they followed the great buffalo herds that roamed the Dakota plains. From the buffalo they got everything they needed: food, tools, weapons, and skins for clothing and tents. In the late 1800s, European settlers came to the Dakotas. They hunted down the vast buffalo herds. Even worse, they forced the Lakota to live in a small area of land called a reservation. This meant that the Lakota could no longer follow the remaining buffalo, and so the Indians began to starve.

Some Lakota danced the Ghost Dance, a new religious ceremony. They believed this would cause the white invaders to disappear forever. The white overseers of the reservation feared an Indian uprising. They found an excuse to arrest Sitting Bull, the chief of one Lakota clan. Guns were drawn and nine people, including Sitting Bull, were killed.

The families of Sitting Bull's clan were so frightened by this that about 40 of them ran away from the reservation. They joined up with other bands of Lakota who were hiding in the Badlands. The United States Seventh Cavalry pursued them. On December 29, 1890, soldiers surrounded about 340 Lakota at Wounded Knee Creek. Even though most of the Lakota were unarmed, the cavalrymen set up four rapid-fire cannon on a rise that overlooked the Indian camp.

A nervous brave fired his rifle. The cavalrymen began firing. They set off their cannon. The battle took only a few minutes.

About 30 soldiers died at Wounded Knee. No one knows exactly how many Sioux died. Not all the corpses were buried together, but one large grave in what is now the town of Wounded Knee holds the bodies of 146 Sioux men, women and children.

Native Americans have been treated unjustly by whites many times since the United States became a nation. Agreements have been broken, lands taken and many people killed — probably numbering in the hundreds of thousands. For most of these crimes, no one has ever been tried and no evidence remains. Too few people know about this terrible part of American history.

Wounded Knee is important because there is actual proof of what happened there. All Americans need to learn more about the history of this violence. Only with increased understanding will every citizen receive equal justice in future generations. As Chief Sitting Bull himself said, "Let us put our minds together and see what life we will make for our children."

31

Optional memorial of

St. Sylvester I
pope (died 335)

After nearly 300 years of persecution, Christians could finally practice their faith. The emperor Constantine had declared that Christians could worship freely. He made Sunday a weekly holiday.

Around this time, in the year 314, Pope Sylvester was elected to office. Sylvester was a Roman. Not much else is known about his personal life. He remained pope for 21 years. Constantine was a powerful friend. He gave Sylvester property and helped him build churches. One of his gifts was the famous Lateran basilica (November 9).It had been a palace, but then it became the cathedral of Rome.

During the time that Sylvester was pope, the Council of Nicea was held in Bithynia (in what is now Turkey). More than 220 bishops attended. Sylvester did not attend the council himself, but he probably had a hand in shaping the way it was organized. Nicea was the first of many such gatherings. Like every council since, Nicea was called so that church leaders could seek God's will in a time of special challenge.

The Council of Nicea was modeled after the meetings of the Roman senate, where everyone present had an opportunity to give an opinion on whatever issue was being discussed. The council prepared the Nicene Creed, a statement of Christian beliefs that we recite at Mass.

St. Sylvester's Day comes on the last day of the year. In many countries, New Year's Eve is called "Sylvester night," and people who celebrate it are "sylvesters." According to folklore, after Pope Sylvester died he was put in charge of the clock that runs the universe. He became known as Father Time.

The real Pope Sylvester called every day of the year a feast day. Each new day brings us closer to perfection. Sylvester knew that the coming of Christ means the end of time and the beginning of eternity.

> Glory to God in highest heaven,
>   Who unto us a Child has given.
> With angels sing in joy and mirth:
>   A glad new year to all the earth!

Jewish Days

Rosh Hashanah
The Head of the Year
The first and second day of Tishri, the seventh month

Seven is a special number. For the Jewish people, the seventh day of each week is the holy day, the Sabbath. And the seventh month is also special. It is filled with festivals.

The first month of the Jewish year is in springtime. The seventh month is in early fall. Rosh Hashanah, the new year, begins on the first day of the seventh month, at the new moon. Rosh Hashanah literally means the "head of the year." Because the Jewish calendar depends on the moon, Rosh Hashanah can fall anywhere between early September and early October. It is a joyful day, but it is also a day when Jews spend time in profound reflection and prayer. It begins a ten-day period called the "Days of Awe," which end with Yom Kippur, the Day of Atonement. Rosh Hashanah and Yom Kippur are known as the "High Holy Days."

During this time, Jews all over the world congregate in the synagogue. They examine their lives and the actions of the community. As a community, they confess their sins and ask for forgiveness. According to tradition, on Yom Kippur God's judgment will be sealed in the book of life for another year.

The first day of Rosh Hashanah lasts from sunset to sunset, as do all Jewish days. After prayers, the family gathers for a meal. Everyone who can afford it dresses in new clothes for the new year. On the table is a loaf of *hallah* (a rich egg bread served each Sabbath). Tonight's *hallah* may be baked in a spiral, a symbol of hope for a full year and a long life. Apples are dipped in honey in a prayer for sweetness in the year ahead. Some families eat a traditional dish called *tzimmes,* a sweet stew made from prunes, carrots, sweet potatoes and sometimes meat.

In the evening people go to the synagogue. One of the prayers of this season is, "Remember us for life, O King who delights in life, and inscribe us in the book of life."

The next day, during the synagogue service, a shofar is blown. A shofar is a ram's horn with the tip cut off so that it can make a great, loud sound. A shofar called the Jews together when God gave them the Law on Mount Sinai. Tradition has it that the Messiah will sound a shofar to raise the dead. Now its haunting sound is heard to call the people to remembrance and repentance.

Yom Kippur
The Day of Atonement
The tenth day of Tishri, the seventh month

The Sabbath that comes every week is the holiest day of the Jewish year. But Yom Kippur is called the "Sabbath of Sabbaths." It symbolizes the renewal of the covenant between God and the Jewish people. This day completes a time of special prayer called the Days of Awe. These days began on Rosh Hashanah.

According to tradition, on Rosh Hashanah God opens the book of life. Today God's judgment about each person's conduct over the past year is sealed in the book, and the book is closed for another year. During the past ten days, Jews have asked pardon of all whom they have wronged. They have tried to forgive anyone who has hurt them. Disputes have been settled if at all possible.

Jewish days begin and end at sunset. On the day before Yom Kippur, a late-afternoon meal is eaten. After that, everyone — except children under 13 and persons not physically able — fasts completely from sunset until after sunset of the following day. Fasting honors the solemnity of this day and the divine gift of life.

As the evening service begins, the scrolls of the Torah, the first five books of the scriptures, are taken from their resting place. The leader of song, who is called a cantor, sings the haunting chant called *Kol nidre*, a prayer first said in times of persecution centuries ago.

The next day, services last from morning until just after sunset. The congregation prays for forgiveness for every kind of sin. The Book of Jonah is read. It tells the story of a prophet who himself needed forgiveness. Stories are told about Jews who died for their faith. Then the memorial prayers for the dead are chanted.

In the evening, when the first three stars appear in the sky, everyone stands. With one voice they affirm that God is one and that the Lord is their God. A single long note is blown on the shofar (the ram's horn), and Yom Kippur is over.

Upon returning home, people break their fast with a joyful meal. This very night some people will begin building the harvest booth for the celebration of Sukkot, only a few days away.

Sukkot

The Festival of Booths
From the 15th to the 21st day of Tishri, the seventh month

The somber, reflective time of the Jewish High Holy Days is over. Yom Kippur brought forgiveness from God. Now, five days later, at the full moon, Jews begin the festival of Sukkot (su-KOT), the festival of booths. Sukkot is also called "the season of our joy" and "the festival of ingathering." It lasts a full week.

At Sukkot, people obey the biblical command to live for seven days in huts. Each family or congregation constructs a shelter, usually with wooden slats and boughs from trees. (In Hebrew, this is called a *sukkah*. The plural of *sukkah* is *sukkot*.) As they build and decorate these beautiful booths, the people recall the 40 years when the Jews, wandering in the desert, put together *sukkot* each evening. They also remember how, at the harvest moon, farmers build shelters in the fields so they

can continue to gather the crops. These booths are sometimes called "harvest homes."

Each *sukkah* must be built and decorated with natural materials. Its roof must be open enough that the sky can be seen through it. This symbolizes the openness between God and humanity. The shelter is decorated with harvest bounty, such as grape clusters, corn, vines and gourds. To stand in a sukkah is to surround oneself with creation. At one time every Jewish family built its own. Now sometimes the *sukkah* is built on the grounds of the synagogue.

Sukkot is a season of fun and blessings. One special blessing involves willow and myrtle branches and the fruit of the citron tree (which looks like a large, bumpy lemon). The fruit and branches represent all God's creation. People march in processions while singing the psalms and waving their branches: "Hosanna! Blessed is the one who comes in the name of the Lord." (Psalm 118:25–26)

Jewish mystics taught that the ancestors, beginning with Sarah and Abraham, come to visit the *sukkah* each evening. According to tradition, the Messiah will come at Sukkot and welcome all creation into God's *sukkah*.

Sukkot, coming after the reconciling work of Yom Kippur, is a time of hospitality. Families visit each other, sharing cake and wine or a festive meal. As with all Jewish holidays, the poor and all who do not have their own sukkah are welcomed in. This practice of hospitality reminds everyone that God's sukkah will be a house of prayer for all peoples.

Sh'mini Atzeret

The Eighth Day of Solemn Assembly
The 22nd day of Tishri, the seventh month

In the fall, Jews celebrate the harvest festival of Sukkot for seven days. In many Jewish communities, Sh'mini Atzeret, the eighth day of solemn assembly, completes Sukkot. The Torah, the books of the law for living as a Jew, instructs people to linger with God for one more day, an eighth day.

The special thing about today is that Jews all over the world begin to pray for rain to fall on Israel. Next year's spring crops will depend on winter moisture.

Sh'mini Atzeret is a day of rest like a Sabbath, so no work is done today. Tomorrow will be Simhat Torah, another special day.

Simhat Torah
Rejoicing in the Law
The 23rd day of Tishri, the seventh month

Simhat Torah means "rejoicing in the Torah." It has become one of the most joyful days of the Jewish year.

Simhat Torah is unique among Jewish holidays. The others are celebrations of the seasons or of great events. Simhat Torah honors the Torah — the first five books of the Hebrew Scriptures.

The Torah provides a framework of laws for living daily life as a Jew. After the fall of Jerusalem in the year 70, the Jews were scattered all over the world. Because of the Torah, they were still able to live a shared life as Jews, whatever country they found themselves in.

At every synagogue, the entire Torah is read over a year of weekly services. On Simhat Torah, the cycle ends and then begins all over again. The final words of the Book of Deuteronomy are read aloud, ending in "Israel." Then the first words of Genesis are read, "In the beginning." This starts the story of creation. The circle is eternal. This is cause for joy and thanksgiving.

Each synagogue has its own hand-lettered Torah scrolls. On Simhat Torah, everyone sings and dances around the synagogue. The Torah scrolls are passed from one person to another. Children wave flags printed with miniature scrolls. The procession circles the synagogue seven times. The special seventh month that began with Rosh Hashanah draws to a close.

Hanukkah
The Feast of Dedication
From the 25th day of Kislev, the ninth month, until the second or third day of Tevet, the tenth month

In the year 175 BCE, the tyrant king Antiochus IV of Syria took over the land of Israel. He ordered the Jewish people to stop observing Jewish customs and the Jewish law. He wanted everyone to adopt Greek culture and customs. He stripped the temple of its treasures and installed idols there. He even allowed wild pigs, which the Jews believe to be unclean, to rummage in their holy place.

Some Jewish people went along with this in order to fit in with the Greek-speaking Syrians, who were wealthier and better educated than they were. So they wore Greek clothing, they changed their Jewish names to Greek names, and they worshiped the Greek gods.

But some Jews refused to give up the Jewish way of life. Many were arrested and killed by Antiochus. Others went into hiding to keep the faith alive. But a young Jew named Judah, of the family of the Maccabees (August 1), led a band of guerrilla soldiers and reclaimed the city of Jerusalem.

The people decided to dedicate the temple anew with an eight-day feast. This was the first Hanukkah, a word that means "dedication." They scrubbed every inch of the temple. They did their best to restore its beauty so that they could again offer sacrifice to God.

According to a legend, within the temple they found a hidden store of the blessed oil used to keep the sanctuary lamp burning. They rekindled the lamp, but there was only enough oil to burn for a day. To prepare more oil, eight days would be needed. And yet during the eight-day period, the lamp kept burning.

To remember the miracle, Jewish families light an eight-branched candlestick in their homes during Hanukkah. Each evening at twilight one more candle is lighted until, on the eighth day of Hanukkah, all eight lights are burning, plus a ninth light that is used to light the others.

Everyone in the family takes a turn lighting the candles. The candlestick is put in a window so that the great power of God can be seen. Special foods cooked in oil are served. *Latkes,* potato pancakes, and *sufganiyot,* doughnuts, are Hanukkah treats. A game is played with a spinning top, the *dreidel.*

Hanukkah comes when the days are shortest in the Northern Hemisphere. This is also when the moon is at its darkest phase (look for the crescent moon in the east before sunrise when Hanukkah begins, then just after sunset in the west as the days of Hanukkah end). It takes great faith for people to keep their way of life when they see their neighbors behaving otherwise. This kind of faith is a light in the midst of darkness.

Tu b'Shvat
The New Year of Trees
The 15th day of Shvat, the eleventh month

In Israel, winters are rainy and mild, and summers are bone dry. By the middle of winter, trees begin to bud. This is cause for a day of rejoicing. Tu b'Shvat (Too buh-SHVAT) means "15th of (the month of) Shvat." Today, at the full moon, the almond trees are in bloom and the Jewish Arbor Day is celebrated.

In a desert land like Israel, trees are appreciated for the beauty and shade they provide as much as for the food they produce. In modern-day Israel, trees give even more bounty than they did in ancient times. The harvest includes avocados, olives, citrus, dates, almonds, peaches and pomegranates.

Some families plant a tree when someone dies or when someone is born. Cedars are planted for boys, cypresses for girls. Children tend their own trees until they and their tree are both grown. When the child eventually gets married, branches from the tree are cut to make poles to hold the wedding canopy.

Now, schoolchildren plant trees everywhere throughout Israel on Tu b'Shvat. Afterward, they dance to celebrate the coming of spring.

Purim
The Feast of Lots
The 14th day of Adar, the twelfth month

The coming of spring was celebrated in all ancient lands. For centuries, Purim (POOR-im), the most cheerful of Jewish holidays, has been a celebration of Jewish survival, of the victory of life over death.

The story of Purim is told in the Book of Esther. This is one of the all-time great love stories. It makes wonderful reading. It is set in Persia, in what is now Iran.

Ahasuerus the king was rather absent-minded and allowed his chief minister Haman almost unlimited power. Haman expected everyone to bow to the king. Only one person refused: a Jew named Mordecai, who had once protected the king from a plot against his life. Haman decided to take revenge on Mordecai and on all the Jews in the kingdom. He persuaded the king to massacre them. Then he drew lots (called, in Hebrew, *purim*) to decide on the day of slaughter.

Haman didn't know that the queen, Esther, was Jewish. Esther fasted and prayed for three days to get up the courage to ask the king to save her people. When Esther told King Ahasuerus all about Haman's plans, he realized that Haman was evil. The king hanged Haman on the gallows that Haman had built for Mordecai.

Purim is celebrated on the 14th day of the Hebrew month of Adar, at the full moon, one month before Passover. In years when a second month of Adar is added to the year, Purim falls in the second Adar. Many Jews begin the celebration by fasting beforehand, like Esther did. Then they gather to hear the story. Every time the name Haman is said, people shake noisemakers to drown out the sound. Some people write Haman's name on their shoes so they can stomp on it.

Children dress up in costume and act out the story. Then a lavish family dinner is served. Gifts of food are sent to relatives and the poor so that everyone can take part in the feasting. Afterward, people eat *hamantaschen,* special three-cornered pastries, which are said to be shaped like Haman's hat, his pockets or even his ears.

Pesach

The Festival of Passover
From the 15th to the 21st or 22nd day of Nisan,
the first month

Pesach, also called Passover or the festival of unleavened bread, is the great freedom festival of the Jewish people. It begins on the 15th of the month of Nisan, at the full moon, and continues for seven or eight days. It is the springtime remembrance and celebration of the deliverance of the Jews from slavery and their covenant with God. This is the story of the very foundation of the Jewish people.

The name Passover calls to mind that the firstborn children of the Egyptians, even firstborn pets and farm animals, were destroyed by the tenth plague, the angel of death (Exodus 12:1–14). But the angel passed by the Jewish families, who were kept as slaves by the Egyptians. The angel could recognize the Jewish homes because the blood of a lamb marked their doors. When Pharaoh saw the dead, he let the Jews leave Egypt. They passed over into freedom.

At the Seder meal of Pesach, this great story is retold as part of the Jewish liturgy. Special foods and customs bring the story to life. The most important food is *matzah,* which is unleavened bread. The Jews left Egypt in such great haste that they did not have time to wait for their bread dough to rise before they baked it.

There are other ritual foods of Passover. Bitter herbs, such as horseradish root, are eaten to recall bitter slavery. Fresh spring greens, such as lettuce and parsley, are dipped in salt water, representing the tears of the people. *Haroset,* a mixture of chopped fruits, nuts, spices and wine, reminds each family of the bricks and mortar used by the slaves in their forced labor. The shankbone of a lamb is put on the table as a sign of the blood that protected the firstborn on the terrible last night of their enslavement. A roasted egg serves as a symbol of rebirth.

At the Seder meal, the youngest child asks, "Why is this night different from all other nights?"

The answer to this question is the story of Passover. A special cup of wine is set aside for the prophet Elijah, who will someday return to prepare the world for the Messiah. The front door is opened to welcome Elijah. Perhaps the prophet is there, standing in the spring moonlight.

Celebrating Pesach is not just a history lesson. Rather, it is a living event, a mystery to be entered into, an experience here and now of God's gift of freedom. The Passover meal ends with the call, "Next year in Jerusalem!" Next year may all people be free!

Yom Hashoah

The Day of the Destruction
The 27th day of Nisan, the first month

Today will be a quiet day in the nation of Israel. The banks, theaters, schools and most businesses will be closed. At memorial services in Israel and around the world today, the stories of Holocaust victims will be told. Their cultures will be remembered. Psalms will be sung and candles lit.

On the Jewish calendar, today is the 27th day of the month of Nisan. This is Yom Hashoah (yahm ha-SHO-ah), the "Day of the Destruction." Unlike the other days described here, Yom Hashoah is a day that has been named in recent times. It is a day to remember the Holocaust.

In ancient times, a holocaust was a sacrifice that was totally consumed by fire. In the twentieth century, the word has taken on a grim new meaning. It refers to the systematic killing by the Nazis of six million Jews of Europe. While the Holocaust was taking place in Europe, the other nations of the world looked away.

Shavuot

The Festival of Weeks
The sixth, and in some places the seventh, day of Sivan,
the third month

After the Jewish slaves escaped from Egypt, they journeyed until they came to Mount Sinai. Moses went up the mountain to meet God. The people kept vigil for Moses to return. When he came down from his time with God, he brought with him the Torah, God's holy law.

Shavuot (shuh-voo-OAT), one of the oldest of all Jewish festivals, is a celebration of this great gift of God. The word Shavuot means "weeks." Shavuot falls seven weeks — a week of weeks — after Pesach. Shavuot brings Pesach to a joyful conclusion.

In Israel, this is summer harvest time. The wheat is ready for reaping at Shavuot. In ancient Israel, rejoicing farmers carried their baskets of firstfruits in a procession through the streets of Jerusalem. Today, in Jewish communities all over the world, homes and synagogues are decorated with springtime greenery and flowers. Shavuot is also called Yom ha-Bikkurim, the festival of firstfruits. The first crops are being gathered — strawberries, cherries, peas and asparagus. The lean days of winter are turning into the plentiful days of summer.

Tisha b'Av
The ninth day of Av, the fifth month

The Temple in Jerusalem was the center of life. It was built on a mount, which many believe is the meeting of the divine and earthly worlds. Built by King Solomon, the son of David, the Temple contained the Holy of Holies where God dwelled. The Temple contained the ark, the symbol of God's presence.

The Temple stood for nearly four centuries. It was destroyed by King Nebuchadnezzar, who sent the Jews into exile in Babylon. Centuries later the Temple was rebuilt on its old foundations. In the year 70 it was destroyed again, this time by the Romans. The Jews were scattered all over the world.

All that remains of this great temple is its western wall. Tisha b'Av (tish-uh buh-AV), the ninth day of the Jewish summer month of Av, is set aside as a fast day to mourn the destruction of the two Temples.

The ark that holds the Torah scrolls in the synagogue is draped in the colors of mourning today. Passages are read from the Book of Jeremiah. This prophet lived during the destruction of the first Temple. The mournful poetry of the Book of Lamentations is also chanted today.

Other tragedies in Jewish history are remembered on this day. For example, all Jews living in England were expelled from their country in the thirteenth century. The same thing happened to Spanish Jews two hundred years later. With these and other events in mind, many Jews keep today with a solemn fast from sunset to sunset.

Muslim Days

Muslim New Year
The first day of Muharram, the first month

The Muslim calendar is used in Iran, Turkey, Arabia, Egypt, Pakistan, and certain parts of India and Malaysia. In the Muslim calendar, months last from one new moon to another. There are 12 months in the year.

The length of time from one new moon to the next is 29 ½ days, so the 12 months of the Muslim year add up to 354 days. That's 11¼ days short of the 365 ¼-day solar calendar. This means that the Muslim New Year (like every Muslim holiday) comes 11 or 12 days earlier each year on the Western calendar. In about 30 years, it's back to where it started.

Awwal Muharram (the first day of the Muslim month of *Muharram*) begins the year. However, the arrival of the new year is not a reason for rejoicing. People worship quietly on this day. The month is devoted to mourning the dead. Young boys have the task of tending family graves and strewing marigolds or rose petals over them. Fresh palm fronds are tied to tombstones. Because palm trees stay green even in the hottest weather, they are symbols of eternal life.

Muhammad, the founder of Islam, fled from the Arabian city of Mecca in the Western year 622. He was escaping from enemies who wanted to assassinate him. Many of his followers joined him in the city of Medina, where they were able to worship freely.

Muhammad's journey, called the *Hegira,* was the first major event in the history of Islam. Muslims use this event to date the beginning of their calendar, just as Christians count their years beginning with the birth of Christ. The Western year 622 is considered by Muslims the year 1. But because Islamic years are 11 days shorter than Western years, the Islamic year 1421 will begin in the Western year 2000.

Ramadan
the ninth month of the Muslim year

Muslims hold this month sacred. In Islamic countries, Ramadan is devoted to fasting and prayer. For these 29 or 30 days, Muslims may not eat or drink from sunup to sundown. In most nations the month is pronounced RAHM-uh-dahn, but in Pakistan and India it is pronounced RAHM-zahn.

An hour before sunrise each day, sirens call people to breakfast. According to tradition, the day's fast begins "when it is light enough to tell a white thread from a black one."

The fasting is accompanied with prayer to God for pardon. Everyone fasts together. This makes it easier to do, but it also shows that people need each other in the path of holiness. Fasting during Ramadan helps Muslims to be more aware of the sufferings of the poor. Fasting is also a way to honor the month when Muhammad, the founder of Islam, received its holy book, the Koran.

Keeping the fast is a serious obligation. It is one of the five "pillars of Islam." Everyone, except very young children and very old or sick people, observes the fast.

In years past, when most Muslims lived in small villages, during the days of Ramadan they could pray, rest and study the Koran. But in modern cities, work must go on as usual. This makes fasting more of a challenge.

People listen for the sirens that blow at sundown, when the day's fasting ends. In some cities, when the sirens sound, traffic comes to a dead stop. People jump from their cars and run to tea or lemonade stands. Colored lights are strung up over courtyards. People try to be especially friendly and helpful to each other.

When the month of Ramadan ends and the month of Shawwal begins, the fast is over and the great feast of Id al-Fit'r begins.

Id al-Fit'r

Feast of the Breaking of the Fast
The first day of Shawwal, the tenth month

At the end of the Muslim month of Ramadan, people gather on their rooftops at twilight. They search the sky for the new moon. When the crescent is visible, the fasting of Ramadan is finally over. Id al-Fit'r begins, a three-day feast.

Id al-Fit'r is one of two great festivals prescribed by the prophet Muhammad, the founder of Islam. Muslims all over the world keep it. If weather permits, prayers and a sermon are held outdoors, with vast crowds attending. People make donations to charity and care for the tombs of the dead. Families visit, exchange gifts and settle misunderstandings. People dress up in new clothes. They stroll in the streets, hugging each other and expressing wishes for good crops and good health.

Id al-Fit'r is especially a day for children. Little girls are dressed in brand new satin dresses of bright purple, pink or blue. Boys go to the mosque to worship alongside their fathers. Candy sellers roam the streets. Turkish children receive candy made of gelatin covered with powdered sugar. (This candy is sometimes called "Turkish delight.") In Pakistan, children eat *sawaeen*. It looks like spaghetti, but it's sweet and flavored with almonds, pistachio nuts and dates. In front of the Great Mosque of Delhi in India, children ride on a wooden ferris wheel turned by hand.

The prayer and fasting and forgiveness of Ramadan bring peace and renewal to families, to neighborhoods, even to the world. So when Ramadan is past, everything seems new and fresh. That makes Id al-Fit'r the favorite holiday of many Muslim people.

Id al-Adha

Feast of the Sacrifice
The tenth day of Dhul-Hijjah, the twelfth month

Id al-Adha honors Abraham (March 16), the father of the Muslim peoples through his son Ishmael, and the father of the Jews through his son Isaac. Christians also call Abraham their father in faith. No wonder the name Abraham means "father"!

The holy book of Islam, the Koran, tells a story of Abraham's obedience to God. Abraham was willing to sacrifice his beloved son Ishmael when he thought God had commanded it. Then a voice told him to sacrifice a ram instead.

To honor this day, Muslim families sacrifice an animal to eat. Prosperous families cook extra food so that everyone will have a share in the celebration. A third of the food goes to the household, another third to relatives in the area, and the remainder to the poor. No one is turned away.

The prophet Muhammad taught that a sacred shrine in the city of Mecca in Arabia was built by Abraham and his son Ishmael. One of the five "pillars of Islam" that every Muslim must perform is to make a *hadj,* a pilgrimage, to Mecca. Hundreds of thousands of people are in Mecca to celebrate during this feast.

At one time Muslims made great sacrifices to get to Mecca. Caravans came through the deserts and mountains of central Africa. (Piles of loose stones along trails still mark the burial places of those who died along the way.) People traveled from Persia, India, Malaya and China by ship.

Muslim people also came from Albania, Bosnia, Turkey and Syria by rail. They suffered from hunger, thirst and exhaustion. Most people were old before they could afford to make the journey and become a *"hadj"* (the name given to someone who has been to Mecca). When they returned to their homeland, they were entitled to wear a green turban to set them apart from other people.

Nowadays, pilgrims fly to Mecca or come in ships, although for most people it still is a once-in-a-lifetime experience. During their stay, pilgrims worship and give alms. Believers from all nations and races gather together to pray and to visit the sacred places of Islam.

Suggested Reading

The following is a selection of recently published materials, with a special focus on items that might be useful for teachers and their students.

Ball, Ann. *Modern Saints: Their Lives and Faces,* 2 vols. Rockford IL: Tan Books and Publishers, Inc., 1983. This useful pair of volumes provides otherwise hard-to-locate stories of contemporary saints and of persons proposed for canonization.

Carmody, Denise Lardner. *Biblical Woman: Contemporary Reflections on Scriptural Texts.* New York: Crossroad, 1989. Paperback. Insights on selected scripture passages are presented by an author with a strong understanding of women's issues and of theology as well.

DeSola Chervin, Ronda. *Treasury of Women Saints.* Ann Arbor MI: Servant Publications, 1991. A compact and comprehensive book, this paperback contains over 200 entries.

Dooley, Kate. *The Saints Book.* Ramsey NJ: Paulist Press, 1981. This illustrated paperback outlines the lives of saints whose stories may hold special appeal for young people.

Foley, Leonard. *Saint of the Day: Lives and Lessons for Saints and Feasts of the New Missal.* Cincinnati: St. Anthony Messenger Press, 1990. Brief, lively biographies of the saints of the Roman calendar, with quotes and reflections, makes this a highly recommended work.

Jegen, Carol Frances, ed. *Mary According to Women.* Kansas City MO: Leaven Press, 1985. This valuable book is filled with reflections on Mary in regard to contemporary issues of justice and ministry.

Metford, J. C. J. *Dictionary of Christian Lore and Legend.* London: Thames and Hudson, 1983. This paperback provides a quick classroom reference tool for information about symbols, saints, biblical figures and more.

Newland, Mary Reed. *The Hebrew Scriptures: The Biblical Story of God's Promise to Israel and Us.* Winona MN: St. Mary's Press, 1990. This highly readable, high school religion text can enliven the study of scripture for personal reflection as well; includes timetables and questions for review.

Pennington, M. Basil. *Through the Year with the Saints: A Daily Companion for Private or Liturgical Prayer.* New York: Doubleday and Company, 1987. Wonderful reflections and quotes make this paperbound resource useful for daily study.

Pochocki Marbach, Ethel. *Saints of the Season for Children.* Cincinnati: St. Anthony Messenger Press, 1989. This illustrated paperback is an assortment of delightful prose and poetry designed to help young children get to know the saints.

Twomey, Mark J. *A Parade of Saints.* Collegeville MN: The Liturgical Press, 1991. Skillfully written for young people in a way that respects their intelligence, this attractively illustrated book belongs in every religious education classroom.

Van Straalen, Alice. *The Book of Holidays around the World.* New York: E. P. Dutton, 1986. A compact and beautiful desk reference, this book provides lore about a holiday for each day of the year; includes all sorts of intriguing oddities.

Walsh, Michael, ed. *Butler's Lives of the Saints: Concise Edition.* San Francisco: HarperCollins, 1991. A revised and updated paperback, this work includes one saint for each day of the year.

White, Kristin E. *A Guide to the Saints.* New York: Ivy Books, 1991. A quick reference guide to many saints.

An Illustrated History of the Church, translated by John Drury. Minneapolis: Winston Press, 1980. This ten-volume set for young people is brightly illustrated and eminently readable. Places the saints and important movements in the church within their historical context.

Saints and Feast Days: Lives of the Saints with a Calendar and Ways to Celebrate. Chicago: Loyola University Press, 1985. Designed for upper grade or high school students, this practical book is adapted from the *Christ Our Life* religion series.

Bibliography
General Sources

Adam, Adolph. *The Liturgical Year: Its History and Its Meaning after the Reform of the Liturgy.* New York: Pueblo Publishing Company, 1979.

Boadt, Lawrence. *Reading the Old Testament: An Introduction.* New York: Paulist Press, 1984.

Burghardt, Walter. *Saints and Sanctity.* Englewood Cliffs NJ: Prentice Hall, Inc., 1965.

Chase's Annual Events: The Day-by-Day Directory to 1992. Chicago: Contemporary Books, Inc., 1991.

Coulson, John, ed. The Saints: A Concise Biographical Dictionary. New York: Hawthorn Books, Inc., 1965.

Cowie, Leonard W. The Reformation. New York: The John Day Company, 1968.

Deen, Edith. Great Women of the Christian Faith. New York: Harper and Brothers Publishers, 1959.

Delaney, John J. Dictionary of Saints. Garden City NY: Doubleday and Company, 1980.

_____, ed. Saints for All Seasons: Personal Portraits of Favorite Saints by Twenty Outstanding Catholic Authors. Garden City NY: Doubleday and Company, 1978.

Donnelly, Doris, ed. Mary, Woman of Nazareth: Biblical and Theological Perspectives. New York: Paulist Press, 1989.

Epstein, Sam and Beryl. European Folk Festivals: A Holiday Book. Champaign IL: Garrard Publishing Company, 1968.

Flannery, Austin. The Saints in Season: A Companion to the Lectionary. Northport NY: Costello Publishing Company, Inc., 1976.

Halton, Thomas, ed. Message of the Fathers of the Church, series. Wilmington DE: Michael Glazier, Inc.

Harper, Howard V. Days and Customs of All Faiths. New York: Fleet Publishing Company, 1957.

Kalberer, Augustine. Lives of the Saints: Daily Readings. Chicago: Franciscan Herald Press, 1975.

Kleinz, John P. The Who's Who of Heaven: Saints for All Seasons. Westminster MD: Christian Classics, 1987.

Knowles, Leo. Saints Who Spoke English. St. Paul: Carillon Books, 1979.

Koulomzin, Sophie, The Orthodox Christian Church through the Ages, revised edition. New York: Metropolitan Council on Public Communication, Russian Orthodox Church of America, 1963.

McBride, Alfred. The Story of the Church: Peak Moments from Pentecost to the Year 2000. Cincinnati: St. Anthony Messenger Press, 1983.

McGill, Mary E. Introducing the Saints, 2 vols. St. Meinrad IN: The Grail Publications, 1952.

Miles, Clement A. Christmas Customs and Traditions. New York: Dover Publications, Inc., 1976.

Myers, Robert J. Celebrations: The Complete Book of American Holidays. Garden City NY: Doubleday and Company, 1972.

Nelson, Gertrud Mueller. To Dance with God: Family Rituals and Community Celebrations. New York: Paulist Press, 1986.

Powers, Mala. Follow the Year: A Family Celebration of Christian Holidays. San Francisco: Harper and Row, Inc., 1985.

Sheed, F. J. Saints Are Not Sad: Forty Biographical Portraits. New York: Sheed and Ward, 1949.

Sheridan, John V. Saints in Times of Turmoil. New York: Paulist Press, 1977.

Stevens, Clifford. Portraits of Faith. Huntington IN: Our Sunday Visitor, Inc., 1975.

Talley, Thomas J. The Origins of the Liturgical Year, second edition. Collegeville MN: The Liturgical Press, 1991.

Thompson, Blanche Jennings. Saints of the Byzantine World. New York: Farrar, Straus and Cudahy, 1961.

Thurston, Herbert, and Attwater, Donald, eds. Butler's Lives of the Saints. New York: P. J. Kenedy and Sons, 1956.

Valentine, Mary Hester. Saints for Contemporary Women. Chicago: The Thomas More Press, 1987.

Weiser, Francis X. The Holyday Book. New York: Harcourt Brace and Company, 1956.

Sources for Specific Days

Third Monday in January: Martin Luther King Day
Witherspoon, William R. Martin Luther King, Jr. . . . To the Mountaintop. Garden City NY: Doubleday and Company, 1985.

Second New Moon after the Winter Solstice: Lunar New Year
Brown, Tricia. Chinese New Year. New York: Henry Holt and Company, 1987.

January 27: Angela Merici
Mary St. Paul, Mother. From Desenzano to the Pines. Toronto: MacMillan Company of Canada, Ltd., 1941.

January 30: Mohandas Gandhi
Shahani, Ranjee. Mr. Gandhi. New York: The Macmillan Company, 1961.

February 12: Abraham Lincoln
Greene, Carol. *Abraham Lincoln, President of a Divided Country*. Chicago: Children's Press, 1987.

February 20: Frederick Douglass
Morsbach, Mabel. *The Negro in American Life*. New York: Harcourt Brace and World, Inc., 1966.

McKissack, Patricia and Fredrick. *Frederick Douglass: The Black Lion*. Chicago: Children's Press, 1987.

February 22: George Washington
Hoobler, Dorothy and Thomas. *George Washington and Presidents' Day*. Englewood Cliffs NJ: Silver Press, 1990.

March 2: John and Charles Wesley
Gilles, Anthony E. *The People of Anguish: The Story behind the Reformation*. Cincinnati: St. Anthony Messenger Press, 1987.

March 3: Katharine Drexel
Tarry, Ellen. *Katharine Drexel: Friend of the Neglected*. New York: Farrar, Straus and Cudahy, 1958.

March 10: Harriet Tubman
Ferris, Jeri. *Go Free or Die: A Book about Harriet Tubman*. Minneapolis: Carolrhoda Books, 1988.

May 1: May Day
Chambers, R., ed. *The Book of Days: A Miscellany of Pop Antiquities*. Detroit: Gale Research Company, 1967.

May 6: Henry David Thoreau
Burleigh, Robert. *A Man Named Thoreau*. New York: Atheneum, 1985.

May 13: Julian of Norwich
Jantzen, Grace M. *Julian of Norwich: Mystic and Theologian*. New York: Paulist Press, 1988.

Knowles, David. *The English Mystical Tradition*. New York: Harper and Brothers, 1961.

May 21: Jane Addams
Keller, Gail Faithfull. *Jane Addams*. New York: Thomas Y. Crowell Company, 1971.

May 30: Joan of Arc
Fisher, Aileen. *Jeanne d'Arc*. New York: Thomas Y. Crowell Company, 1970.

June 3: John XXIII
MacEoin, Gary. "John XXIII." In *Saints Are Now: Eight Portraits of Modern Sanctity,* edited by John J. Delaney. Garden City NY: Doubleday and Company, 1981.

Nevins, Albert J. *The Story of Pope John XXIII*. New York: Grosset and Dunlap, 1966.

July 1: Junípero Serra
Dolan, Sean. *Junípero Serra*. New York: Chelsea House Publishers, 1991.

Gleiter, Jan, and Thompson, Kathleen. *Junípero Serra*. Milwaukee: Raintree Publishers, 1989.

August 6 and 9: Hiroshima and Nagasaki Memorial Days
Committee for Compilation of Materials on Damages Caused by the Atomic Bombs in Hiroshima and Nagasaki. *Hiroshima and Nagasaki*. New York: Basic Books, Inc., 1981.

Lifton, Betty Jean. *Return to Hiroshima*. New York: Atheneum, 1970.

August 13: Florence Nightingale
Boyd, Nancy. *Three Victorian Women Who Changed Their World*. New York: Oxford University Press, 1982.

August 14: Maximilian Mary Kolbe
Dewar, Diana. *All for Christ*. New York: Oxford University Press, 1980.

September 18: Dag Hammarskjöld
Hershey, Burnet. *Dag Hammarskjöld, Soldier of Peace*. Chicago: Brittanica Books, 1961.

September 20: Andrew Kim Taegon, Paul Chong Hasang and companions
Kim, Joseph Chang-mun and Chung, John Jae-Sun. *Catholic Korea: Yesterday and Today*. Seoul: Catholic Korea Publishing Company, 1964.

Second Monday in October: Columbus Day
D'Aulaire, Ingrid, and Parin, Edgar. *Columbus*. Garden City NY: Doubleday and Company, 1955.

October 1: Theresa of the Child Jesus
Furlong, Monica. "Thérèse of Lisieux." In *Salt* (May 1990). Chicago: Claretian Publications.

Election Day
Phelan, Mary Kay. *Election Day*. New York: Thomas Y. Crowell Company, 1967.

Fradin, Dennis B. *Voting and Elections*. Chicago: Children's Press, 1985.

November 3: Martin de Porres
Bishop, Claire Huchet. *Martin de Porres, Hero*. Boston: Houghton Mifflin Company, 1954.

November 23: Miguel Agustín Pro
Hanley, Boniface. *No Strangers to Violence, No Strangers to Love*. Notre Dame IN: Ave Maria Press, 1983.

November 29: Dorothy Day
Egan, Eileen. *Dorothy Day and the Permanent Revolution*. Erie PA: Pax Christi USA, 1983.

Miller, William J. "Dorothy Day." In *Saints Are Now: Eight Portraits of Modern Sanctity,* edited by John J. Delaney. Garden City NY: Doubleday and Company, 1981.

December 1: Rosa Parks

Friese, Kai. *Rosa Parks: The Movement Organizes.* Englewood Cliffs NJ: Silver Burdett Press, 1990.

Greenfield, Eloise. *Rosa Parks.* New York: Thomas Y. Crowell Company, 1973.

December 2: Maura Clarke, Ita Ford, Dorothy Kazel, Jean Donovan

Hollyday, Joyce. "Four U. S. Martyrs." In *Cloud of Witnesses,* edited by Jim Wallis and Joyce Hollyday. Maryknoll NY: Orbis Books, 1991.

December 10: Thomas Merton

Collins, David R. *Thomas Merton: Monk with a Mission.* Cincinnati: St. Anthony Messenger Press, 1981.

Stone, Naomi Burton. "Thomas Merton." In *Saints Are Now: Eight Portraits of Modern Sanctity,* edited by John J. Delaney. Garden City NY: Doubleday and Company, 1981.

December 12: Nuestra Señora de Guadalupe

DeCock, Mary. "Our Lady of Guadalupe: Symbol of Liberation?" In *Mary According to Women,* edited by Carol Frances Jegen. Kansas City MO: Leaven Press, 1985.

de Paola, Tomie. *The Lady of Guadalupe.* New York: Holiday House, 1980.

Jewish Holidays

Cuyler, Margery. *Jewish Holidays.* New York: Holt, Rinehart and Winston, 1978.

Greenfield, Howard. *Passover.* New York: Holt Rinehart and Winston, 1982.

_____. *Purim.* New York: Holt Rinehart and Winston, 1982.

_____. *Rosh Hashanah and Yom Kippur.* New York: Holt Rinehart and Winston, 1979.

Morrow, Betty, and Hartman, Louis. *Jewish Holidays.* Champaign IL: Garrard Publishing Company, 1967.

Rockland, Mae Shafter. *The Jewish Party Book.* New York: Schocken Books, 1978.

Smart, Ninian. *The Long Search.* Boston: Little, Brown and Company, 1977.

Waskow, Arthur. *Seasons of Our Joy.* New York: Bantam Books, 1982.

Muslim Holidays

Hobley, Leonard. *Moslems and Islam.* East Sussex, England: Wayland Publishers Ltd., 1979.

Lanz, Robert. *The Land and People of Pakistan.* Philadelphia: J. P. Lippincott Company, 1968.

Additional Resources from Liturgy Training Publications

An Advent Calendar: Fling Wide the Doors. A freestanding, three-dimensional liturgical calendar.

At Home with the Word. Alone or with a group, this annual book encourages you to read and reflect on the Sunday scriptures and on ways by which to carry God's word out into the world to act on it.

At That Time: Cycles and Seasons in the Life of a Christian, edited by James A. Wilde with a Foreword by Mary Perkins Ryan. A meditation on time for the catechumen, the neophyte or the seasoned Christian.

School Year, Church Year: Customs and Decorations for the Classroom, by Peter Mazar. Solid, practical advice on how to keep the liturgical calendar in the Catholic classroom.

Forty Days and Forty Nights: A Lenten Ark Moving Toward Easter. For each day of Lent and the Easter Triduum, windows and doors on Noah's ark reveal the stories of Lent.

Sourcebook for Sundays and Seasons, by Lawrence E. Mick with art by Rita Corbin. For presiders and all who plan parish liturgy. Each Sunday and feast comes with a full set of notes; options for every day of the year are noted.

Take Me Home: Notes on the Church Year for Children, by Christine Kenny-Sheputis with illustrations by Suzanne Novak. A book of reproducible take-home notes on the saints and the seasons, with more than enough for each week of the year.

The Year of Grace Liturgical Calendar. An annual, circular calendar that begins with the first Sunday of Advent each year.

Index